EDUCATION AS A PUBLIC SERVICE

THE AUTHOR

Marten Shipman studied at the London School of Economics after working in the Royal Navy and the Police. After professional training he taught in a secondary modern school in London. From 1961 to 1969 he lectured and was Head of the Sociology Department at Worcester College of Education. From 1969 to 1972 he was Senior Lecturer in Education at the University of Keele, and from 1972 to 1978 he was Director of Research and Statistics for the Inner London Education Authority and visiting Professor of Sociology at the University of Surrey. In 1979 he was appointed Professor of Education at Warwick University. He is the author of several books on the sociology of education and on social research methods.

EDUCATION AS A
PUBLIC SERVICE

MARTEN SHIPMAN

Harper & Row, Publishers
London

Cambridge San Francisco
Hagerstown Mexico City
Philadelphia Sao Paulo
New York Sydney

7114

British Library Cataloguing in Publication Data
Shipman, Marten
    Education as a public service.
    1. Educational sociology
    I. Title
    370.19′3   LC191

    ISBN 0–06–318268–8

Typeset by Inforum Ltd, Portsmouth
Printed and bound by Butler & Tanner Ltd, Frome and London

CONTENTS

INTRODUCTION

All public services fail to meet the hopes placed upon them. Resources are not available to meet all the demands made. Furthermore, those demands increase as the public feels the benefit of improvements in the service. Doctors limit the care they give to the very old. They discourage some categories of patient in order to find time to concentrate on others. Similarly, claims on the time of officials in social security or housing departments are met selectively. Because public services cannot meet total public demand, because their success only increases that demand, those involved have to judge the priority of different claims and allocate their efforts on the basis of that judgement. This selective allocation of time, effort and resources is also exercised by teachers. This book is an attempt to show why this is often a frustrating experience for those involved, whether as politicians, public servants or consumers.

Most books on the organization of the education service are unrealistic. Those describing its administration tend to mislead because they omit the horse-trading behind the legal position. They tend to bore because they omit the excitement of the political basis of decisions about education. At the other extreme are books about that political base, but these also tend to mislead because they deal with abstractions. On the left the focus is on education as part of capitalist, class-based social relations. On the right the focus is on the levelling effects of education under socialism. Most readers, working and voting in an apparently mixed and rather muddled economy, rightly suspect that the reality is messier than the -isms described, and that the discussions of systems, state, ideologies and hegemony say more about the academic mind than the way in which resources are allocated to schools or lessons organized.

This lack of realism is also apparent if the reader is looking for ways forward. Socialist writers may conclude that genuine educational change depends on the overthrow of capitalism. Reactionary writers may conclude that it depends on an acknowledgement of inherited differences. But few politicians and fewer chief education officers are in a position to lead the march to the barricades or to recommend genetic engineering as educational policy. Many writers do, of course, combine description and interpretation and the author is indebted to them. This book deals with education as a public service; that grounds it on the supply side in the political and economic factors that restrict social policy. It also relates education to the demands of parents and students. Supply and demand are brought together in a final section to evaluate the effectiveness of the service provided.

This look at education as one among many related public services, and as a means of satisfying the hopes of parents, may seem divorced from the world of administration, school organization or curriculum. But teachers cannot escape from their involvement in sorting children out on to very different paths towards adult employment and higher education. They face the hopes and fears of parents for their children. These arise from the realization that schooling will affect the chances of getting a good job. Improving the education service only increases the hopes placed upon it because it is meshed into a differentiated division of labour for adults. This prominence of selection is a major force in determining the scope and limits of education as a public service because opportunities are restricted. One child's success can mean that others come second. That unhappy fact of life is known to parents and children, both rich and poor. It is the built-in barrier to attempts to humanize teaching, to innovate and reform.

The clearest view of this problem can be obtained by looking at the career of children during compulsory schooling from the ages of 5 to 16. Apparently undifferentiated groups of infants in the reception class become the separated and very differently skilled groups at 16. During that period the hopes of parents and children have been realized or frustrated. Within the service teachers will have played their part in the selection process. But parents also will have employed very different resources and exercised very different pressures to influence the actions of teachers.

This situation is particularly difficult for teachers, given the diversity that faces them. In a society split into groups with identifiably different prospects, teachers perform this selective, sensitive service without clear guidance, public agreement or even reliable instruments for assessment. Some win and others lose because rewards are limited by the availability of good jobs and of places in high-prestige institutions of higher education. The rewards within education are largely determined outside. Public satisfaction with the service will always be limited by the competitive nature of education as a means of achieving adult status because the emergence of societies from poverty rests on advanced divisions of labour. Whether the role of teachers is viewed as promoting the welfare of individual children, or of society, or as the preservation of the culture, or the quality of the adult workforce, the same dilemma will persist. Some children will be warmed up, some cooled out.

No reform is going to remove this dilemma of scarce opportunities. Chronic unemployment has increased the problem, but it still existed even when the education service was expanding. Indeed, the service is affected more than most social services by what Hirsch (1977) described as the 'hole in the affluent society'. As more people come to enjoy services previously enjoyed by a minority, the enjoyment is decreased. There is a new, expanding service class, which is privileged through its education. But those privileges come as much from being in a minority as from the qualifications that govern entry to white-collar jobs. Once education is a genuine public service the search is on for sources that will once again mark out a minority for promotion, thus defeating the drive to create a sense of community through the provision of a service shared by everyone. Yet that creation of fraternity had been a central principle behind the foundation of the welfare state. There is no natural balance between individual interest and the collective, public good.

A similar problem arises over the position of teachers. The annual salary bill for a large secondary comprehensive school now exceeds £1 million a year. The history of teachers in maintained schools illustrates the tension between a drive to establish teaching as a reasonably paid and respected occupation, and the drive to establish professional status on the basis of conduct, not just financial rewards. The struggle for uniform national salaries, for job security and for an end to unskilled, non-certificated teachers has continued throughout the twentieth century. This lasting campaign was accompanied by pressure to be recognized as a profession. But there are too many teachers for their salaries not to be under the microscope as each year's pay round is settled. Teachers are like a crowd at a football match. A few can stand on tiptoe and get a better view, but if they all stretch up, the advantage disappears with the view. Half a million teachers cannot be privileged or the Treasury would go berserk.

Thus there is frustration built into education as a public service. The tendency for private initiatives to frustrate public policies, and for the latter to disappoint those who initiated them, is reinforced by the way the service is organized. Procedures are largely determined by the weight of previous investment in policies, buildings, personnel and the curriculum. Those who want change have to work against previous decisions which have been incorporated into large-scale and sometimes unresponsive institutions. They also have to overcome the interests of professionals whose careers are mapped out in those institutions.

This book attempts to understand the sources of frustration and hope in the education service. The issues can be illustrated by looking at any of the persisting problems facing teachers, administrators and politicians. Why is a service that spent over £11 billion in 1980–1981, employing some 500,000 teachers in nearly 30,000 institutions, perennially incapable of providing an adequate education for that 'half our future' that are often the despair of teachers and whose prospects deteriorate with increased unemployment? Why was it that the only momentum generated as job prospects declined came from the Manpower Services Commission organized from within the Department of Employment (DoE), and not from the Department of Education and Science (DES)?

Answers to questions within education usually require consideration of outside forces. In this book education is examined as one among many public services. Before starting on that examination a few assumptions have to be made. Whether implicit or explicit, there are models in the minds of authors describing social conditions. Such models direct the search, serve as sources for hunches or hypotheses, account for the evidence selected and presented. At the most elementary level there are one-word descriptions such as 'service', 'partnership', 'decentralized', 'disseminated' or 'diffused'. There are also constructed models which view education as a system or as a series of exchanges wherein the resources held determine the allocation of power. Others link education to economic, political and social factors or to the growth of large-scale public corporations. A selection of such models can be found in the Appendix.

Building a model is a common method of gaining understanding. Mathematical models are the basis of theoretical physics. The model of the DNA molecule was important because it served as the source of hypotheses about the biochemistry of creating and sustaining life. But it isn't only scientists who use models as a source of theorizing. Teachers, parents, politicians and administrators have their own, often implicit models, however crude, of the way the service works. Each group defines the model from its own viewpoint and that definition is reality to the group, serving as a source for guiding its actions. These pictures in the mind may be implicit, incomplete and biased, but they yield some understanding and guide action.

When teachers, advisors, students and parents discuss education, they employ implicit models, however ill-informed and incomplete. But so do academics when they use terms such as education 'system'. Fowler (1974), with political experience inside the DES, sees this as inaccurate given the lack of coordination between different parts. 'System' implies interrelated parts that are not only meshed together but in a detectable, predictable way. Change here will have repercussions there. The whole may be more than the sum of the parts. 'System' implies systematic, systemic wherein the parts are ordered and the working methodical. Shorthands such as 'system', 'service', 'organization' and 'structure' contain implicit assumptions. Their use, like that of theoretical models, may lead to hunches that can be useful in making decisions about education. But the assumptions are still present and the concepts may suggest more rationality than really exists. Similarly Kogan (1975), also with experience within the DES, is cautious about models derived from political science. The 'imagery' gives an impression of precision that does not fit the educational scene. 'Softer and more modest imagery is needed' (Kogan, 1975, p. 23).

The perspective which lies behind the chapters that follow is derived from Maclure (1970). The stress is on tensions as legal, administrative and financial pressures meet professional considerations, procedures and traditions. Maclure (1970) starts by challenging the idea that education is 'controlled'. Like Fowler and Kogan he is wary of suggesting too much precision. The service can be seen as a grid, a net. That net, the education service, depends for its shape and organization on pressure groups pulling away at the corners. On one axis of the grid are financial, legal and administrative controls exercised by central government, the Treasury, the DES, LEAs, churches and so on. On the other axis are professional, academic pressures exercised by teachers, lecturers, researchers, examination boards and so on. Developments are the result of the interaction between these two sets of influences.

To each of the parties within the education service pulling at their corner, can be added external forces. Some of these will come from the Treasury, the Department of Employment, the Manpower Services Commission, the Department of Industry, the universities, independent schools, the European Economic Community, the Commission for Racial Equality, the Equal Opportunities Commission and so on. But others come from parents, employers, trade unions, social workers, youth workers, acting through interest groups both to affect the legal and financial basis of the service and to influence professional practices.

The advantage of this model is that it focuses attention on identifiable groups which are organized to exert influence rather than on detached concepts such as the state, the system or ideologies, which cover up the often messy reality in school or government. It avoids suggestions of cosy consensus among partners. The assumption is that the service works because the conflicts of interest are resolved. Each party fights their corner but along agreed lines. A few radicals on the left and a few privateers on the right do not want to play by the rules, but in most cases there is agreement over how the game should be played, however fierce the conflict during it.

There are three cautions to be aired over the selection of this model to guide the analysis of the education service. First, it is pluralist, based on an assumption that power is dispersed rather than concentrated in the capitalist class, or the state as its agent. Other models assume that power is concentrated and result in different interpretations. Second, like any model used to generate hunches about the working of the service, it should not be mistaken for reality on the ground with all its confusion and change. Third, models suggest rationality in decision-making. They are often presented as flow charts or neat block diagrams. But, in practice, the policy-makers in a public service such as education not only make decisions without the information that would enable them to predict the consequences of their actions, but spend much of their time watching policies being implemented in ways that distort their original intentions. They live with the unintended consequences of their actions.

At this point readers may prefer to turn to the Appendix for a flavour of alternative ways of modelling the service, before proceeding to the chapters describing it. Others may prefer to go straight to the description of education as a public service. In both cases the same caution applies. An author's assumptions hold a book together. Alternative explanations will result if the model is changed. Readers will have their own assumptions. They are invited to be critical.

The book is organized in four parts. In Part One the place of education as one of the many public services forming the welfare state in the late 1940s is established. In Part Two the government, sub-government and finance is described in order to detail the forces for change and inertia in the organization of the service. Part Three focuses on corporative developments and their relation to the professionalism of teachers. In Part Four the factors limiting the achievement of the goals of those who supported the 1944 Education Act are examined, in order to produce the conditions for an evaluation. Parts One and Two are deliberately descriptive to ground the analysis in the legal, administrative and financial base of the education service. But the emphasis throughout is on the actual rather than the formal procedures through which policies are made, implemented and adapted.

PART ONE

EDUCATION AND THE WELFARE STATE

CHAPTER 1

EDUCATION AS A PUBLIC SERVICE

Education is one among many public services. It is administered by local authorities with corporate responsibilities for a range of such services. Its resources come from taxation which also has to pay for competing services. Educational policies and practices can only be fully understood as part of an organization of personal and social services for the public, financed out of their taxes, governed by their elected representatives and administered by public servants. Resource allocation, the cost-effectiveness of developments, the rights and responsibilities of the public that provided the money, and political sensitivity to that public concern are the context in which educational decisions are made.

The end of assured economic growth among the advanced industrial countries, such as Britain, which was accelerated by the oil crisis in 1973, reinforced an already marked change in policies and practices concerning social welfare. In that year the education service received its highest ever share of the Gross National Product. The proportion was then reduced during the next decade. The welfare state may have seemed firmly established a generation after the Beveridge Report of 1942 and the legislation of the Attlee government in the late 1940s, but strains were visible and criticism came from political Left and Right. The tendency to view education in isolation has meant that recent events have usually been analysed without reference to these broader historical changes. Yet they affected the service during periods of expansion as well as contraction, just as they shaped and have changed the welfare state.

The build-up to the welfare state

Three important historical factors shaped the contemporary education service and the remaining public services. The first was the persisting liberal view that government intervention should be restricted. This had both political and economic implications. State intervention in securing individual and communal welfare was restricted. Government expenditure and interference with market forces were limited to dealing with social conditions requiring urgent action. The second factor was the counterpart to the restricted view of the role of the state: there was early and sustained voluntary activity, particularly by the churches. This, and the restricted role given to the state, established a tradition of decentralized control in education and the other welfare services. The third factor was the reluctant realization that general social conditions reduced the impact of any one service. Effective education for example, even regular attendance at school for a few years, depended on adequate income, health and housing.

There are various interpretations of these historical factors that remain influential in the public services. The most comprehensive comparative account of education is provided by Archer (1979). A typical American view of these British traditions (Heidenheimer et al., 1975) selects the structure of political institutions, stressing the reluctance of the Labour Party to use central government power, the view that the role of the state should be limited, and the varied social conditions of the population. Yet all commentators agree that the contemporary organization of public services reflects deep-rooted historical influences.

The urban, industrial society that developed in Britain in the nineteenth century was governed on the principle of minimum interference with market forces. However, by the time of the 1851 Census, when over half the population was living in towns, government was, albeit reluctantly, having to intervene to limit the threat to public health, security and stability resulting from disease, poverty, ignorance and overcrowding. The need for a pure water supply and adequate sanitation, for the institutional care of the sick, orphaned, penniless and mentally ill, for elementary schooling and for controls over building standards, was seen as too pressing to be left to private enterprise and voluntary action, particularly in densely populated towns. Cholera spread among the rich as well as the poor, and crime and riot affected both.

The realization that government had to take an active part in promoting social welfare spread slowly throughout the second half of the century.

Private enterprise could not provide the necessary medical and environmental services. Similarly, the demand for a literate and disciplined workforce could not be met solely by voluntary effort. As early as 1833 government grants were given to the National Society and the British and Foreign School Society which had been organizing elementary schooling for the Church of England and Non-Conformist churches respectively. The Education Act of 1870, which set up school boards to fill the gaps in voluntary provision of elementary schooling, was one of the many steps towards a new philosophy of government intervention to secure services that had not been forthcoming from unaided private enterprise. The start of a maintained sector in education coincided with the origins of the personal and social services that were to be labelled 'the welfare state' after 1945.

As new problems were identified amid the rapid changes of advancing industrialization and urbanization, they were tackled by limited action with specific objectives. But the infrastructure of government was organized after the establishment of public services. After 100 years of such activity dating from the middle of the nineteenth century, there were numerous overlapping services and many gaps between them. The 1902 Education Act simplified administration by placing the responsibility for providing schooling with the county and county borough councils first established in 1888. Some district councils still retained limited responsibilities for education until 1944. It took over 100 years from the time of the first government subsidy to voluntary bodies in education to the Education Act of 1944 which established a unified, comprehensive service. The social services were organized piecemeal in the face of entrenched resistance to government intervention. Only in the spirit generated during the Second World War were synchronized social services organized into a welfare state. Thirty years later, in the 1970s, the pressure to dismantle and privatize these services, including education, was still powerful. This opposition to an interventionist state rested partly on political beliefs about the benefits of individualism and the perils of state intervention, and partly on a determination to limit government expenditure.

The most persistent restriction on the growth of early public services was the financial orthodoxy that persisted until the Second World War. At the end of the nineteenth century, about 12 percent of the Gross National Product went to public services, including defence. Only some 2.5 percent went to the social services. The dominant economic philosophy was that the state should maintain the conditions for private enterprise, with minimum intervention, minimum expenditure and a balanced budget. This was applied to the education service as well as to the other public services. The introduction of 'payment by results' after 1862, whereby teachers were paid according to the standards achieved by their pupils after testing by inspectors, was an extension of the economic philosophy of 'less eligibility' that was the guide to payments under the Poor Law Amendment Act of 1834. Just as the condition of paupers should be made less attractive than that of the lowest paid worker in employment, so elementary schooling was kept as cheap as possible by establishing minimum standards in a limited range of basic subjects.

The tight control over expenditure was only resentfully relaxed at the end of the nineteenth century. Even in the 1980s central government requests for more accountability in the education service are met by objections that a return to 'payment by results' is being threatened. Yet these limits on central government funding were a condition for limiting its part in the organization of schooling. As long as the impact on taxation was kept small, direct controls over teachers could be minimized. There is a trade-off between state aid and state control. Even with the Labour Party as a major force since 1945, big, interventionist government has been opposed. An economic policy of restricted central government funding was seen as a condition of local autonomy. As the proportion of educational expenditure provided by central government grant increased, there was a threat to the local authorities which were responsible for the provision of resources and the working of schools. Some idea of that economic position can be gauged from comparisons with the USA in the 1970s. Whereas in Britain about half of the cost of local services came from central government, the equivalent figure in the USA was one-tenth. If power goes with the purse strings, the threat to local control was obvious.

The second factor was the long tradition of voluntary effort in providing schooling. This ranges from the foundation of grammar schools that have survived for 500 years or more and now flourish as independent schools, to part- and full-time elementary schooling for the poor. The churches, while receiving financial support for the maintenance of their schools, still retain responsibility for buildings and, in the case of 'aided', mostly Catholic schools, for the appointment of staff. There are numerous arrangements for using voluntary organizations and many independent institutions to supplement maintained schooling.

This voluntary action by the churches, by charitable organizations and by benevolent individuals, coupled with the slow and reluctant establishment of central and local government, was only one aspect of a reluctance to accept government control. Her Majesty's Inspectors (HMI), as their title implies, are not administrators legally responsible to a government minister. Teachers are public but not civil servants, and their professional associations and unions defend their right to determine the school curriculum and how it is taught. Public services such as education were often late, mean and restricted in their national organization. However, that delay left voluntary effort with an important part to play. Thus restrictions on the scope of public services were not all loss. Throughout the organization of the social services, government action was premised on the continuation of voluntary work. This might have been inadequate for solving the major problems of overcoming poverty, unemployment, ill health and ignorance, but it was flexible enough to provide help for new problems, to publicize the need for state intervention and facilitate voluntary action. The absence of strong central government protected local initiative. The emphasis on services being effective and cheap, with central government inspection to secure this economy, avoided the need for detailed state intervention. The education service today reflects the benefits of these restrictions. Pre-schooling in particular depends on voluntary help. The way in which schooling is organized remains the responsibility of local authorities not central government. Above all, teachers retain a high degree of responsibility for the curriculum. The early organization of a centralized service might have reduced this local and professional initiative.

The third historical factor in the development of the education service was the recognition of the relationship between schooling and social background. The possibilities for education were limited by the social and medical condition of the mass of the people. The balance between schooling, family circumstances and the availability of work made the achievement of regular school attendance and hence sustained attainment a very slow process. Sickness, unemployment and poverty made schooling an irregular experience for many children until the end of the nineteenth century. The benefits of universal popular schooling were also delayed by gaps in other social services. Sickly and hungry children were liable to obtain spasmodic, inadequate schooling. The 'silent social revolution' described by Lowndes (1937) was the result of many public services adding to the benefits of economic advance.

The recognition that the various public services had to be organized into a coordinated welfare state in order for each to be effective, was only built into legislation after the Second World War. It was one of the many contributions of the Beveridge Report of 1942, which not only stressed the connection between different social services, but based their overall success on the maintenance of full employment. Yet it is easier to recognize the connection between ill health, poor housing, poverty and low attainment in school than to organize comprehensive services. Furthermore, while the connection is apparent among the starving or the homeless, it is less obvious when basic human needs have been met. Yet it persists in the form of inequality and injustice in more affluent societies.

The Education Act of 1870 and the building and staffing of sufficient elementary schools to ensure that all children could have at least a basic education, were the forerunners of later attempts to secure minimum standards of provision for all in many other social services. The experience of maintained elementary schooling also indicated a dilemma in the provision of social welfare. It is relatively easy to define and to deliver minimum standards of education, health and income, but the extension of such provision above a basic minimum is politically and financially controversial. Should the state try to ensure equality of access to the necessary resources for all, or even aim to achieve some equality of attainment, health, income and so on for all, or should individuals be left to decide the level of service they want by paying for privately provided schooling, medical services, houses and insurance? This is a major political issue in all wealthy societies where basic human material needs are judged to be met. The problem is exacerbated by the expense of post-primary schooling, further and higher education, hospitals, state pension schemes and subsidized housing. Difficult choices have to be made. This political and economic dilemma lies behind the debate over the development of education services in Britain as elsewhere. It is also debated within the other personal and social services. At what point should the responsibility of the state cease and private competition for resources be encouraged?

Education in the welfare state

The piecemeal, untidy development of the education and other public services accounts not only for the persistence of local and voluntary effort, but for the diffused, decentralized, often confusing location of control. It is often difficult to find where the power lies between the centre, locality, professionals and voluntary bodies. But that lack of clarity is a condition for limited central government control. Many different interests would unite to oppose government censorship of textbooks, or any attempt to standardize the way reading should be taught in schools. The education service is also linked to the health and other public services. It is increasingly affected by the activities of the Department of Employment. The legal framework of the current service was established as the welfare state was organized at the end of the Second World War. The organization of the education service can only be understood as part of that attempt to provide for welfare from the cradle to the grave. Children's needs are the concern of many services and these share the assumptions underlying the legislation that established the welfare state. The organization of the education service following the 1944 Act was based on the same principles as applied to related public services, and any current stress in that organization can only be understood by reference to the assumptions of those who fashioned it as one part of an ambitious attempt to provide comprehensive welfare services.

The report produced by Sir William Beveridge was important because it outlined a number of welfare measures that would overcome Want, Disease, Ignorance, Squalor and Idleness. While the report is remembered mainly for its recommendation of a comprehensive system of national insurance as a protection against want, this was seen as dependent on accompanying measures to remove the remaining evil 'giants'. After 100 years of piecemeal development, a comprehensive organization for social welfare was spelled out and accepted in principle by the coalition government during the war. The development of the education service was part of this package. The details of the Education Act of 1944 were being drafted as the Beveridge Report was published. The defeat of ignorance through education was seen as one of the broader programmes of social welfare.

Three major principles were incorporated into the Beveridge Report and into the legislation that followed. First, social welfare was indivisible and needed unified social services. Beveridge comments on the social policy recommended in the report:

> The Plan for Social Security is put forward as part of a general programme of social policy. It is one part only of an attack upon five giant evils: upon the physical Want with which it is directly concerned, upon Disease which often causes that Want and brings many other troubles in its train, upon Ignorance which no democracy can afford among its citizens, upon the Squalor which arises mainly through haphazard distribution of industry and population, and upon the Idleness which destroys wealth and corrupts men, whether they are well fed or not, when they are idle.
>
> (Beveridge, 1942, p. 170)

The five evil 'giants' had to be overcome together. The relation between squalor and ignorance has been repeatedly confirmed by the research on educational attainment and social background. But the emphasis through-out the report on the need for full employment has also been confirmed. Once unemployment started to rise in the 1970s, the strains on the educa-tion service grew. By the 1980s further education and secondary schooling were being radically disturbed by the absence of work for many school leavers and by the expedient action being taken by the Manpower Services Commission to provide training and alternatives to idleness. Education cannot be divorced from the other public services because want, disease, squalor and idleness are affected by, and affect, ignorance.

Beveridge gave five reasons why social services depended on the preven-tion of mass unemployment: long-term unemployment was demoralizing; it makes it impossible to decide who is genuinely seeking work; it reduces incentives to get well enough to work; it is a basic source of human unhappiness; the cost of unemployment benefit could make the welfare state insupportable. The maintenance of full employment was seen as a condition for the effective working of the social services, including educa-tion.

A second principle incorporated into the report was the need for positive government action. This was accepted by all political parties immediately after the Second World War. There was to be disagreement over the extent of that intervention, but the principle of minimal state action, which had dominated politics for over a century, was overthrown as the welfare state was organized. This was to be achieved by cooperation between state and individual. Security was to be guaranteed, but in exchange for both service and contributions.

This strengthened role of the state is spelled out in the Education Act of 1944. Part 1, Section 1 (1) defines the duty of the Secretary of State as '. . . to promote the education of the people of England and Wales . . . and to secure the effective execution by local authorities under his control and direction . . . of national policies for providing an education service in every area'. This was a new definition of the role of central government, giving it responsibility for framing national policies and ensuring that local educa-tion authorities implemented them. The education service may be a partnership between central and local government, and the teaching profes-sion may exercise responsibility for the curriculum in schools, but the Act places the ultimate responsibility firmly with central government.

If a comprehensive organization of social services, including the educa-tion service, required positive action by government, there was still the choice between universal and selective policies. Beveridge supported universalism as a third principle whereby services would be used by everyone, regardless of status or income, on similar terms and conditions. There were to be no special conditions for sectional interests. The flat-rate contributions and benefits of the National Insurance Scheme of the 1950s, the National Health Service independent of contributions, uniform family allowance and free secondary education for all, were based on the principle that citizens should have uniform rights in social welfare and should contribute so that benefits were viewed as rights, not charity. The alternative view, wherein needs were identified among particular groups and then met by collective action, was rejected. In practice, the National Insurance Scheme, the National Health Service and the education service were never organized on a purely universal basis. Just as secondary selection ensured the continuation of inequality in education, so national assistance based on a means test was necessary because benefits under the National Insurance Scheme still left families in need of help. Family allowances never fully compensated for the difficulties faced by large families and the National Health Service could never cope with all the demands made on it. Private provision also persisted alongside all these services. Nevertheless, the principle of universalism was central to the welfare state.

Underlying this third universalist principle were three views of social welfare which were spelled out most clearly by Titmuss (1968). They were held by the middle ground in British politics and were sustained in the education service, as elsewhere, for a generation after the Second World War. First, the benefits from the social services were to be obtained as a right. Initially there were flat-rate contributions and flat-rate benefits or free services financed out of taxes. There was not to be a dole, a means test, a stigma attached to receipt. The services were to be available as a right. Education was conceived as three stages through which everyone would pass, just as free health services were to be available to all. Nothing split the post-war Labour governments more than the introduction of charges into social services, for this meant that the poor had to apply for them to be waived and that was stigmatizing.

Second, the universalist principle was supported as integrative. Benefits of right meant that all shared a service. The 'cradle to the grave' label for the welfare state summed up not only the universality of the services, but their community use. In the clinics, the primary schools, the hospitals and through pensions, the feeling of belonging would be promoted. This would extend not only to the users, but to their relation to the officials. The service offered was to be flexible, sensitive to the needs of individuals and to local communities. These were common services promoted for universal use, organized in a humane fashion and creating a sense of national unity.

Third, the welfare state was to be egalitarian and redistributive in its impact. To Titmuss, a Fabian socialist, welfare was redistribution. As economic growth created inequalities or unemployment, so social services should ensure that the poor were compensated for any disruption. Once again this applied to education as to the other services. There was to be equality of educational opportunity. Shared schooling would ensure that poor and rich alike received their chance to move into higher education and hence into high-prestige occupations. But it would also promote a fairer, more fraternal society. This fraternity was assumed to be important, not only because of the war-time spirit of the 1940s, but because of the memory of the dole, the means test, the workhouse and the poor law. The new services were to be used without shame, staffed by humane professionals in an open administration.

Writing in that spirit in the 1980s is difficult. It is a different world for all, regardless of political leaning. The feeling of community, of belonging, of togetherness, was not a dream for many during the war, and this fraternal feeling persisted afterwards; 'If for warfare, why not for welfare' captures that feeling. One wing of the Labour Party had always maintained that 'socialism is about community as well as equality' (Titmuss, 1968). The welfare state came from a demand for 'one society' without two separate nations in youth, employment, sickness or old age. Such a feeling for community was shared by many Conservatives such as Boyle, Minister of Education from 1962 to 1964. There were always those who wanted to attack the underlying causes of inequality and those who disliked social services for undermining self-help and private initiative. But for 20 years the centre supported universalism.

The strength of universalism as a principle behind social policy is that it diminishes the influence of sectional interests. It encourages fraternity. But its weaknesses appear once some sections of the society become visibly disadvantaged. An emphasis on common interests and obligations was no comfort for the Black population at the end of the 1960s or the unskilled working class at any date. From the end of the 1960s the pressure for specific policies aimed at identified social or ethnic groups weakened the universalist basis of post-war social policy.

There was another problem for universalism in educational policy. Kirp (1979) has compared American policies, with their explicit aim of reducing racial inequalities, with British inexplicitness. In Britain doing nothing, or doing good by stealth, was a deliberate policy. Blacks were not identified for positive discrimination. Indeed, after 1973 there were no national statistics on the numbers of ethnic minorities in schools. There is reluctance to identify the disadvantaged and to aim policies specifically at the alleviation of their social condition. Inexplicitness and universalism were features of educational and social policy in Britain. Both involved a reluctance to identify deprived groups and to act to improve their lot in comparison with that of others. That could stigmatize, and avoiding stigma was a funda-mental concern of Beveridge and of legislation in the 1940s and 1950s.

The hope that lay behind the post-1944 legislation also incorporated a belief in the power of good social conditions to produce good people. To Titmuss, social deviation, like crime, was a social ill, not a social problem. Provide a healthy environment and health would be restored to the body politic. This may now seem naive, but it is important for understanding how the education service in particular became vulnerable to disillusion-ment. Education was the service that could provide the right environment at impressionable ages. That feeling persists through the Plowden Report of 1967. The education service had more to lose than other public services because it contained the hopes of parents and politicians alike, who wanted to believe that schooling was not only the way to promote talent but was the road to universal betterment and community spirit. A taste of that faith can be seen in this statement from a Workers' Education Association pamphlet following the Education Act of 1944: 'For the finest war memorial we can erect will be a generation with the light of knowledge in their eyes' (Shearman, 1944).

Many chapters in this book are concerned with the events that under-mined the confidence of the founders of the welfare state. Their beliefs were too vague, too romantic, too idealized. They were concerned too much with society as a vague notion and not enough with the reality of the distribution of power between groups. The urge to reward private initiative and success proved stronger than the drive to use welfare as redistribution. 'You've never had it so good' came, ironically, at a time when the end of economic recovery was in sight. It also marked the end of the spirit of the Beveridge Report. The professionals and the officials who were employed to expand the service, turned out to be concerned with establishing their own control over their own working conditions. The drive for credentials that would enable them to preserve the client–official relation that Titmuss regretted also affected education directly. Accusations of unresponsiveness, inflated bureaucracies and restricted professionalism that were common in the

1970s, were a long way from the integration and the shared humanity that were seen as a hope of the welfare state in the 1940s.

It is too simple to see the reaction against universalism in public policy as solely government inspired. It took place under both Labour and Conservative administrations. It was preceded, and accompanied by, individual action. The urge to buy better housing, better medical care and higher pensions was not confined to a minority. The urge to provide a better education and more secure future for one's children was even stronger. Thus, just as education was the most vulnerable service because of the hopes pinned on it, so it was most open to parental manoeuvring to get the best. It is misleading to see this only in the strength of the independent schools. It was present in the maintained sector in comprehensive as well as maintained schools, in access to sixth forms and to higher education. Wealth helped, but so did a knowledge of the way the service worked. The poor remained poor while the new service class, which included professionals and administrators in the public services, strengthened the prospects of their children (Goldthorpe, 1980).

The way in which the personal and social services were being used, and their implementation by private initiatives, meant that universalism in practice was being circumvented by the enterprise of groups who knew how to use such services in the most advantageous way, and who had the money to supplement the benefits received. Those who gave political priority to attaining more equality, looked to greater selectivity in the social services to ensure that available resources were channelled to the groups which needed them most. Others argued that individual enterprise was to be valued. Private medicine and education, and tax-efficient insurance schemes flourished on one side, while positive discrimination was pressed from the other. By 1970, universalism was cracking under the squeeze. The universality of public services had also failed to remove gross geographical and social class differences in the provision of such services. General practitioners, hospital beds and good housing, were more plentiful in the South. Just as opportunities for private initiatives enable richer consumers to buy services, so staff in the public services were free to concentrate where they were needed least. This further break in universalism came in education as elsewhere (Taylor and Ayres, 1969). In a liberal society there was freedom for both the employees and clients of public services to create inequality, and after 25 years of the welfare state this was well researched.

For those who wanted not greater equality but reward for effort and excellence, the evidence on the working of the social services was disturbing. High taxation to fund flat-rate benefits and universally available services reduced incentives to work hard and save money. Health service costs rose alarmingly, but the poor still experienced more sickness and higher mortality rates. If relative poverty had persisted, despite the social security system, it was an indication of wasteful policies that were encouraging indolence. If easily identifiable groups of children from the working class and from immigrant families were failing to benefit from new schools and more teachers, it was just one symptom of a wider failure to detect and reward intelligence and industry. By the end of the 1960s, the Right as well as the Left were questioning the assumptions of the welfare state. The former was pressing for the recognition of enterprise and merit, while the latter pressed for positive discrimination to bring support to those who needed it most.

The right-wing view has been expressed mainly through the Institute of Economic Affairs, organized in 1957 and directed by Ralph Harris and Arthur Seldon. The Institute, through publications on most aspects of the welfare state, has pressed for more choice between private and state services. Its publications range from economic analyses of the social services, ways of increasing choice and getting better value for money in services such as housing and education, to surveys on public preferences in paying for such services (see, for example, Harris and Seldon, 1979). The left-wing view was clearly expressed by Richard Titmuss (1968) in *Commitment to Welfare*. The choice for social policy is not between selective and universal, but concerns the organization of universalist services that would serve as a base for positive discrimination towards those whose needs were greatest. Universal provision is necessary to ensure the involvement of all in the social services, but selective help is also required for those in need and this should also be recognized as a right not a charity.

The controversy within education was particularly acute because the evidence on the persistence of inequality of opportunity had accumulated during the 1950s and 1960s. Floud et al. (1956), Little and Westergaard (1964), Douglas (1964), the National Children's Bureau (1972) as well as the Crowther (1959), Newsom (1963) and Robbins (1963) Reports, confirmed that increased expenditure on schooling had not improved the relative chances of working-class children in obtaining places in selective schools, or access to higher education. Left-wing writers such as Benn and Simon (1970) pressed for an acceleration in the movement to fully comprehensive secondary schooling. Right-wing writers such as Cox and Dyson (1969a, b, 1970) and Cox and Boyson (1975, 1977) pressed for a return to a more traditional curriculum where the emphasis was on order and the attainment of basic skills.

In government the transition from Crosland as Secretary of State for Education between 1965 and 1967, to Mulley from 1975 to 1976, and from Boyle from 1962 to 1964 to Thatcher from 1970 to 1974, reflected the way the Labour and Conservative governments took increasingly opposed views over education as a public service. Consensus in the 1960s had been replaced by marked opposition in the 1970s. Such a separation of views occurred in every social service as the persistence of Beveridge's five giants was recognized, despite the steadily increasing share of the GNP allocated to public services. In absolute terms the population had become more affluent. But the affluent society contained within it groups whose chances of a good life remained significantly worse than the rest. Social and educational policy in the 1970s was directed at solving this persisting problem, but there was no political agreement on how this should be done. Indeed, the rediscovery of relative poverty at the end of the 1960s coincided with a polarization of political views over education as well as the other social services.

The response to the persistence of inequality of educational opportunity came in the Plowden Report of 1967 and its recommendation for positive discrimination. But this again was part of a package of measures taken to provide special help for particular groups, rather than continuing to rely on the provision of universalist services. By the end of the 1960s, concern over the accumulated evidence on the persistence of poverty from writers such as Atkinson (1969) and Abel-Smith and Townsend (1965), and organizations such as the Child Poverty Action Group, was increased by the need to provide services in those areas of the country where there had been heavy immigration from the New Commonwealth in the mid-1960s. Much of the evidence was concerned with the multiple deprivation facing families in the inner cities, where immigrants had settled in order to find work. The government's response was the Urban Programme, announced by the Prime Minister in 1968, which has continued through many changes into the 1980s.

Edwards and Batley (1978) trace the Urban Programme to the 'rediscovery of poverty' in the latter half of the 1960s and to the government's response to Powell's vision in 1968 of '. . . the River Tiber foaming with much blood. . .'. The evidence of continuing poverty and inequality within the welfare state had accumulated in services other than education. The Seebowm Report (1969) on the social services and the Milner Holland Report

(1965) on housing in London had reached similar conclusions about the persistence of relative deprivation. The Urban Programme was a response to the concern about this persistence of poverty and inequality, just as the Educational Priority Areas (EPA) projects were a response to inequality in education.

The programmes that were established spanned many social services, and included the Community Development Project, the General Improvement Areas, Housing Action Areas, Urban Aid, up to the Inner City Partnerships at the end of the 1970s. These programmes were premised on the need for positive discrimination in favour of identifiable groups who lived in poverty, rather than relying on general improvements brought about by the welfare state. This not only represented a break in the Beveridge principle of universalism but, as Jordan (1973) argued, this switch to identifying specific groups to receive extra resources, was a return to poor law principles. It might concentrate resources where they were needed most, but it would not necessarily improve the services for the poor generally. Indeed, it could lead to abandoning universal welfare provision in favour of selective aid, thus cutting public expenditure and returning the responsibility for welfare to individual enterprise.

The acceptance of positive discrimination within the education service came after the Plowden Report of 1967. But, as with the remainder of the Urban Programme, the resources employed were small, there was a danger of stigmatizing areas, schools and teachers as 'EPAs' and, even more important, of small-scale efforts at positive descrimination concealing the need for more extensive action to reduce inequality (Shipman, 1980). The identification of areas for special treatment has also been shown to be wasteful. Thus in education, Barnes and Lucas (1975) have shown how area-based projects fail to affect the majority of the poor who live in areas not identified as deprived.

It is, however, too easy to dismiss the Urban Programme and the Educational Priority Areas projects as unimportant, or as deflecting attention from more fundamental reforms that were required to affect poverty or inequality. Compared with the extra resources that go to the children of the rich as they enter the top streams in selective schools, sixth forms and higher education, the amount made available to the poor may have been derisory. The amount of positive discrimination that was possible in providing better buildings or more suitable curricula in schools in poor areas, or the extra money for teachers who taught there, was small. Nevertheless, the principle that available resources should be allocated to areas, schools or teachers where there was the greatest poverty remained the most visible policy in education across the 1970s, as it did in the other public services. Jenny Lee, discussing the purposes of the National Health Service at its 20th Anniversary Conference, said: '. . . to ensure that everybody in the country, irrespective of means, age, sex or occupation, should have equal opportunity to benefit from the best and most up-to-date medical and allied services available' (National Health Service, 1968). That could have been said about any social service.

When the Department of Education and Science recommended new policies for education, or when education committees sat down to allocate resources within county halls, positive discrimination was often in the mind of the decision-makers, but so were the thoughts of promoting increased competition, building bridges to the private sector and making parents pay. In both cases the emphasis was selective. Selectivity spread in all social services in the 1970s. In education, as elsewhere, there had been faith in investment across the board to raise standards. Building new schools, lowering pupil–teacher ratios and improving the pay, conditions and training of teachers, would raise attainment and create improved opportunities for all. But this belief was eroded by the failure of increased investment to reduce inequalities in attainment. Throughout the social services in the 1970s, it became policy to identify specific needs and allocate resources to meet them rather than investing in the hope of universal advancement.

There were costs involved in such a switch in policy. Resources for inner-city areas were no longer available for use elsewhere. While the economy was in good shape, the redistribution of resources was not too painful, for all got bigger, if unequal, shares. But the move to selectivity in the social services preceded a series of economic crises. As the 1970s progressed, even marginal redistribution meant that more spent in one area led to less in another. This was to reinforce the position of those who challenged universal social services and who pressed for less state intervention to secure more personal responsibility for welfare.

There was a final concern about the welfare state that affected the education service as well as the remaining services. Administrators, professionals, auxiliary workers, clerical and public service manual workers became powerful interest groups. By 1980 there were over one million full- and part-time employees in the education service. Every teacher was matched by a non-teaching employee. The bureaucrats, the schoolkeepers and the teachers organized to exert political pressure. The definition of service was hardly fraternal. It was a service run by experts with only a reluctant acceptance of the right of the public to a small voice in decision-making. Yet the 1944 Education Act spelled out the duty of LEAs to the community and to meeting the needs of the local population.

The welfare state replaced the free market in the provision of health, education and other services. The poor could obtain schooling or housing without the need to pay or to accept charity. The material benefits accrued. But there was no planned involvement of consumers in the running of the services or the allocation of the resources. Direct participation was not discussed as a possibility in the Beveridge Report, neither was it built into the legislation that followed. Priorities were determined by experts. When pressure for participation built up in the 1970s, it met entrenched professional opposition.

Defining the extent to which it is desirable for the state to provide services rather than allowing them to be bought out of private income, remains an important political question. The Elizabethan poor law was disputed on the same principles as national superannuation schemes are disputed today. The change has come in the level at which personal and social needs are satisfied. The provision of shelter and food concerns one period, public health and elementary education another, and the availability of transplant surgery and higher education the next. Welfare from the cradle to the grave still leaves open the debate over the level at which child benefits and death grants should be satisfied through government provision. Rising aspirations ensure the continuation of the political debate over the best way to allocate resources to secure personal and social welfare. But such resources have to be collected through taxes and many prefer to leave more provision to individual enterprise.

Rising aspirations also account for the persistence of relative poverty, low educational attainment, low standards of housing, low pensions and poor health among identifiable groups of the population. In absolute terms we are healthier, richer and better educated and housed than our grandparents. But there are still tragic cases of groups that suffer from ill health, poverty, lack of marketable skills and squalor. There is hardship among plenty and it is made less bearable by the knowledge that others are better off. In the early days, after the implementation of the Beveridge Report, it was assumed that the rush to obtain medical care, spectacles and dental treatment would die down once immediate and urgent cases were treated and that demand would then fall. But by the late 1960s, Crossman (1969), from his experience in government, confirmed the suspicion that the provision of services actually stimulated demand, rather then the demand producing the supply according to economic orthodoxy. This is all for the best. Once you know what it is like to see or hear properly, to be fit, or to have no worries about paying the rent or electricity, or about old age, you raise your sights about the quality of life you expect. The poor were aspiring to a little of the life that was taken for granted by the rich.

It is wrong to ignore the benefits that education brings. Halsey et al. (1980) have shown how the maintained schools in Britain have given formal academic schooling to large numbers of children from homes where there had been no such tradition. In 1968–1969 nearly half of all school leavers had no examination passes. Ten years later this figure had fallen to one-sixth. Halsey and his colleagues also claim that there has been a dissemination of culture through the maintained schools, not just the maintenance of a cultural monopoly by wealthier groups. But these authors also confirm the persistence of inequality. Amid a general social advance, the wealthy and the expanded numbers of civil servants and professionals who man the welfare state have maintained their position of privilege through the effective use of public services such as education, and by using private insurance, health and schooling.

The response of the political Left to this situation has been to press for genuine universalism in the provision of public services. According to Richard Titmuss, universally provided services were a necessary base to ensure that selective services could be provided as a right. To the political Right, the way forward was to give more responsibility for welfare to the individual. After the general election of 1979, the Conservative government started to move towards the opportunity state, trying to limit the scope of public services and increasing that of privately purchased services. This action was preceded by a series of cuts by the Labour government to limit the growth of public expenditure. The 1975 and 1976 White Papers on public expenditure, and the additional cuts made to satisfy the International Monetary Fund in 1976, when they were asked to loan money in the financial crisis of that year, provide the background of the change of policy since 1979. The significance of these preceding cuts for the education service is that they started in the year when the 'Great Debate' was launched by the Labour Prime Minister, James Callaghan.

Thus education has been organized within social services that have been the centre of a continuing debate over means and ends. Universalism may have been dominant from 1945 until the mid-1960s, but the meritocratic, opportunity-orientated view that came to the fore in the 1970s and 1980s also has a long history. In education, as in other social services, the different philosophies remain unreconciled. There are deep political differences between those who support universal, state-administered social services, in which all pay and all benefit, and those who prefer only a safety net provided through taxation, with individuals free to pay for their own medical, educational or social services.

These differences are visible not only between the major political parties but also within each party. The Labour Party, for example, has always had an idealist and a meritocratic wing (Barker, 1972). In the early years of this century men like Will Thorne, a member of the Social Democratic Federation and founder of the Gasworkers and General Labourers' Union, supported universalism within the newly formed Labour Party. There should be fair shares for all and in education this meant a free, national, secular education up to university entry for everyone. On the other wing of the party was Sydney Webb, a Fabian and founder of the London School of Economics, who supported a meritocracy and saw education as 'the capacity catching machine'. These differences survive today in education, as they do when Socialists or Tories or Liberals or Social Democrats consider policies for social services.

Finally, just as there are differences within, as well as between, political parties over the philosophy for social services, so there is frequently a gap between rhetoric and practice. The welfare state is criticized for reducing services to a lowest common denominator, yet it contains practices that penalize the poor and benefit the rich. Field (1981), for example, has identified tax allowances, company welfare arrangements, welfare financed from unearned income, private market welfare and 'traditional benefit' systems as ways in which the welfare state is used to sustain inequality. Each enables the rich to benefit at a price that is reduced through tax allowances. In a similar way, education can be bought, and even within the maintained sector poor children tend to leave school at the earliest opportunity, while the children of the rich stay on for the most expensive part of schooling in the sixth forms, and then enter even more costly higher education. In terms of the redistribution of resources affected by public services, the flow is still to the rich rather than to the poor. Even in the welfare state the opportunities are not taken by those whose children need them most.

When education is viewed as one public service among many, the importance of the drift away from universalism is highlighted. Until the mid-1960s it was possible to believe that increased investment in schools would lead to the implementation of the 1944 Education Act and to raised levels of attainment among all groups. Increase the resources, and the professionals would ensure that standards rose. More resources would mean a better education for all. The available evidence does not support this.

Inequality persisted in education as in all public services. By the time of the Plowden Report of 1967, it was necessary to acknowledge that the children of semi- and unskilled workers were not benefiting as were their more fortunate peers. Since then the focus has been shifted to Blacks, to girls, to children of one-parent families and to other disadvantaged groups. Pumping in extra resources did not promote universal improvement. It became necessary to be selective in allocation and to think more about the way in which resources, particularly teachers, should be used.

Evaluating education as a public service

This book describes the way in which education is organized as a public service; it also evaluates the effectiveness of that organization. In practice, no neutral description is possible. Behind the most factual versions of the government of education lie assumptions that account for the selection and presentation of the content. Here, one question is asked as the start of this evaluation. Does the organization of the education service help or hinder the achievement of the ideals of those who framed the 1944 Education Act? R. A. Butler (1944) described the bill at its second reading as the first of the government's measures of social reform. The education service is still organized on the basis of that Act. The achievement of those post-war ideals remains a tough but relevant test of that organization.

The three principles of the Beveridge Report yield the ideals that were supposed to be achieved in social services such as education. The services were to be universalistic, serving general not sectional interests. They were to be comprehensive so that none of the evil giants remained to stop the defeat of the rest. They were to be organized by the state, but in a way that did not stifle incentive, opportunity or responsibility, leaving room for the encouragement of voluntary action by individuals.

These ideals incorporate important practical questions about benefits and costs. Universalism included assumptions about equality of opportunity. Comprehensiveness meant that there should be coordination not competition between public services. The emphasis on individual responsibility alongside state intervention assumed an open relationship between those responsible within the education service and those dependent upon it. The ideals form a framework for examining effectiveness in delivering a service that has national importance and on which parents pin their hopes for their children.

Such an evaluation contains the more conventional but more restricted questions about the standards attained, cost-effectiveness and account-ability. The universalism and comprehensiveness were seen as ways of ensuring that the potential of all the population, not just the more wealthy sections, was realized. The effectiveness of the service was to be measured by the raised attainment of all social groups. But it was also to be an accountable service, treating the public who depended on it as responsible and active, not as passive recipients. By asking the questions that led to the organization of education after 1944 we not only incorporate current concerns; we can place education in the context of the satisfaction of other social needs that Beveridge saw as the condition for the fulfilment of each.

PART TWO

THE ORGANIZATION OF EDUCATION

INTRODUCTION

In Part One the focus was on the public service context within which the principles and the legal framework of the education service were established after 1944. In Part Two the capacity of the organization to deliver the service intended is examined. This is a tough test, for the service was organized to achieve liberal and comprehensive ideals at a time when these seemed reliable and realistic. Many social and economic changes since 1944 have weakened the feeling of fraternity that lay behind the establishment of the welfare state.

Chapters 2, 3 and 4 look at the government of education, its financing as one of the public services and the 'sub-government' – the array of interest groups which are consulted on a routine basis or which press their case on local and central government. These accounts are largely descriptive. This is intentional; the division of formal responsibility in the service has to be understood before the strengths and weaknesses of actual practice can be analysed. Those working relationships are examined in Part Three.

The descriptions in Part Two are based on a pluralist model of the education service, assuming that power is dispersed. A different model would be likely to alter the level at which relations were viewed and, as a consequence, the distribution of power. A partnership between central and local government on the one hand, and the teachers on the other, may be an adequate description of the way discussions are carried out in education, but it can conceal the way they serve identifiable political purposes. All the partners may support existing social relations. Another model might bring these into focus and show them to be repressive.

CHAPTER 2

THE GOVERNMENT OF EDUCATION

The legislation that created the social services in the 1940s marked the end of minimal state intervention in securing individual welfare. The state was no longer to be restricted to helping those in distress, but was to act positively to overcome want, disease, ignorance, squalor and idleness. The intention was to promote integration, a sense of community and individual responsibility, but through action by central government. The education service was organized as a national system, locally administered. Welfare was conceived as indivisible and government was given the responsibility of securing comprehensive and coherent social services.

Looking back at this policy it is easy to see the possibility of creating services in which people had little say. The rapid completion of a welfare state, particularly during or immediately after a world war, required a reversal of policies of minimal government intervention. Comprehensive social services were organized rapidly during the acute financial crisis of the post-war reconstruction period. It was a remarkable achievement, producing an efficient administration backed by an enthusiastic public.

With some 10 million persons involved in education in any one year, it is a triumph of administrative procedures that those involved need not worry about the service being delivered at the right place, by the right people, at the right time with suitable resources. But the world around education changes rapidly. The communal needs and rights that were incorporated into the Education Act of 1944 are not the same in the 1980s, although the organization has changed little. Even more important, the size of the enterprise, the organized strength of the one million people who work within it and the fluctuating balance between central and local government made it difficult to meet the hopes that were built into education as a public service in 1944.

Two aspects of the government of education form the thread through this chapter. First, it is difficult to identify not only the levers of change, but also who is pulling them. Interpretations vary from a cosy partnership (Dent, 1982) to a repressive capitalist state apparatus (Holloway and Picciotto, 1978). Some authors see the teachers forcing changes against the wishes of the public (Cox and Marks, 1982), while others see the DES working to establish the programme for change (Salter and Tapper, 1981). But one feature stands out. For all the emphasis placed on the responsibilities of the Secretary of State for Education in the 1944 Act, it is a service that is not easy to change because many parties can exert influence at the centre, in county or town halls, or in the schools and colleges. They may all play by the same rules which may support social, economic and political arrangements, but the different partners press their own, often conflicting interests and the horse-trading for better and for worse inhibits speedy unilateral action.

The second aspect is that the partners not only act as bulwarks against rapid change, but they have made it difficult for outsiders to exert influence. At any one time, one of the partners may exert a dominant influence. There may be disagreement over the agenda for debate, but rarely over the procedures for settlement. The service has not been the centre of intense political interest. There have been disputes and the courts have been involved. The partners have established working relations that have secured cooperation in running the service. But that institutionalization of procedures tends to be exclusive. The difficulty in finding levers to affect change is often due to the way agreements among the partners have created procedures that are opaque.

Central government

The assumption that the education service should have strong central government was in line with the thinking that launched the post-1945 welfare state. The 1944 Education Act makes it clear that the Secretary of State has 'the duty . . . to secure the effective execution by the local authorities under his control and direction, of the national policy for providing a varied and comprehensive educational service in every area' (Education Act 1944, Section 1). This was opposed in the country and in Parliament as it made the Minister a dictator. But the amendment in the House of Commons to remove the words 'under his control and direction' was defeated. The leader of the Liberal Party stated that it was vital that the Minister should be armed with full power and authority to force education authorities up to one common level (Dent, 1944). Thus a strong central government position was clearly intended. The Explanatory Memorandum of 1943 defended an increase in power and authority at the centre as 'a recognition of the principle that the public system of education, though administered locally, is the nation's concern, the full benefits of which should be equally available to all alike, wherever their homes may be' (Gosden, 1966). There may be claims for partnership, for freedom for LEAs and for teacher autonomy, but the legal position remains in line with the centralist assumptions behind the public services in general. There was to be positive central government intervention and it was to be exercised to promote equality.

The 1944 Education Act gives the Secretary of State the duty of promoting the education of the people of England and Wales. He or she is responsible to Parliament. These responsibilities are exercised through the DES. The Secretary of State not only has oversight of local authorities, but must take the initiative in framing national policies. However, the bulk of the Act is not concerned with spelling out these responsibilities, but with the duties of local authorities. These are not delegated to them by the Secretary of State, but are laid down in the Acts that form the legal basis of the education service. The service is organized on the assumption that the Secretary of State will not exercise detailed control and direction.

The Secretary of State does not provide schools and colleges, nor employ teachers or prescribe textbooks or curricula. He or she can try to influence by issuing circulars, by asking Her Majesty's Inspectors (HMI) to report on curricula, teaching methods and the organization of schools, and on the way things are working out on the ground. The Secretary of State can speak out on behalf of education and try to influence the direction of affairs through the media. He or she can instruct the officials in the DES to work out ways of trying to move the service in a particular direction. He or she speaks for education in the Cabinet and bids for resources. The style adopted by different Secretaries of State varies. Both Boyle and Crosland gave priority to obtaining resources for education and saw their role as Secretary of State as one of fighting its corner against the Treasury and other spending departments (Kogan, 1971). Gordon Walker, however, saw the job as one of adapting departmental bids to achieve agreement in Cabinet in line with government policies (Gordon Walker, 1969). In practice many had little time to even get to know the job. Since 1944 the average tenure of

Secretaries of State has been two years and of the last ten, six have served for less than two years.

The Secretary of State can identify areas for development and place duties on local authorities. He or she has powers under Local Government Acts to withhold grants if reasonable standards of provision are not maintained. But when these policies relate to the running of schools, the Secretary of State has to carry the local authorities with him or her, for they have the duty, under the 1944 Act, to secure the provision of the schooling and they employ the teachers. They pass decisions about school management to governors of schools through articles of government. In turn, governors leave many decisions to the teachers. The source of decisions that move the service often lies far from the Secretary of State and the DES.

There are three powerful controls exercised by the Secretary of State over educational provision. The most general of these is financial and is dealt with in Chapter 3. The second is the control over the building programme. This consists of regulations laying down standards for school buildings and limits to their cost. The DES also receives bids for school building every year. The need for the work is examined and a final list of projects is approved in line with the public expenditure agreed in advance with the Treasury. The DES does not provide the money for this building; it sanctions the loans that the local authorities have to raise.

This control over the building programme is a potent, long-term instrument when used to push a particular policy. For example, in 1974 when Prentice, the Labour Secretary of State, published Circular 4/74 requiring local authorities to produce plans for comprehensive secondary schooling, it was followed by a refusal to grant loan sanction for secondary school building that was not for a comprehensive reorganization. The building programme was being used to stop any building for grammar or secondary modern schools. Prentice argued that this was a legitimate use of loan sanctions. This is a central government control that applies in all public services. But in education it provides a powerful central control in a service where local autonomy is often seen as paramount.

The third control exercised by central government over the education service is in determining the numbers of teachers in training. The 1944 Education Act places the responsibility for ensuring that there are sufficient teachers with the Secretary of State. This gives the Secretary direct control over the number of places in the colleges of education and training establishments in the public sector. In 1977, for example, Shirley Williams published a list of 22 colleges that would have to close in order to reduce the total number of teachers in training to avoid excessive unemployment as school rolls fell during the 1980s.

These central government controls over the education service are concerned with money, buildings and teacher numbers. HMI may bring back to the DES details of the way these resources are being used to educate children and influence teachers in their schools or on in-service courses, but the Department is above all a provider of resources and not the authority on textbooks, curricula or pedagogy. An ex-Permanent Secretary at the DES saw his role as listening, reflecting, advising, explaining and administering (Pile, 1979).

In a memorandum to the Expenditure Committee of the House of Commons in 1975, the DES described its planning as 'resource orientated, being concerned with options of scale, organisation and cost, rather than educational content' (House of Commons Expenditure Committee, 1976). Later, in giving evidence to this committee, Sir William Pile, the Permanent Secretary at the DES, elaborated on this by showing that the Department did go beyond 'the sheer mechanical business of calculating costs and scale of things'. But he pointed out that the law assigns responsibility for the curriculum, apart from religious instruction, to people other than the Secretary of State. Sir Toby Weaver, giving evidence to the same committee, maintained that the system depended on those involved acting sensibly. Were this not to be the case, the Secretary of State would find some way of intervening in curriculum matters. But central government planning of the education service is essentially about resources.

Both Kogan (1978), with experience as an administrator within the DES, and Fowler (1979), an ex-Minister of State at the DES, have stressed that education has rarely been the subject of debate at Cabinet level. Educational policy interests government in the same way as it concerns planners inside the DES – only when resources are being considered. It is the need to cut expenditure that usually brings education to the attention of government, and not concern about what is being learned or how it is being taught. Kogan and Fowler also confirm the rarity of Parliamentary debate over the content of education. The refusal of the Secretary of State to answer Parliamentary questions about the curriculum of particular schools is another indicator of this paradox whereby there is responsibility to '. . . promote the education of the people. . .', but the Secretary of State does not have the legal right to determine the content of education and in the phrase first used by a Minister of Education, is not expected to enter 'the secret garden of the curriculum'. Looking back at his time as Secretary of State,

Crosland described central government's role in this way: '. . . the only influence is an indirect one that is exercised through HMIs, through DES participation in the Schools Council, and through Government sponsored research projects like the one on comprehensive education. The nearer one comes to the professional content of education, the more indirect the Minister's influence is, and I am sure this is right' (Kogan, 1971).

These limitations in the part played by the DES provided relaxed rather than positive government for 30 years after 1944. Change was introduced but over long periods of time by building up financial and legal constraints on the old arrangements while encouraging the new. With occasional hiccups the partnership held. Twenty years after the decisive step was taken by central government to complete comprehensive secondary schooling, there are still LEAs with grammar schools and one with no comprehensive schools at all. When the first break came in the indivisibility of social welfare – the rise in unemployment, particularly among the young, in the late 1970s – the education service could not respond rapidly and action was taken through the Department of Employment and the Manpower Services Commission. A balance of interests secures harmony but not pace.

The second feature of the government of education – its exclusiveness – aggravates the problem of generating momentum. The Secretary of State is responsible, through the DES, for a service that is tight-knit compared with other government departments. The DES has few executive functions, no extensive regional organization and is the smallest of the big spending government departments. There are some 3000 staff in Elizabeth House built over Waterloo Station, and these include about 500 HMIs. The partnership with the local authorities and the teachers' unions gives the DES a closed circle for consultation. It is rarely faced with sudden crises that require immediate reallocation of funds or emergency measures. Current patterns of spending can be assumed to have set the pattern for the longer term. It is easy to project the numbers of children in school at all ages up to 16, once they have arrived in the infants' schools at five. Even when economies have to be made, the debate often centres on items such as transport, school meals and milk, where savings can be made without affecting the number of teachers or the size of the classes. It has been possible for central government to concentrate on providing resources to the education service without being intimately involved in the way those resources are being used in schools or colleges to educate children.

The Organization for Economic Cooperation and Development (OECD), 1975) produced three major criticisms of the planning procedures of the

DES in 1975: it was seen as too secretive, it reacted to existing trends rather than actively considering new patterns, and it was too narrow in its view of education, ignoring the actions of other government departments and failing to consider the wider role of education in modern society. In the 1975–1976 session, the Expenditure Committee of the House of Commons took 'Policy-making in the Department of Education and Science' as its subject. Evidence given by critics of the DES confirmed the OECD view that planning just reacted to trends, particularly the relation between numbers of pupils and the buildings required. Pile and his fellow administrators from the DES did not deny this view. In a service where the local authorities allocated resources to the schools and the teachers determined the curriculum, the DES was inevitably concerned with resources. It was being criticized for restricting its role within the limits insisted on by its 'partners' in the local authorities and schools, and by the 1944 Education Act. The LEA and teachers' witnesses at the Expenditure Committee rejected criticisms about the narrow material concern of central government planning in education because they denied the right of central government to be concerned with the curriculum or the organization of individual schools. They complained of a lack of consultation by the DES, even though Pile stated that the 'door of Elizabeth House is open'. But they did not want the Department engaged in forward planning that included the relation between education and social justice or equality, or the boundaries between education and health and social security, or between education and employment. The OECD and members of Parliament might see these areas as the key to educational planning. The partners saw them as their concern, not those of central government.

The recommendations of the Expenditure Committee have not been implemented. The professed neutrality of the DES had unfortunate implications for those outside the partnership. It has given rise to the OECD accusation that the DES is secretive and its procedures closed to public scrutiny. Cuthbert (1981) has argued that the stance of neutrality is either deception or self-deception. By giving priority to providing resources and playing down its responsibilities for promoting the development of the service, the DES confirms ongoing policies and excludes alternatives that might be supported by those outside the partnership. Claiming to be politically neutral the administrators can maintain confidentiality. By concentrating on keeping things going and claiming to leave the determination of the content of education to the teachers, the DES could avoid involvement in public debate over the direction in which the service could be moved.

It is clear that the Secretary of State and the DES were on a hiding-to-nothing in this controversy over the Department's planning role in the late 1970s. By confirming its passive role, it invited accusations of dereliction of duty and of excessive secrecy. But once it began to take a more active role at the end of the decade, it was accused of conspiracy to take over powers that belonged to the teachers (Lawton, 1980). The passive position allowed local initiatives to flourish as long as the service received extra resources each year. There is, of course, no guarantee that central planning would be any more effective in adjusting the service to changed economic or demographic conditions than would the accumulation of many local decisions. There is also no evidence that the absence of a strong central government had secured local democratic decision-making. Indeed, central government intervention has often been justified as a way of securing individual and communal rights. The Education Act of 1980 gives the public access to information about schools. That has been increased by the publication of HMI reports on school inspections since 1982. Race relations and sex differentiation have been the subject of legislation. The Education Act of 1981 promised a new deal for those with learning difficulties and special needs.

Given the duty of the Secretary of State to promote the education of the people, a claim to neutrality by the DES was sure to produce anomalies in the role. The idealism at the top can be seen in Kogan's interviews with Sir Edward Boyle and Anthony Crosland on their time as Secretary of State (Kogan, 1971). It can also be seen in Kogan's interviews with chief education officers (CEOs) (Kogan and van der Eyken, 1973; Bush and Kogan, 1982). In central and local government there is a concern with education as a means to a better life for all, and particularly for the poor. Crosland emphasized social justice as a principle guiding him in his stay at the DES. Boyle, in his forward to the Newsom Report of 1963, stressed that all children should have equal opportunity to develop their talents. Both Boyle and Crosland wanted an end to the waste of talent that was built into selective secondary schooling. These two represented the middle ground of political life, carrying Beveridge principles through the 1960s.

Unfortunately, 40 years after education became a public service as part of the welfare state, gross inequalities remain. Good intentions among those who govern the service have not markedly improved the prospects of the poor (Halsey et al., 1980). It is difficult to reconcile idealism with an emphasis on keeping the service running, on sustaining agreement among the partners when the chances of the children of the poor were not being improved.

The secrecy condemned by the OECD and the House of Commons Expenditure Committee is also difficult to reconcile with idealism. The evidence on the persistence of inequality and the waste of talent has been published regularly for 30 years. If the officials that worked on the *Yellow Book* in the early 1970s were concerned with the effectiveness of the schools, confidentiality meant that the public was denied information that would have secured an informed debate. The welfare state was built on an assumption that the public would be treated as responsible. Yet, with a few honourable exceptions such as the Inner London Education Authority, many local authorities kept evidence on attainment in schools confidential, even though that information might have helped parents to avoid an inferior education for their children. When central government introduced the 1980 Education Act listing the information that should be made public by local authorities and teachers on their schools, there was an outcry from the professionals concerned. In the face of evidence that idealism was not working out in practice, restricted and confidential planning fed the suspicion that the organization of the service was not meeting the ideals incorporated into the 1944 Act that defined it. The flow of DES publications after 1975 did keep the service under the spotlight. Many of these publications opened up controversial issues, such as mixed-ability grouping. The HMI assessments of the adverse effects of cuts on the service were also published (DES, 1981b, 1982d). The DES, especially through the Assessment of Performance Unit, and HMI were keeping both the profession and the public better informed at the start of the 1980s. Reports of school inspections were being published. Central government was intervening and this was resented.

Since 1971 the DES has shown more interest in directly influencing the curriculum. The Green Paper of 1977 (DES, 1977) in particular ushered in the concept of accountability and was followed up by a number of HMI documents on the curriculum published under the generic title *Matters of Concern*; by surveys of primary (DES, 1978b), secondary (DES, 1979b) and infant schooling (DES, 1982a); and by the setting-up of the Assessment of Performance Unit. The implementation of changes in the content of education is usually left to the school authorities and to the teachers. The government uses its control of resources and legislates to secure local authority plans for developments such as comprehensive schooling, but does not determine what goes on in those schools. It can raise the school-leaving age but do no more than make suggestions for the use of the extra year. It can provide money for an expansion of nursery schooling, but leaves the possibility of using that expansion to give deprived groups a chance of keeping up with their more favoured peers to the staff. Similarly, when rising unemployment created a need for fresh approaches to the education of the 16–19 age-group, the initiatives were left to the Manpower Services Commission and the impact on the curriculum lower down the secondary schools was left to teachers to realize.

The change in the DES role can be traced back to the early 1970s. The *Yellow Book* on which Prime Minister James Callaghan based his speech at Ruskin College in 1976, had been produced within the DES earlier that year. It has never been published, although extracts were reproduced in the *Times Educational Supplement* (1976) and copies were distributed within the DES and the Schools Council. Clearly, although reluctant to take an active part in determining the curriculum of schools, officials of the DES were sufficiently concerned at developments to work on a most critical document. The launching of the Great Debate by Callaghan in 1976 meant a sudden exposure of education to public scrutiny and through the very active follow-up by HMI and the DES the service was under pressure to become concerned with curriculum matters and with the accountability of teachers to their public.

The pressure from the DES can be seen as a continuation of the historical role of central government in strengthening voluntary participation in education through legislation and financial support (Silver, 1980). It can be seen as a shift in the balance between the partners, or as an attempt by central government to give parents and employers a partnership position. It has usually been seen as a conspiracy to secure central government control over the curriculum (Lawton, 1980) or as an attempt by the DES bureaucracy to mobilize support for a service more tightly geared to the economy (Salter and Tapper, 1981). Holloway and Picciotto (1978) see it as an instrument for the repression of the working class. Yet it is also a political response to public disquiet that was detected in the early 1970s. This was the period when selective secondary schooling became an exception, freeing the primary schools from the need to prepare for 11+ testing and facing articulate middle-class parents with the prospect of having to use the comprehensive schools. By 1976, anxieties were increased by the Black Papers, the publication of *Teaching Styles and Pupil Progress* (Bennett, 1976) and the tribunal on the William Tyndale School (Auld Report, 1976). Politicians probably detected votes in this anxiety. The progressive educational coalition collapsed under the attack (Jones, 1983). The Great Debate was launched by a Labour Prime Minister – James Callaghan. Shirley

Williams, the Secretary of State who organized the debate, later became a leading Social Democrat. The debate was continued under the Conservatives into the 1980s. Such political interest is not conspiratorial or clandestine. Political action at the centre was an attempt to meet perceived public concern. Such activity also increased within local authorities. There was nothing underhand about this. Politicians acting politically are doing their job.

The local education authorities

The statutory duties of the local education authorities (LEAs) under section 7 of the 1944 Act are '. . . to contribute towards the spiritual, moral, mental and physical development of the community by securing that efficient education shall be available to meet the needs of the population of their area'. These duties reflect the idealism behind the Act. The organization of the service was to be responsive to local community needs and to the rights of citizens. There is no mention of participation. The problems in the central government role also apply to LEAs. Community and individual interests were to be served by strong action in government. But in practice LEAs may have only limited capacity for influencing education in schools, and the processes of decision-making in town and county halls are rarely open to public scrutiny or influence.

The LEAs still carry two important responsibilities for meeting communal needs. First, as with all local government, the LEAs are essential to local democracy. Locally administered services are under the ultimate control of elected members who are close to the communities which elected them. They bring local knowledge and interests into government. Second, LEAs protect local diversity against national pressures for standard services. In education the model of a 'national service locally administered' is defended because it encompasses ideals such as equality of opportunity (Brighouse, 1979). Local variations in provisions and practice are necessary to obtain different opportunities in very different localities. That is the advantage of local authority provision: it secures the chance of making the spiritual, moral, mental and physical development suitable to local conditions and responsive to local demands.

The bulk of the 1944 Education Act is devoted to spelling out the way in which the national service should be locally administered. The LEAs build and maintain the county schools and the one-third of schools provided by voluntary, usually religious bodies. The LEAs usually appoint and always pay the teachers. They allocate resources to the schools. Over the years these local authorities have often developed distinctive styles of administration and forms of school organization. Cross a local government boundary and you may find different ages of transfer between schools, whether from primary to secondary, primary to middle or middle to secondary. There are sixth forms in schools, consortia of schools, tertiary and sixth-form colleges. Some LEAs pioneered comprehensive secondary schooling, while others doggedly fought for the survival of their grammar schools.

The Local Government Act of 1972 reduced the number of local authorities in England and Wales from 146 to 104. The elected councils of these authorities deal with all matters of local government. But there has to be an education committee. This committee appoints a number of sub-committees for sectors such as schools, further education and special education. These have a regular cycle of meetings to develop policies, bid for resources, deal with problems and receive reports on the working of the service from administrators and inspectors or advisors. At meetings of these sub-committees and of the education committee itself, politicians debate and make decisions. Officers attend, advise and answer questions. But the final decisions are taken by the political members, however influential officers may be in advance. Committees may include representatives of teachers' professional associations and other co-opted experts, but there is always a majority of elected members. Behind these public committees there will be policy committees and party groups where the lines to be pursued will be worked out in advance.

The chairman of the education committee usually joins the chairmen of other major committees of the local authority on a policy and resources or a general purposes committee, which has the tasks of coordinating policies and allocating resources within the authority as a whole. These committees contain the key political members and can exercise power through their control over funding. Local government reorganization in 1972 speeded up the establishment of powerful policy committees which control finances and prepare budgets. This change has meant that the education committee is now more limited in the freedom it can exercise in developing the service as the case of other services is pressed. But there still has to be an education committee and that was an important victory for the service during the reorganization of local government.

The chief education officer (CEO) or director of education serves as head of the salaried officers of the local education authority. These are usually organized into branches corresponding to the sub-committees of the education committee, so that the chairman of each sub-committee and the assistant education officer, who heads the branch, can work together. Once again there is a great variety in the way the chief education officer and his officers carry out their work. Some, like Clegg in the old West Riding of Yorkshire, seem to have exercised considerable influence over policy. But such influence was probably curtailed in the 1970s. First, local government reorganization in the 1970s brought the chief education officer into a corporate management team under the chief executive of the authority. The power of the education officer was probably reduced. Day-to-day responsibility for the education service was liable to be fragmented as management responsibilities in the council were redistributed.

The most disturbing case came with the resignation of Williams, Chief Education Officer of Avon, in 1976. Williams reports that 'The management of the education service is fragmented between so many committees and administrative departments of the council that there is no united or effective direction of it' (Bush and Kogan, 1982). At the other extreme there are LEAs in which corporate management has had little impact. But Bush and Kogan point to falling rolls, financial stringency and reduced certainty about the place of education as a force for good, as further factors facing the CEOs in 1980 compared with those interviewed in 1972. The CEOs no longer felt secure at the centre of a web of relationships. Within county and town halls, within central government and within the governing bodies of schools, which enjoyed increased independence, there were pressures reducing the predictability and certainty in the education officers' positions.

The second factor was that in many authorities there has also been a tendency for local politics to consolidate along national party lines. Since reorganization in 1974, party political control seems to have increased (Jennings, 1977). Simultaneously the views of the two major parties on secondary education in particular diverged. This politicization of LEAs put the officers under closer scrutiny from politicians at the same time that they were subject to corporate management, hence restricting their freedom of action. It is dangerous to generalize. The experience of the London boroughs or of Manchester may have differed widely from that in many shire counties. But in all LEAs the final masters are the politicians and they are elected to take the decisions. There should be no surprise if they act politically in order to exercise power. Academics are fond of concluding extensive analyses with a surprised statement of the political nature of educational decisions. Yet that is what politicians are expected and expect to do.

The political differences within local authorities can exist within, as well as between, political parties. Within a Labour group in particular there is liable to be a left wing, usually a young group, conflicting with experienced seniors. The debates here are likely to be fought out in private, are often bitter, and concern principles and their consequences for schooling which can be more contrasting than those between different political parties. In 1981, local government elections brought many of these differences into the open as more radical groups took over committees from their middle-of-the-road colleagues. Such conflicts are a persisting feature where there is party political control in local government and where party groups decide policies before committees meet.

The internal disputes within LEAs only rarely disturb the smooth running of the service. Schools are staffed, funded and repaired, cleaned, supported and advised in predictable ways year after year. Indeed, the investment in buildings, in staff, in procedures and support services establishes a pattern that can usually only be changed at the margin. The financial reasons for this are described in Chapter 3. But there are also political checks and balances. Chief education officers listen to their political masters, but also to the organized teachers. They receive feedback from the schools, from advisors or inspectors. They can caution either politicians or professionals by reference to the other. A further check on freedom of action comes from parents and the various pressure groups that press diverse interests on politicians, teachers and officers. Finally, LEAs operate within the law and in continual relation with central government. They have responsibility for the everyday working of maintained schools and colleges. But the form-filling and the telephone calls and the meetings between the DES and LEAs act as an ongoing constraint, for legal and financial obligations have to be satisfied.

Despite the strength of these constraints there is local variety in both the organization of schooling and in the way resources are allocated to schools. As spending was constrained in the 1980s, the differences between the LEAs widened. The Inner London Education Authority estimated the cost per child in primary school as £1025 and in secondary school as £1427 in 1982–1983. Newham, with more non-white children and children born abroad, more in low socioeconomic groups, more in poor housing and more in large families, planned to spend £824 and £1124 respectively. The figures for Lancashire were £561 and £842 (Chartered Institute of Public Finance and Accountancy, 1982). Spending on books and teaching materials was £38 per child in ILEA primary schools and £69 in secondary schools. In

Newham it was £23 and £41, and in Lancashire £14 and £28, respectively. This confirmed earlier evidence (Taylor and Ayres, 1969; Byrne et al., 1975) of wide variations in provision, which were not necessarily related to the social disadvantages faced by different LEAs.

Where then does this diversity in provision leave the claim that local government in education secures the chance of meeting local community needs? Does it enable local democracy to flourish and to feed local views into the administration of the service? In the key area of equality of opportunity the variations do not support these claims. The high-spending LEAs are not necessarily those facing most social deprivation. Yet, on the positive side there have been striking local innovations. The reorganization of secondary schooling on comprehensive lines came from within LEAs in advance of, even despite opposition from, central government. Above all, the alternatives to local government are unpromising. A national service devolved to local boards, as with the provision of gas, electricity or water, would be very unlikely to be responsive to communal needs as sensitive as those spiritual, moral, mental and physical aspects spelled out in the 1944 Education Act. Democratic participation is at least possible under local government. The key lies in the responsiveness of local politicians, professionals and education officers to local interests. That is the subject of Part Three of this book.

There are similarities between the central and local government of education when the capacity for exerting pressure for change is examined. The balance of interests between the influential parties may be even more marked at local level. The organized teachers may have been excluded from some central government decision-making in the 1980s but their cooperation has still to be obtained at the local level. There have, for example, been successful union actions to stop cuts in services by LEAs. Within county or town halls, formal and informal discussions and committees of politicians, administrators and teachers' union representatives ensure that professional views are heard. Much of the bargaining power of teachers may have been lost when they are in surplus, but they still determine what goes on in their schools. From the outside it is difficult to get into the local authority decision-making network, or even to get a clear picture of it. Pre-meetings, senior member groups, policy sub-committees and regular contacts by phone, at formal gatherings and informal events all serve to exclude outsiders.

This balance of insider interests also controls the scope of any one party to act positively. Many interests have to be squared and all the groups involved have 'constituencies' to be consulted. Politicians judge the response of their local electorate. Education officers assess the impact on the administration, on the response of the DES, the legal position and the financial implications. Union secretaries gauge the views of their members. All have an appreciation of public responses. Even if there is agreement on a way forward, the implementation of the agreed policy is liable to be unpredictable. From senior to junior, administrators will adjust the action required. Inspectors and advisors will interpret it. Teachers will adapt it to their own particular school circumstances. There is a strength in this adaptation to local conditions; it facilitates small-scale innovation. But the balance of interests and the scope for adaptation make it very difficult to get rapid change if external conditions make this essential.

In the description of central–local government relations which follows there are many examples of the anxiety that LEAs are under threat. The 1960s saw the LEAs delivering a service, receiving increasing resources and governed by familiar partnerships with central government, with the organized teachers, and represented on quangos such as the Schools Council, which was organized on partnership lines. The 1980s are less cosy, yet the local initiatives continue. Indeed, Brighouse and Hainsworth (1983), both chief education officers, have argued that partnership, with LEAs leading local professionals and listening to local communities, is the only viable system. Local government remains responsible for running the schools and colleges and for developing them to meet communal needs.

Relations between the central and local government of education

With the education service taking over half of the spending of local authorities, it is inevitable that it will be hit hard as central government tries to align expenditure on the public services to the state of the economy. While resources are plentiful, local authorities can be left to innovate. With contraction, attempts to limit local spending hit the education service hard because it is the biggest local spender. There has always been tension between central government and local authorities, even when the money available was increasing year by year. Nor were local authorities necessarily the weaker party. Many took and sustained an independent line on comprehensivization (James, 1980). The Secretary of State has only the powers that an Act of Parliament bestows, and interpretations of them in the courts can often favour local authorities. Thus Tameside's decision to restore selection for secondary schooling in 1976 was upheld in the courts because the authority was not judged to have acted unreasonably. Fifteen years after Circular 10/65 requested LEAs to submit plans for comprehensive reorganization within one year, there were still authorities which had not reorganized.

In retrospect, the end of the freedom of LEAs to push ahead with their own policies was signalled by Circular 10/65, despite its lack of bite. Once the economic recession deepened in the late 1970s, LEA dependence on economy-minded central governments ensured that local freedom would be restricted. Fiske (1980b) and Kogan (1978) date the end of political consensus over education to the mid-1960s. Hunter (1983) gives 1974 as the watershed for education. Pattison (1979), looking back at the opposition of the London Borough of Sutton to the DES in the 1960s and 1970s, concluded that a determined LEA could resist successfully. Legislation and financial penalties could finally stop an LEA developing a local service out of line with central government wishes. But towards the end of the 1970s the power of central government to overcome resolute local resistance was limited. In the 1980s, however, CEOs such as Fiske (1980b) and Tomlinson (1981) were raising the alarm over a rapid shift of power to the centre, generated largely through financial controls. But the Secretary of State also rejected LEA plans for the reorganization of secondary schooling in Manchester and Croydon in the early 1980s and was using his powers to increase central control. In the late 1970s, the Social Science Research Council set up a panel which funded research and reviews of the literature in this area. In 1981, the Society of Education Officers was so concerned that it appointed a working party and commissioned a special paper (Bush, 1982). These concerns followed a series of official reports and committees on the structure of local government. Bush lists 42 books, articles and reports on the topic of central–local relations published between 1974 and 1982.

The advantages of a 'national system locally administered' can be seen in initiatives taken, especially where massive capital for building was not required. The development of middle schools, the Leicestershire scheme for secondary reorganization, the use of tertiary colleges, are examples of local initiatives. LEAs such as Coventry pioneered comprehensive schooling before government action in 1965, and new patterns of education for the under-19 group with mass unemployment in the 1980s. These local initiatives involved ideas and political will, as well as bricks and teachers. The advantage of not having a fixed location for control over the education service is that these ideas percolate upwards and along as well as downwards. A development in one school can be spread to neighbouring schools by local advisors or by being adopted as a policy for development within the LEA. Her Majesty's Inspectors can take the ideas back to the DES. Boyle, looking back at his days as Minister of Education, saw this as the justification for the concept of partnership between central and local government. Without it, local initiatives would be restricted. But the benefits of local enterprise over the costs of variations between local authorities depend on that enterprise being sustained. It is not necessarily beneficial to limit central government influence to providing resources and advice. If local authorities are unable to respond to a crisis such as massive juvenile unemployment, central government action might be necessary. Adapting the service during a period of contraction meant squeezing the savings out of falling school rolls; this course of action was limited unless teachers were to be sacked. Once local adaptation could not match local changes in employment, the pressure on central government to intervene built up. In the 1980s that adaptation was organized from the centre by the Manpower Services Commission, usually bypassing the LEAs.

This division of responsibility left the CEOs free to develop local schooling in a distinctive way (Kogan and van der Eyken, 1973). This was in the light of broad national policies. Each local authority was developing a distinctive form of secondary schooling, but all were moving slowly to the ending of rigid early selection. The CEOs did not feel inhibited by central pressure. They could develop in their own way and encourage the staffs of schools to innovate. But they were aware of the direction of national policies through the advocacy of the Minister. Crosland saw the task of the Minister as building up morale and impetus in the service (Kogan, 1971). He saw that teachers and local authorities needed to know the direction in which the government wanted the service to move. His job was to use the press, the conferences, Parliament and all the platforms available to spread the feeling that things were moving. The CEOs supported this view of the Minister's role; they did not want a weak Minister or one that was passive. Within broad policies being pushed from the centre, they could develop their own local response. One of those interviewed stated that they carried 'the thrust of innovation'. This is not incompatible with momentum generated from a strong Secretary of State. Knowing the direction of national policies helped in planning distinctive local services. At the start of the 1970s, national and local interests were still compatible.

The change in this gentle relationship by the end of the 1970s, with the LEAs steadily building local services under a persuasive, but benign, central government, is summarized by Fiske, then the CEO for Manchester, who stressed the powerlessness of the LEAs (Fiske, 1980b). A situation had developed in which power had been so dispersed that the centre might have to be strengthened by legislation in order to restore accountability in decision-making. It would be better to increase central government control over the service than to face LEAs with responsibilities which they had no power to implement. Tomlinson (1981) similarly diagnosed a situation where effective local planning was the casualty, but he recommended a counter-attack rather than an acceptance of greater central government power. As Chairman of the Schools Council, as well as CEO for Cheshire, he concentrated on the increase of central government influence rather than the lack of power in local government. That influence had to be countered by a united front of LEAs and teachers, gaining the support of parents to strike back at central government. An ex-president of the Society of Education Officers and a former CEO summed it up as 'too tough at the top' of an LEA as the strains piled up in the 1970s (Cooke, 1980).

The shift in the position of CEOs has been illustrated in the contrast between those CEOs interviewed in the early 1970s (Kogan and van der Eyken, 1973) and those interviewed at the end of the decade (Bush and Kogan, 1982). The vigorous political control and the reorganization of local government, which brought CEOs into corporate management teams, were, by the end of the 1970s, seen as causing their authority to be undermined. To Kogan, the end of the consensus over education increased the power of local politicians facing unrest among reluctant ratepayers. Similarly, Burgess (1982) maintains that not only has the Secretary of State for Education come to claim to know best in matters that should not be his concern, but also he has allowed power over education to be centralized in the hands of the Secretary of State for Employment.

The roots of this concern with reduced local freedom through financial stringency, stretch beyond the education service and have a long history. The debate is over money that should go to the public sector and how it should be allocated within that sector, given the state of the economy. Successive Labour and Conservative governments decided to limit their public sector growth at the end of the 1970s, and as a big spender education became the prime target. But this alignment of public services to economic activity is not new. The Geddes 'axe', wielded to cut educational and other public spending in the early 1920s, is only the best remembered because teachers' salaries were cut. For 150 years central government has looked anxiously at spending on maintained education in relation to the economy. It has also been concerned with the consistency of local provision (Silver,

1980). There are very different standards in different local authorities (Taylor and Ayres, 1969; Byrne, 1974; Byrne et al., 1975). Between schools within homogeneous groupings in the same LEA, often twice as much was being spent per pupil in one secondary school as in another, and up to six times as much between primary schools (Hough, 1981).

The decisions about the allocation of resources to education, to different LEAs, and from there to schools are political. The problem in the 1980s was that the cuts in local authority expenditure stretched back to 1975. Between then and 1981, local expenditure fell by 21 percent, while central government expenditure increased by 8 percent (Association of County Councils, 1982). Much of the difference is accounted for by decreased capital expenditure within education as rolls fell and new building was not needed, but as the screw was tightened further, many believed that the only solution lay in central government taking over local responsibilities as LEAs could no longer meet them. If such centralization was the only solution, then the obvious target would be the salaries of teachers, which accounted for most of the money spent by local authorities.

This situation in the 1980s may be just another correction in the local–central balance of power. Ranson (1981) has outlined three shifts in this location of power since 1945. Throughout the 1950s, central government gave a strong lead in education, continuing the pre-war tradition of elaborate codes of guidance and using specific grants that could be audited easily to check that expenditure went where central government intended. In the financial climate of the 1960s and early 1970s, LEAs gained power at the expense of the centre, while teachers established their claim to control the curriculum. Thus the shift that followed in the late 1970s can be seen as a restoration of the balance rather than a new development. More profound in its implication was the shift in attitude towards public services in general. Selectivity and payment in the provision of services, support for private schools, medicine and insurance, and the emphasis on individual rather than collective responsibility were signals of a new departure.

It is difficult to distinguish direct political influence from the consequences of economic action. Looking at the legislation there is a case that central government was continuing the policy of limiting excessive variations in provision. The Rate Support Grant had encouraged diversity. The new Block Grant from 1981, with grant-related expenditure calculated centrally and serving as a norm towards which high- and low-spending authorities can be pressed, continued the historical policy of ensuring consistency. It is certainly likely to support increased expenditure among 'under-spending' authorities (Crispin, 1980). Similarly, the Education Act of 1980 altered the balance of power by giving parents more information about schools and more say on some governing bodies. But from the local authority view these are minor influences compared with the effects of financial constraints.

There are also indirect consequences of financial cuts that force decision-making towards the centre. First, there are decisions that can no longer be made within schools by headteachers and staff. As school rolls fall, staff are not replaced as they leave. If there are no replacements, the curriculum can only be preserved if there is local authority action. A school could lose all its mathematics teachers and still have to lose more staff. The decision to redeploy has to be made by the LEA. As recruitment may not be possible there has to be movement of staff to save key areas of the curriculum. Any new appointments to the authority are used to maintain a balance of staff across all schools so that there are enough specialist staff in short supply to preserve the basic curriculum of the schools. Thus staffing by a curriculum worked out in town or county halls replaces the system of appointments to fill vacancies as they occur in schools. To achieve this many LEAs have completed surveys of the staffing of their secondary schools. The appointment, deployment, promotion and in-service training of teachers is centralized, as is curriculum planning. The teachers may be involved in the discussions over the parts of the curriculum that are essential and over the procedures for redeployment, but the decision-making has moved away from schools. Sayer (1980) has pointed out that LEAs are increasingly compelled to treat teachers as personnel, manpower or a global teaching force and to intervene in the determination of conditions of service. Further, information in HMI surveys has enabled individual LEAs to see how their standards match against national ones (DES 1978b, 1979b).

Established procedures involving the LEAs are also pushed towards the centre. There is no point in LEA and teacher representatives agreeing on the level of teachers' salaries if the Treasury has decided in advance that public sector wage settlements are to be fixed at a lower level. Once again the necessary information is often not available to local authorities and to the teachers' unions. During expansion, decisions can be made locally because the extra resources will be available. During contraction, only central government can find those resources.

Fowler (1979) has described this situation as 'disjointed decrementalism'. Options for actions shrink and all that is possible is to prune away bits here to save pieces there. But LEAs have statutory obligations. They cannot prune transport, heating or the upkeep of buildings very far before running foul of Health and Safety at Work regulations. They have to provide student grants. Their moral obligations towards handicapped children, careers education and English as a Second Language teaching reinforce their legal commitments. The ability to prune in order to obtain savings is short-lived. It is in any case a solution for no-growth, level funding, but not for decreasing expenditure year after year. Parliament has to take action to release LEAs from statutory obligations such as the provision of subsidized meals. Thereafter further legislation will be needed to free resources. Thus power tends to flow towards the centre. Schools cannot cope with reduced capitation and the need to lose staff, and refer back to county hall. LEAs cannot maintain their legal and moral obligations and refer to central government. If central government maintains the pressure for more economies, no 'disjointed decrementalism' will suffice. Class sizes, the range of subjects offered and the existence of many schools come under threat.

The economic stringency that makes it difficult for decisions to be taken in schools or in county or town halls reinforces any political moves to strengthen the hand of central government. The lack of control over what went on in schools was a political issue by the mid-1970s. This concern was expressed in the Green Paper of 1977 which was the government's response to the Great Debate. There was substance in this concern. In 1979 the government published *Local Authority Arrangements for the School Curriculum* (DES, 1979a). This was based on answers from LEAs to Circular 14/77. While the bulk of the information on the school curriculum is of doubtful value, the sections on the information available to LEAs showed a remarkable ignorance. Legally the LEAs were responsible for the curriculum, yet many seemed to have little information on it and even stated they did not require any. Once secondary school rolls began to fall in the 1980s they had to acquire this information very quickly to be able to help schools to obtain or maintain the specialist staff required. But the position at the end of the 1970s was unsatisfactory and central government pressure to ensure that LEAs were in a position to exercise their responsibilities was understandable.

The way the Secretary of State has increased central influence has, however, been unfortunate. As LEAs tried to reorganize in order to cope with falling school rolls, they faced the prospect of plans being rejected, as in Manchester and Croydon. Costs were increased by the need to introduce new plans and to cope with the delay in finding a solution. Hunter (1983)

couples this increase in central government control with support for training rather than education, as defined by the Manpower Services Commission, and with restriction of entry into higher education as signs of central
government restriction on the freedom of LEAs.

Over the years since 1944, central government influence may have
increased. But a strong central state was recommended in the Beveridge
Report and was incorporated into the 1944 Education Act. Up to the
mid-1970s the absence of a single power centre enabled local initiatives to be
taken while central government still had a hand on the reins. Teachers had
been able to experiment in modest ways within the constraints imposed by
public examinations. As contraction replaced expansion, more decisions
were forced back to county or town halls, or to central government. Some of
that ebbing to the centre may have been deliberate policy. Much was the
incidental result of contraction. It still left most procedures diffused. That
diffusion not only avoided dominance by central or local government, or by
the teachers, but it continued to make it difficult to affect rapid changes.
The organization of education, through its diffusion, has been resistant to
rapid change.

The 1944 Act established the legal basis for an expanded service. It now
spends over £10 billion a year. The service is delivered efficiently. The
balance in the partnership, the diversity of represented interests and local
government democracy avoid both domination by the centre and excessive
local variation. Scope is secured for innovation in schools and colleges. The
cost is in the inertia built up. The service is difficult to drive in a new
direction or at a faster pace. Nor does the diversity guarantee that all
interests are represented. The momentum generated may result in efficient
delivery, but the result may still be to benefit sectional interests. Certainly
the poor have not benefited as was anticipated in the 1940s. Now it is
increasingly difficult to shift the service, for the resources invested have
created a pattern of delivery that is hard to change. Checks and balances
limit dictatorship by central government, but they also inhibit essential
adaptation as the world outside education changes. The words of the 1943
Explanatory Memoranda make clear the assumptions behind the 1944
Education Act, which remains the legal basis of the service. Central government was to have power because it was necessary to secure that the full
benefits of the public system of education should be available to all alike,
'wherever their homes may be' (Gosden, 1966).

CHAPTER 3

THE FINANCE OF EDUCATION

The ease with which adaptation and development can be organized within education during expansive periods, and the loss of momentum upon contraction, are partly the consequence of the diffusion of influence among central and local government, the teaching profession and the interests that these serve. But a major factor in inhibiting adaptation to changing demands arises from the structure of finance within the education service. This is not just the direct result of shortages in money. It arises both from the position of education within the public services and from the allocation of resources within the service. These financial constraints are the subject of this chapter.

Eight factors make it difficult for the education service to escape the full rigour of scrutiny for economies and to retain the scope for adaptation and development. First, education is involved in the difficulties faced by successive governments in funding public services from a weak economy. Second, it competes for available resources with other services both at Cabinet and local government level. Third, it has been hard hit by attempts to control government spending. Fourth, education is very expensive and consequently is scrutinized closely as a major item of public expenditure. Fifth, education has to obtain its resources in competition not only with other central and local services, but with competing sectors within the service itself. Sixth, the weight of previous commitments largely determines future developments and makes anything bar marginal changes unlikely. Seventh, the service is labour intensive and any flexibility has to be obtained by changes in the budget for teachers. Eighth, the difficulties during contraction are very different in central government, county or town halls, or in the schools and colleges.

There is an obvious connection between the wealth produced in a nation and the level of material wants that can be satisfied. Two hundred years ago Britain could not have supported any advanced social services. Today, the debate is over the difficulty of supporting inflation-proofed pensions. In all societies, at all levels of development, decisions have to be made about the distribution of wealth and welfare. The resources received by a school are dependent on numerous decisions in government departments, in Cabinet and in county halls. Political and financial decisions are inseparable. Decisions affecting tax levels, defence, social services or overseas aid are relevant to the resources claimed by and allocated to education. Because it is one among many public services it is affected by the problem common to all mixed economies, that of attaining a balance between expenditure in the private and public sectors. Because it is one of the most expensive services, education is often caught in the ebb and flow through which governments alter that balance.

Paying for public services in a weak economy

The rising trend of expenditure on services provided by central and local government is clear throughout the twentieth century. Taken as a percentage of Gross National Product it rose from about 9 percent in 1890 (Peacock and Wiseman, 1961) to about 58 percent in 1975. It is wise to be wary of such figures. There are many very different definitions of 'public spending'. The definition used here includes all current and capital payments, including transfers such as social security benefits. Thus expenditure on goods and services alone takes under one-half of the total spending by government. This figure is also 'at factor cost', excluding indirect taxes and adding in subsidies. Using market prices, and including indirect taxes but excluding subsidies, the figure for 1975 drops to around 50 percent. The important point is that on the same definition there has been a rise during this century on the amount spent by government from under 10 to over 50 percent. Putting it the other way round, the proportion of the national cake spent through the market by firms and individuals fell from 90 to under 50 percent. In real terms the United Kingdom GNP in 1975 was about three times as large as in 1890. With such growth there could still be private affluence with less public squalor. The ease with which governments can increase public expenditure depends on a healthy economy.

Throughout the post-war period in Britain, the organization of the welfare state came with an often ailing economy. The series of crises separated by periods of growth has been justifiably called the 'stop–go' economy. As early as 1958 Thorneycroft resigned from the Conservative government over the level of public spending. Since then, alongside the concern over the balance of payments, the level of the pound sterling and inflation, there has been anxiety over the level of public expenditure. The 'stop–go' in public expenditure has not been the responsibility of any one political party when in power. In the late 1960s there was a sharp rise in government spending under the Wilson Labour government, but in 1968 Jenkins introduced cuts and proposed limited future growth. The Heath Conservative government of 1970 was determined to make cuts in public services, but by 1971 major increases in government spending were planned.

The pattern was now repeated in even more dramatic fashion. In 1973 further public spending cuts were introduced. Later in the year, after the massive oil price rise in October and the three-day week, further cuts were announced. The new Wilson government which came into office in 1974 agreed to heavy cuts in 1976 as a condition of a loan from the International Monetary Fund. Three times in 1976 there were announcements of more cuts in public spending. The new Conservative government, elected in 1979, cut further. However, the succession of cuts was more an attempt to limit growth in public spending than to reduce it. Beneath the cries of anguish over the harshness of Healey and the first years of Howe, lay the steady growth in the proportion of available resources which continued going into the public as distinct from the private sector. From 1979 to 1983 the proportion of the GNP going to public spending continued to increase. At the end of the 1970s Labour as well as Conservative politicians were concerned that the trend should be checked, for the percentage going to the public sector, having fallen during the 1950s, rose in the 1960s from 42 to 50 percent and was still accelerating. In a stagnating economy, with rising inflation and a level of investment in the productive sector of the economy that was below that of Britain's competitors, the resources going to social services were bound to be scrutinized critically.

The dilemma of government is that there are many pressures for an increase in public spending, particularly on social services, making it politically risky to attempt cutbacks. The Conservative government at the end of the 1950s was unpopular after it had cut public expenditure. The decision to reverse this policy had led to the resignation of Thorneycroft. In 1961, a Treasury committee under Lord Plowden had recommended that public expenditure should never be undertaken without regard to the state of the economy, and that there should be planning ahead on a five-year basis whereby the government would determine the total level of public expenditure in line with economic activity. Individual government departments would then compete for their share. This system was finally adopted with the creation of the Public Expenditure Survey Committee (PESC). Because the rate of economic growth was consistently overestimated, the adoption of this forward planning coincided with a decade of very rapid growth in public expenditure.

There are four ways in which the money for public spending can be raised. About three-quarters comes from taxation; 90 percent of this is raised by central government, the rest come from local rates. By far the biggest charge on rates is the payment of teachers and the education service is visibly the big spender among local authority services. In practice over one-half of the money for local government is provided by a grant from central government and this money, although calculated after the Cabinet has considered bids from all the spending departments, is not earmarked and can, in theory, be allocated to any services within local government as each council decides.

The second way of raising money to pay for public services is to charge for them as they are used. The money raised in this way is, however, small. For example, charges made for health and personal social services in the mid-1970s accounted for only 2 percent of the total cost. The biggest single contributor is rents from council housing. However, the scope for charges is small, since most services have been designed to be free. They would need to be reorganized in order to facilitate payments for services and the collection is itself costly. National Insurance contributions are taxes not charges, as they are compulsory.

With the surge in spending on public services from the mid-1960s to the mid-1970s governments were faced with the problem that public spending exceeded the revenue available from taxation and charges. Yet raising taxation further would have been politically unpopular and might have inhibited effort in the private sector of the economy. To cover the gap between government income and expenditure, the government borrowed money. It has always done this to finance capital projects, but in the 1970s the public sector borrowing requirement, mostly met by selling gilt-edged securities to the public, rose to around £7000 million in 1976. This had risen to £13,500 million by 1980. This produced two difficulties. First, this borrowing was expensive and the national debt was increased, thus laying up interest payments for the future. Second, the government sold securities to obtain private savings, often through insurance companies, by keeping the rate of interest it offered high. Thus heavy borrowing meant heavy interest on money borrowed by industry. Both Healey for the Labour government, and Howe for the Conservatives in the late 1970s, attempted to reduce this growth in public borrowing to take the strain off the private sector.

The remaining way open to the government to bridge the gap between spending and income is to create credit for itself. This avoids the politically unpopular steps of raising charges or taxes, and avoids too much competition for borrowed money between government and private industry, thus restricting rises in interest rates. The government can expand the money supply by printing Treasury bills and selling them to the banks. This method is used to ensure a smooth supply of funds for government spending when tax receipts come in unevenly. But at a time when prices were already rising and production stagnating, this creation of money led to further inflation. By the end of the 1970s this method of financing government expenditure had been rejected by the Conservative Party. On regaining office in 1979 the Thatcher government began to cut back borrowing to finance public expenditure and adopted a monetarist policy aimed at severely limiting the creation of new money to finance the gap between income and expenditure. To achieve this there were cuts in public expenditure on top of those introduced by the preceding Labour government. Both governments attempted to limit their own spending. Both were trying to reduce direct taxation on incomes. Both were committed to reducing the rate of inflation, with the limits on credit creation that this necessitated. There were very different philosophies behind the steps taken by each; the balance between the steps taken differed. But there was agreement that public spending had to be aligned to economic activity. Following a decade during which public spending had exceeded growth, there had to be some cutting back.

Competition between services for resources

A few public services such as sanitation can be easily judged for effectiveness, but most have no easily definable criteria of success. Furthermore, improving absolute standards of provision will not necessarily improve the relative position of some sections of the population. However good the service provided, some groups will always be worse off than others. These groups can exert political pressure and are the subject of public concern. The provision of services shows people what they have been missing and their aspirations justifiably rise. But the satisfaction of the rising demand for public services also depends on the strength of the economy. Some redistribution of the good things of life can be affected by collective action under a socialist government, but in Britain a majority seem to prefer the promise of a higher standard of living with inequality under capitalism, to the promise of equal shares through a centrally planned economy. Given this political choice, governments have to organize first the allocation of available resources between the public and private sectors of the economy, and after that between the different public services. At local government level corporate government involves similar decisions over the allocation of resources to competing services.

When the competition between services such as education and health, social security and housing is considered, the late 1960s once again can be seen as the critical years for the welfare state. Before then the run-down in expenditure on defence balanced the rise in public spending. Between 1955 and 1970 defence expenditure was reduced from 9 to less than 6 percent of the GNP. Thereafter further cuts were politically controversial. Consequently, just as social services spending was accelerating there was no scope for further compensating savings on defence. After 1979 defence expenditure was deliberately increased in a sickly economy, thus squeezing the other services harder.

Competition for funds was built into the way the different social services grew between 1965 and 1975. The rapid rise in the proportion going to education was partly the consequence of rising numbers in schools, particularly from 1960 to 1975. But this was also the time when the number of people over 65 was rising, yet the proportional increase in spending on the health services was modest, particularly as the fastest growing age-group was the over-75s who make heavy demands on the social services and health service. Part of the reason for the proportionately larger share of expenditure going to education was the increase in the number of pupils staying on at school and going on to higher education. These are the expensive sectors of the service. In a competitive situation for public money, any rise in the proportion going to any one service is unlikely to be sustained. The claims for education got weaker once new schools had been built while hospitals got older. This point is important in understanding why the education service was a target for economies in the late 1970s. Falling school rolls were only one factor. The expansion had been sustained long enough for competitors for resources to have established an increasingly strong case. The planning methods adopted by the government in the 1970s enabled the Cabinet to decide priorities between services, just as corporate management did in reorganized local authorities after 1974. Furthermore, by the latter half of the 1970s, governments had devised more effective ways of checking public spending during times of inflation.

No relief is anticipated from this pressure on the education service by the remaining public services. Indeed, the number of births has not risen as fast in the 1980s as was expected, given the increased numbers of women, born in the period 1955–1965, reaching fertile ages. Thus the demands on education will not increase as a result of increased intakes. The expansion, if it comes, is likely to be from the involvement of expensive 16–19-year-olds. But other services will have rising demands on the public purse. The health service is under steadily increasing demand from the elderly, and the new state pension scheme introduced in 1978 will result in increased spending until well into the 21st century. Unless the economy recovers, the pressure on available resources will increase and the run-down in North Sea oil may bring back balance of payment problems.

Controlling public expenditure

Governments that were concerned to control public expenditure in Britain in the 1950s were faced with three sets of related problems. First, there was no machinery to ensure that an increase in spending by one government department was compensated by contraction in another. Second, local authorities were heavy spenders on social services. This applied particularly to education, which is a national service locally administered. Thus central government economies might still leave heavy spending locally. Finally, by the 1970s rapid inflation made forward planning difficult. In services such as education, where most of the money went to paying teachers and other staff, unanticipated wage rises often meant higher costs than those planned.

The concern of Treasury ministers and officials at the end of the 1950s about the level of public expenditure led to a new system of planning after the Plowden Report of 1961. The new system, PESC, not only ensured that the Cabinet could decide priorities after reviewing all bids from spending departments, but also increased Treasury influence. The Treasury was responsible for informing departments of the economic assumptions to be used in preparing spending forecasts, for collecting in the bids from the various departments, and for preparing the report on the economy that would be considered by ministers when deciding where the spending should occur. The Treasury officials have been described by Heclo and Wildavsky (1974) as a small, select club. They come from similar backgrounds, schools and Oxbridge. The senior officials in the spending departments such as the DES or the DHSS have often spent much of their civil service career in the Treasury. In the spending departments the Treasury worked to get a firmer grip. This effort continued into the 1980s. Most of the intervening failure to align spending and government income was due to overestimating economic growth. By the 1980s, however, government controls over public sector expenditure were formidable.

The forward planning of public expenditure is undertaken annually as a rolling programme. The final decisions are made by the Cabinet between June and November each year, after considering the spending proposed by government departments and the likely rate of economic growth. PESC consists of a series of negotiations between spending departments and the Treasury. The latter aggregates the departmental submissions and presents the package to the Cabinet. The White Paper on public expenditure is published when final decisions have been made and shows how much each service can expect to receive in each of the following five years.

Throughout 20 years of development since 1961 the PESC system has provided the machinery for planning and controlling public spending. Possibly even more important, it made spending departments cost-conscious. It established that public spending should be restricted in line with economic performance. By 1980 the prospects were of sustained restrictions following those introduced by both Labour and Conservative governments in the second half of the 1970s. This often meant cutting programmes which were assumed to be secure by ministers and officials in spending departments. Financing the social services in a period of sustained economic contraction took planning procedures into new territory.

It would be useless for central government to plan public sector expenditure if local authorities were able to spend without limit. In reality the amount that can be raised by local rates is limited, and between 1951 and 1975, while local authorities spent more, they became more dependent on central government grants. The amount of local government expenditure covered by the Rate Support Grant rose from one-third to nearly two-thirds of the total. By the 1980s this trend had been reversed. In 1983–1984 only 51 percent of local revenue came from central grants. Just as there has been 30 years of effort to control the expansion of public sector expenditure, so there has been a parallel effort to support local government spending while keeping it under control. In 1959 the grant was changed from a percentage to a block, which put a ceiling on expenditure. But local authorities could still exceed the grant and in 1981 a new Block Grant was announced, which is designed to further restrain and discipline authorities that were considered to be overspending. At central and local government levels there has been over a quarter of a century of effort to control the public sector as economic growth slowed.

Up to the financial year 1980–1981 money had been given to local authorities through the Rate Support Grant. Once ministers knew the level of public expenditure for the forthcoming year, they started negotiations with the local authorities over the size of this grant. The major part was distributed according to the needs faced by the authorities, compensating them for differences in expenditure per head needed to provide standards of services. It is doubtful if the complicated calculations actually resulted in this needs element reflecting genuine local needs (Burgin, 1978). From the view of central government the Rate Support Grant did little to discourage big spenders and the new Block Grant introduced in 1981 was designed to bring these authorities into line.

The basis of the new Block Grant is an assessment of how much local authority services should cost. This Grant-Related Expenditure (GRE) is calculated to enable each authority to provide a typical standard of service. The grant from central government is calculated to bridge the gap between this GRE and the rateable resources available to the authority. Thus high spending is discouraged because expenditure above GRE would have to be raised by borrowing or by increased rates. However, the 1980 Local Government Planning and Land Act gave the government power to influence the level of rates which could be raised by local authorities. If a local rate exceeded a national uniform rate established by the Secretary of State for the Environment, the grant from central government could be reduced.

The impact of these new arrangements became apparent when the Department of the Environment published the grants for 1981–1982. Three-quarters of all local authorities lost grant compared with the previous year. The London boroughs did worst of all, while the county councils came out best. The public expenditure White Paper of February 1983 showed a continuing squeeze on pay and prices. Pay rises were assumed to be pegged at $3\frac{1}{2}$ percent and prices at 4 percent. Spending on education was to remain stable in cash terms, being £12,147 million in 1983–1984 and £12,780 million in 1985–1986. The assumptions for education were of further cuts in the school meals budget and a loss of 800,000 surplus school places. The number of teachers in schools had been 441,000 in 1978–1979, 420,000 in 1981–1982 and was assumed to fall to 380,000–385,000 by 1985–1986.

The problem of financing programmes during rapid inflation became a major concern in the 1970s. Every year government departments and local authorities had to find more money to pay for labour and materials that cost more than anticipated. The problem did not only arise from the tendency to underestimate the forthcoming rises in costs and wages. When there are arrangements for claiming extra money after overspending in money terms there was no incentive to keep such costs down. From 1965 to 1975, local authority spending, particularly on education, housing and personal social services, took an increasing share of total public expenditure. During the economic crises from 1973 onwards, this trend was reversed by the imposition of cash limits. Instead of deciding on the amount to which original estimates would be raised by supplementary payments after the rises have taken place, government fixed the ceiling in cash terms in advance. Most importantly, the Rate Support Grant, which provided the major part of money available to local authorities, was subjected to such limits. Controlling expenditure was now easier, for the limits on supplementation could be fixed at a level that assumed modest rates of inflation. The new Block Grant was a further measure to limit local spending. Ironically it was central rather than local government that failed to cut its expenditure, largely because of sustained defence spending and the rising cost of unemployment benefit.

The impact of these government measures to plan and control public expenditure has been felt in every social service, and particularly in education where rises in teachers' pay have tended to be larger than anticipated. Cash limits were introduced under a Labour government and used for cutting back public services from 1974 onwards. Cash limits also hit hard because of the tendency for governments, intentionally or not, to be as over-optimistic about the forthcoming rate of inflation as they had been about the rate of economic growth. Overestimating the strength of the economy enabled governments to accelerate the growth of public services up to the mid-1970s. Underestimating the rate of inflation thereafter enabled them to reduce it. If local authorities face 15 percent inflation through wage and other cost rises, while the amount to which original estimates can be raised is limited to 10 percent, there will have to be either a rise in local authority borrowing, a rise in the rates or a cutback in services.

The visibility of expenditure on education

In 1833, Parliament granted £20,000 to religious bodies to build schools for the poor. By 1864 the government was so concerned about the money allocated that payment by results was introduced, making the grant per pupil dependent on him or her reaching a sufficient standard as assessed by Her Majesty's Inspectors. By 1982–1983 the total bill for the education service was over £12 billion. Up to the Second World War the proportion of the GNP going to the education service was 2.6 percent. By 1975 it was 7.6 percent. Since then education has received less of the national cake. The public expenditure White Paper of 1983 forecast spending on education at constant prices to be the same in 1983–1984 as in 1979–1980. But other public services were receiving more in real terms. Social security expenditure, for example, jumped by 19 percent. But at over £12 billion in the years from 1982 to 1986, education was still a very big spender. For local authorities it was by far the largest single item of expenditure.

Thus, at national and local levels the cost of education was of immediate concern to Treasury and treasurers. The reason for this can be seen in the costs of schooling. A 1000-strong London comprehensive school would have had a salary bill for teachers of nearly £1 million in 1982–1983. The cost per pupil would have been over £1500 in inner London. Inevitably the annual pay round for teachers was of acute interest to central and local governments. The Treasury would also be concerned. When half a million teachers negotiate a pay rise the economic consequences are great. A few can negotiate without acute interest being shown. A fraction of a per cent makes a big difference when it is multiplied by 500,000.

The competition at different levels

Four-fifths of the money for education is spent by local authorities. They employ the staff who account for 75 percent of the money spent each year. But the larger part of this money comes in the form of a grant from central government. While central government does not control local government current expenditure directly, it monitors the way the money is spent and in constraining local authority spending is really controlling the finances of education.

Every year there are cycles of resource allocation at four different levels before teachers can be sure of the resources that will be available to them at the start of the academic year in September. First, the available national resources have to be allocated to the different public services and the amount of central government tax income to go to local authorities has to be decided. Second, local authorities, having added the anticipated income from the local rate to the grant to be received from central government, decide how to divide the money available between locally provided services. Third, the money allocated to the education service has to be shared out between the various sectors within it. Fourth, decisions have to be made within schools about the use to be made of the available resources. In the case of universities, central government money is allocated through the University Grants Committee, not the local authorities.

Within the committees, working parties and informal meetings that make recommendations about allocation at these four levels there are large numbers of politicians, administrators, inspectors, professional associations and other interest groups pressing claims for favoured services. Heclo and Wildavsky's (1974) description of the annual Public Expenditure Survey Committee was not about objectives, flow charts and path analyses, but about horse-trading. It is not the production of sets of options to be decided at one big meeting, but continuous informal and formal contracts between the Treasury and the spending departments, and between central and local government. The Cabinet, when considering the pattern of expenditure for the next financial year in the summer of each year, takes about four months to reach its conclusions. Ministers fight to maintain the spending of their department. They depend on their officials to prepare a strong case to defend that spending. The decisions are not arrived at by voting but by settling priorities, by give and take across a table where the spending ministers face each other, and face the Chancellor and Prime Minister.

Similar sequences occur in local government. The Association of Metropolitan Authorities (AMA) or the Association of County Councils (ACC) will have already put their case to central government at the Consultative Council for Local Government Finance. The spending departments within each authority prepare bids for available resources. The chief executive and his senior management team then thrash out proposals or options for spending. The local politicians on the policy and resources committee, who include the chairmen of the major committees such as education, social services, housing, planning, finance and establishment, and the council leaders, decide on the final proposals that will be ratified by the full council. Once again, officers brief their political members to preserve the resources available to their departments. Committee chairmen work with each other and their officers, holding out here, giving way there, until agreement is reached.

With education remaining the biggest single item of local authority expenditure and pupil numbers being the dominant factor in calculating the education GRE, the effects of falling rolls will be an important factor throughout the 1980s and early 1990s. Once the grant has been received from central government it is spent through decisions made by each council. Even though there is an education GRE, just as there was a separately calculated element in the Rate Support Grant for the education service, there is no necessity for education at the local level to receive the sum calculated by central government. That is a decision for local corporate decision-making. Education may lose or gain in the local bargaining.

Within the education department of a local authority the total estimated expenditure for the year will be broken down into page after page of different headings. Primary and secondary school branches will want their share of the total, but so will further and adult education, the youth service and special education. The bids from these sectors will have been aggregated into the total education bid after yet another series of horse-trading sessions. As with central government, professional associations, trade unions, parent groups and a variety of pressure groups will be actively seeking support for particular policies and the resources to back them. Some of this will be voiced through advisory or consultative committees; this is usually the way the professional associations are heard. But a lot more will come through lobbying, informal meetings and the mass media.

The allocation of resources to schools completes the cycle for the education service. In some local authorities the money is earmarked for specific aspects of the work of the school. In others the staff are allowed virement so that money for books and academic equipment and so on may be used interchangeably. In others money is given as a block, banked by the school and spent after internal consultation. But regardless of where this responsibility for allocation lies, decisions between competing options have to be made within schools just as they were in the Public Expenditure Survey Committee, in Cabinet, through corporate management in town and county halls, and within education departments.

Local authorities have little room for financial manoeuvres. Much of their spending arises from legislation over which they have no control. Standards of provision in housing, health, education and so on are determined centrally, and local authorities have to take the necessary action. A typical example is the Health and Safety at Work legislation. To bring schools, hospitals, colleges and offices up to standard, the authorities had to spend large sums in providing fire escapes, replacing dangerous materials and providing new safety facilities. Even when resources are being cut, obligations are increased. The authorities are set up by Parliament. They can only spend money in ways that are authorized by statute. District auditors, who are employees of central government, check on this and on whether any local spending has been 'unreasonable'. Local rates cannot be raised easily and since 1980 this can lead to a reduction in the grant received from central government. Burgess and Travers (1980) have argued that the consequence of the inadequacy of the local rate as a source of revenue has led to a dependence on central government money, which means that local government is accountable to the government not to its own electors. The scope for local initiative is limited. The consequences for the public and for professionals such as teachers can be frustrating. Local authorities are not only unable to find the money to solve pressing local problems, but they are frequently unable to predict the resources that will be available in future. They wait to see how much money will come annually from central government and for statutes that will enable them to act to solve local matters, such as the form entries for schools with falling rolls. Parents and teachers blame the authority for procrastinating. But frequently an answer depends on a decision from central government.

The weight of previous investment

The secret to the working of a service such as education lies in the marginal nature of projected changes. Education is planned incrementally. There is no wholesale shake-up each year, but a bit on here compensating for a bit off there, the amount of trading-off depending on whether resources are being cut or increased. Cancelling school transport in the first week of term saves enough to finance the holidays for the physically handicapped. Stopping the payments for double-entry to public examinations by the authority allows a few extra staff for the new nursery school to be appointed. This sounds undramatic. But the size of previous investments in the service makes any drama unlikely. A new school built in one year will need a build-up in staff in future years. Colleges, schools, institutes, youth centres and education departments have to be staffed. Every year marginal changes are made, but the bulk of the services continues as before. This occurs at all levels. The Cabinet may decide that some resources can be shifted from education to health. A few primary schools are closed and fewer teachers appointed because births fell five years previously. Courses for the 16–19-year olds in the local further education college get a few more staff because numbers there are still increasing. A secondary school closes down its classics course as the sole teacher retires. At all levels minor changes are being made, but there is an inertia within big enterprises such as an education service which leads to incrementalism or, in contraction, decrementalism.

One criticism made of the DES has been that it does not plan ahead by first deciding on educational objectives and then assessing the means available for attaining them. Instead it concerns itself mainly with maintaining the present arrangements efficiently. However, there have been attempts to plan ahead. *Education: A Framework for Expansion* (DES, 1972) was the result of an attempt within the Department to move towards Planning, Analysis and Review System (PAR) with its emphasis on objectives, inputs and outputs. But this was overtaken in the following year by the oil crisis and a lot of work must have been wasted.

The DES has a relatively easy job projecting the level of expenditure necessary to keep the service running. Once children are born it is possible to project the numbers who will enter school at five. Projections for 15 years ahead can be accurate. From thereon staying-on rates and the proportion entering further and higher education make it more difficult, but the task is easy compared with that of estimating the demand for health services, social security benefits or housing.

Incrementalism – adding a bit here and subtracting there – instead of planning by objections may seem amateurish, but it is the easiest way to proceed at all levels. It makes a teacher's job possible. When teaching staff are concerned about the coming year it is over one or two staff out of a total of 50, or a small percentage change in capitation. If objectives were determined anew each year and radical measures taken to achieve them in a short time, the teaching force and the administration would be jittery. There would have to be redundancies, recruitment of new staff with new skills, redeployment and a reorganization of responsibilities and allowances. In this sense incrementalism, or muddling through, suits those already employed and gives them a stake in the status quo. Those working in public services have an interest in restricting change. They are not forced to be responsive to a market where consumers dominate.

In practice, the mass of investment in buildings and staff ties up most of the resources made available for the education service. Pressed by the House of Commons Expenditure Committee (1976), the Permanent Secretary at the DES gave priority to 'roofs over heads' in the school building programme, even though this may result in rich areas which were receiving population getting the new schools rather than run-down areas where the need may have been greater. But that priority results from the statutory duty to provide education for all. If all that is left, even in times of expansion, is marginal because of previous investment, the scope for carrying out policies other than 'roofs over heads' is limited, unless there is to be radical upheaval. This does not mean that there is no policy or principle. Politicians fight elections with promises about education. Central government has to fulfil its obligations to secure statutory schooling for all. It has also supported a policy of positive discrimination through the Urban Programme and in education since the end of the 1960s. Local authorities have pressed on towards comprehensive schooling, or have opposed central government pressure to move in this direction, despite the ban on any building not for comprehensivization. But the inertia resulting from previous decisions is strong.

Throughout the planning of public expenditure, decisions are made at the margin. All but the last few percent have been committed by previous decisions. This occurs at all levels of expenditure. The DES cuts a little of the budgets of the Research Councils and finds a little for training more mathematics teachers. One LEA replaces the retiring advisor for classics with one for the 16–19 age-group. A primary headteacher cancels the annual outing and takes out a subscription to *The Wonderful World of Nature*. In each case the bulk of resources goes to ongoing commitments.

Within each LEA the preparation of the estimates for the forthcoming year will end with decisions by committee. Before then there will have been lengthy discussions among the assistant education officers responsible for the various branches of the education authority. Schools, further education establishments, general purposes, planning or sites and buildings, and special education sub-committees will all submit proposals for spending. The finance department will be involved and the county or metropolitan authority treasurer consulted. The chief education officer will be in contact with the chairman of the education committee and the chairmen of the other sub-committees. There may be discussion with advisory committees of teachers. The education officer will have regular meetings with other chief officers of the authority as part of the corporate planning machinery. The estimates which finally go to the education committee will have been the subject of detailed giving and taking within the education department, between officers and politicians, and between the department and other departments of the local authority. An example of estimates from the Inner

Table 1 Estimated expenditure on primary education within ILEA, 1983–1984

	1981–82 Actual £	1982–83 Original estimate £	1983–84 Estimate £	Increase or decrease over 1982–83 original estimate £
EXPENDITURE				
1. Teaching staff	96,284,208	86,259,000	93,061,000 +	6,802,000
2. Non-teaching staff	27,470,335	24,921,000	26,899,000 +	1,978,000
3. Premises				
(a) General maintenance and upkeep	21,667,800	25,232,000	24,426,000 −	806,000
(b) Maintenance of properties purchased for redevelopment	159,712	478,000	306,000 −	172,000
4. School allowances and equipment	5,613,743	5,209,000	5,559,000 +	350,000
5. Discretionary allowances	—	8,680,000	9,290,000 +	610,000
6. Other expenses	1,610,475	1,311,000	1,515,000 +	204,000
7. Debt charges	7,710,927	7,291,000	7,312,000 +	21,000
Total direct expenditure	160,517,200	159,381,000	168,368,000 +	8,987,000

*Staff numbers FTE (excluding allocated charges)

		†		
Teachers	8,713		8,706 –	7
Clerical	442		433 –	9
Media resources officers	23		23	—
Nursery assistants	634		651 +	17
Schoolkeepers	774		777 +	3
Cleaners	1,499		1497 –	2
General attendants	7		8 +	1
Primary helpers	693		672 –	21
Casual assistants	231		231	—
	13,016		12,998 –	18

* Basic staff only. Additional staff are provided under the alternative use of resources scheme.

† Average number for financial year derived from school year numbers.

Source: Inner London Education Authority, *Capital and Revenue Estimates, 1983–84.* London: ILEA, 1983.

Table 2 Estimated expenditures on secondary education within ILEA, 1983–1984

1981–82 Actual £	1982–83 Original estimate £	EXPENDITURE	1983–84 Estimate £	Increase or decrease over 1982–83 original estimate £
		EXPENDITURE		
		A. Day schools		
126,067,285	113,792,000	1. Teaching staff	118,768,000 +	4,976,000
32,023,191	29,678,000	2. Non-teaching staff	32,680,000 +	3,002,000
		3. Premises		
25,619,576	27,125,000	(a) General maintenance and upkeep ..	29,049,000 +	1,924,000
		(b) Maintenance of properties purchased for		
189,818	464,000	redevelopment	291,000 −	173,000
10,296,690	10,536,000	4. School allowances and equipment ..	10,595,000 +	59,000
7,303,128	7,303,000	5. Discretionary allowances	7,690,000 +	387,000
3,858,128	4,240,000	6. Other expenses	4,997,000 +	757,000
9,443,950	9,260,000	7. Debt charges	8,860,000 −	400,000
207,498,638	202,398,000		212,930,000 +	10,532,000

Staff numbers FTE (excluding allocated charges)

			†	
Teachers	..	..	10,797	10,464 −	333
Administrative and clerical	..		593	601 +	8
Library staff	..	..	180	170 −	10
Media resources officers	..		171	164 −	7
General assistants	..	..	170	167 −	3
Bursarial and child care	..		20	20	—
Laboratory and workshop technicians			824	833 +	9
Schoolkeepers	..	..	783	770 −	13
Cleaners	..	..	1,671	1,601 −	70
Casual assistants	..	..	166	166	—
Domestic and maintenance staff	..		91	93 +	2
Courier drivers	..	..	4	4	—
			15,470	15,053 −	417

* Basic staff only. Additional staff are provided under the alternative use of resources scheme.
† Average number for financial year derived from school year numbers.

Source: Inner London Education Authority, *Capital and Revenue Estimates, 1983–84.* London: ILEA, 1983.

London Education Authority is shown in *Tables* 1 and 2.

It is unlikely, particularly when the money available is expected to increase in the next financial year, that many specific items of expenditure will be scrutinized. The basis of next year's estimates will be last year's expenditure. The easiest way is to exercise what Birley (1970), himself an ex-deputy director of education, has described as 'habitual spending'. Freed from the necessity of making a profit, it is easiest to assume that everything spent last year should be spent this year and to start planning for extra or reduced expenditure from that basis. To Birley this is 'unreflecting', but it simplifies a very time-consuming job which has to be done alongside other pressing issues. Changing existing practices involves detailed analysis. A proposal for even a minor reduction in the budget for something like supporting teachers going on courses will raise objections somewhere in the department. It will be pointed out that such a reduction will create a demand for short as against long courses, increase the cost of the authority's own in-service work, break an agreement with the teachers and will in any case achieve only minor savings given the chances of recouping the money through the further education pool. The weight of events makes it easiest to repeat last year's pattern. Furthermore, a look at the estimates listed in *Tables* 1 and 2 will show that even these detailed estimates contain only broad headings. 'Aid to pupils' may be examined as a possible source for savings, but someone will have to produce a detailed breakdown of the numerous items under this heading, and each will be defended as essential. It is far easier to nod through each item year after year.

Tables 1 and 2 show estimated expenditure on primary and secondary schools within the Inner London Education Authority for the year 1983–1984. The first feature of both tables is the large proportion of the money allocated to paying teachers. The number in primary and secondary schools dropped by 340, but expenditure on teachers' salaries rose by nearly £12 million to £212 million. The weight of previous investment is also clear. Debt charges and the maintenance of buildings at £65 million were almost twice that allocated to allowances for organizing the learning at £33 million.

Across the Inner London Education Authority as a whole, salaries and wages, and the large items for the maintenance of buildings and debt charges, made up 79 percent of total expenditure. Labour costs of support services were also high. Out of £42 million to be spent on school meals, £28 million went to pay 5575 staff. The total amount for wages and salaries was £588 million out of a total of £925 million. The total amount allocated to school, headteachers' and governors' allowances was estimated to be only £63 million.

The inescapable nature of previous investment in buildings and staff stands out from these estimates. Buildings had often lasted over 100 years. They have to be heated, lit, maintained and debt charges paid. Once appointed staff could stay for over 40 years. Thus a decision to invest in new premises, a new support service or new staff can lock in resources for years to come. That is easy to manage with expansion. But in a period of sustained contraction, past decisions not only limit present and future policies, but the inescapable nature of many commitments means that economies have to be made somewhere else in the services provided.

The dominance of wages and salaries

A basic fact of life of the education service is that about two-thirds of expenditure is on wages and salaries, mainly to about half a million teachers. The inertia in the service, which can be seen as beneficial or harmful, follows from this through the following factors:

1   There is little scope for saving staff through technical advances. The teachers' unions have small class sizes as their top priority and pupil–teacher ratios fell nationally in every year up to 1982, in periods of both expansion and contraction.

2   It is easy to expand the teaching force, but difficult to contract it. It is also difficult to move teachers between schools or to retrain them to cover for shortages in specialist skills or for new needs that arise.

3   Teachers' pay is negotiated nationally but the agreement is binding on local authorities, however rich or poor. While economies may be possible in running schools, teachers' pay is beyond the control of their employers.

4   Some two-thirds of all expenditure within education is on wages and salaries. After allowing for the maintenance of buildings, the debt charges on the capital borrowed to pay for them and inescapable commitments due to legislation, less than 10 percent is left for buying books, other teaching materials and the essentials for running a school.

This situation can be appreciated from looking at *Tables* 1 and 2 where the amount spent on teachers is overwhelming. For England and Wales in 1982–1983, spending on books, educational and physical education equipment, stationery and materials was £19 per child for primary schools and £34 for secondary schools, yet the average cost per child was £649 and £903 respectively (Chartered Institute of Public Finance and Accountancy, 1982).

The problems arising from the structure of educational costs become a major headache in times of contraction. If cuts cannot be achieved by small savings in the biggest item – the salaries of teachers – there have to be big savings in the small items. If the cuts continue there is a point at which the amount spent on books and curriculum materials will be reduced to a level where education, however good the teachers, will be undermined. The response to the cuts at the end of the 1970s was to cut recruitment and the numbers training to be teachers, and to offer generous terms for early retirement. But these measures take time. Meanwhile, the essential tools of education had to be cut. With the total resources allocated to education fixed by rigid cash limits, the Clegg award to teachers faced local authorities with a major problem. No cut in the quality of the service could save the money needed. The government was determined not to provide extra resources. Raising the rates through a special levy half-way through the year would have been unpopular at any time, but with high unemployment, depressed industry and falling retail sales, the ability of individuals and firms to pay anything extra was limited. After 1980 there were penalties for high-spending local authorities.

The problem of high labour costs in the education service does not arise only with cuts in the money available. Level spending with falling school rolls in the 1970s had already produced tensions, for the problem is there at all times. In expansive times more teachers are appointed to staff new developments; they remain in service through good and bad times, whether they are effective at their job or not. During contraction teachers still have to be paid and something else has to be cut to compensate. But there is also a tendency for expenditure to rise without the encouragement of an expansive central government. The introduction of a block grant in 1959 was cal- culated to control expenditure by stating a sum of money in place of the percentage grant which imposed no ceiling. But in the form of the Rate Support Grant from 1967, the amount going to each local authority depended on calculations of 'needs' and 'resources'. Governments used this grant to alter the resources available to different types of local authority. Thus in the early 1970s, inner-city local authorities were favoured at the expense of the shire counties. Any increase in the level of grant to an authority was liable to be spent on employing teachers to staff new developments. Any reduction elsewhere was met by economies but not in staffing, due to the pressure from the teachers' unions and the consensus that smaller classes were a priority. Thus while national expenditure on education could be stable in real terms, the numbers of teachers could be increasing, thus building up pressure at the margin of educational spending and storing up problems for periods in which there were cuts.

The figures in *Tables* 1 and 2 confirm that the education service can respond to new demand only through changes within the teaching force. The annual figures produced by the Chartered Institute of Public Accountants confirm this for all local authorities. Even if new resources are made available through taxation or by redistribution from other public services, the developments made possible will mean appointing more teachers. If there are no new resources, some new developments may be possible through redeployment. But there is likely to be resistance from teachers' unions. If the education service has to lose resources, the savings from anything bar the salaries and wages bill are minute. By not replacing staff, there can be some economy, but this will be resisted as it will be a cut in the service, resented by public and professionals. Moreover there comes a time when a policy of no recruitment, even with early retirement, still leaves a deficit. From thereon redundancies are the only option if national or local taxation is not increased.

The problems associated with the high labour costs in education do not end with the consequent inflexibility in resource allocation. A policy of no recruitment leaves thousands of newly trained teachers unemployed. Many of these will have the skills required for a service that has to change with the times. Meanwhile the existing teaching force digs in to weather the storm. Proposals for change, or for redeployment, become a threat. The teaching force gets older. But this not only poses problems for new developments that become pressing; it aggravates the financial problem even further. Teachers get annual increments – the older the teacher, the higher his or her salary. Thus a policy of no recruitment raises the average cost per teacher. A sustained policy of no growth or of cuts would require continual cuts in the total number of teachers regardless of school rolls or the relation between teachers' salaries and inflation. The education service is organized for receiving increasing resources. Contraction hits it hard because the largest item of expenditure cannot be cut easily.

The problems raised by the high labour costs are increased by the power of the universal principle behind the allocation of resources and particularly in the payment of teachers. There has been a shortage of mathematics and science teachers for almost 40 years. Yet the principle that all similarly qualified teachers of whatever subject should be paid the same at entry has made it impossible to attract such specialists by offering them extra money. There have been extra payments for teachers working in schools serving deprived areas but these have been for all teachers in the schools concerned. Similarly, with the exception of additional money for a first degree, there has been no financial incentive for teachers to update their skills through taking higher degrees or other in-service courses. Since 1944 a succession of problems has arisen as the world outside the schools has changed. Each of these increased the pressure for selectivity. But the salary structure which dominated the finance of education remained universalistic and this principle still guides the Burnham Committee where the salary structure is negotiated.

When the service is contracting and economies have to be made, the resistance to selectivity adds to the pressures for decision-making to be more centralized. The first question to the National Union of Teachers' (NUT) witnesses at the Expenditure Committee of the House of Commons in 1976 was about possible consultation by the DES over cuts in expenditure (House of Commons Expenditure Committee, 1976). The NUT's view was that there was no clash between their union and professional functions. Max Morris, an ex-President of the NUT, expressed it this way: 'Every improvement in teachers' conditions is inevitably an improvement in the education of the children in our schools. Equally every improvement in educational conditions within schools improves teachers' conditions. The two things go together like that.' Pressed by the committee about their response to being consulted about cuts in the service given this view, the reply of Fred Jarvis, the NUT General Secretary was that the union was '. . . not in the business of robbing Peter to pay Paul'. To the Expenditure Committee there was a clash between the union's demand to be consulted and this refusal to consider redistributing resources in order to make economies. Sir Anthony Mayer asked: 'Is there not therefore an inherent and inevitable conflict between your activities as a professional organisation upholding the interests of the teaching profession and your desire to give advice to a government department which by its very nature must choose priorities and cannot always give you more of everything?' But the union representatives were adamant: they were not in business to order priorities either within the service or between it and other services.

This resistance to involvement in cutting the service, even as pupil numbers were falling fast, is understandable. If conditions for teachers and the education of children are inseparable, it is legitimate to fight for more of everything, including more and better paid teachers, even when the amount of money available is being cut. But this means that the decisions have to be made back in county or town halls, or by central government. Once financial constraints over local government tightened at the start of the 1980s, decisions about the allocation and reallocation of shrinking resources were forced back to central government. Economic pressures were reinforcing political tendencies to centralize decision-making in a contracting service. Someone had to rob Peter to pay Paul and the selectivity involved in that transfer violated the universalistic foundations on which education and the other public services had been built.

By the early 1980s teachers were complaining that they were being starved of the necessary resources to do the job. Similarly CEOs were complaining that they were no longer in a position to exercise their responsibilities. No doubt the successive Secretaries of State for Education pressed the same case in Cabinet. The strain was increased throughout the service by the roll-on effect of investment during expansion in earlier decades. This strain not only resulted from the cutback in expenditure on education; it was made worse by the progressive ending of grants received by LEAs under various intervention programmes which had proliferated in the 1960s and 1970s. Money had been given to inner cities in particular. Yet these were just the authorities under most pressure in the early 1980s. This money had, for example, gone to employ more teachers in schools, as under Section 11 of the Local Government Act 1966, or to pay teachers extra money for meeting difficult conditions. But there had also been the establishment of an infrastructure around the schools to help with the problems of areas facing multiply deprived populations. Here too teachers and other support staff were appointed, often on tenured posts from money that was withdrawn once the programmes were phased out. Such staff had still to be paid and, once the programme was withdrawn, from an education budget that was already too small to support existing school provision. Growth in one period is paid for in the next.

The finances of the education service have been dominated by the combination of high labour costs, the weight of previous commitments and assumptions of continuing growth. These add to the pain of contraction because they built up momentum during the good years. The slow-down in growth, at a time when wages and salaries account for over two-thirds of the money spent and when appointments can commit expenditure for 40 years ahead, means redistributing resources in ways that are unacceptable in a service dedicated to consistency of provision, standard terms of service and investment to raise the level of education for all. In practice higher education is too expensive not to be selective, but the rhetoric remains. These financial strains alter the balance of power within the service. More decisions have to be taken outside the schools because many involve taking from one sector of the service in order to support others.

The strains at different levels of the service

The annual cycle of financial events depends on a flow of information between the schools, local authorities and central government. The most important set of information for the education service concerns numbers. The DES will prepare its estimates in relation to the numbers expected over the next four years. The Department of the Environment will calculate the education element of the grant for local authorities after counting heads. The LEAs will be estimating where students will be in the following school year. At all levels there is a problem in reconciling these figures. When the projected numbers from local authorities are added up, they may not tally with those calculated by central government. In many areas migration will make accurate projection difficult. Local education authorities will ask school staff to calculate how many pupils are expected in the following year. This is particularly difficult for children over 16 and individual school estimates, when added up, usually exceed the local authority projections. At all levels there has to be reconciliation. But there will also be disappointment. The cake is of finite size; demands on it are infinite.

The number of decisions that have to be made, at different levels, before the allocation of resources for the following financial year can be made, accounts for the frustration in schools at the slowness with which decisions are made in county halls. Early in the calendar year a school's staff want to know how many teachers and how much money they will have next September. But the education department in county hall is waiting for the allocation to the LEA. This has to wait for the level of the grant to local authorities to be decided by central government, and for the council to agree on the local rate that can be raised. But the former has to wait for the completion of the Public Expenditure Survey. In 1981 the White Paper on public expenditure concluding the central government exercise only appeared in March. As schools wait for the LEA, they wait for the council who wait to hear from government about their block grant. This process is complicated by the fact that the school year runs from September, while the financial year runs from April. The wonder is not that the decisions are often late, but that they are made at all. With a succession of economic crises leading to often unexpected cuts imposed from the centre, spending departments, county halls and education departments work with the anxiety that planning will have to be undone, and promises broken through decisions made further up the line. The difficulty in allowing for inflation adds a further complication.

It is not only the timing of the allocation of resources that creates different problems in government and in schools. *Table 3* gives figures for England showing pupils, qualified teachers and pupil–teacher ratios in maintained primary and secondary schools (January rolls). This national picture looks healthy as pupil–teacher ratios have fallen.

Table 3 Numbers of pupils, qualified teachers and pupil–teacher ratios in maintained primary and secondary schools in England, 1974–1982

Year	Primary schools			Secondary schools		
	Pupils	Qualified teachers	Pupil–teacher ratio within schools	Pupils	Qualified teachers	Pupil–teacher ratio within schools
1982	3,922,809	174,240	22.5	3,798,000	228,397	16.6
1981	4,098,730	181,310	22.6	3,839,858	230,928	16.6
1980	4,285,586	188,616	22.7	3,866,102	232,457	16.6
1979	4,444,538	192,462	23.1	3,872,036	231,404	16.7
1978	4,570,797	193,521	23.6	3,851,271	227,379	16.9
1977	4,704,011	197,056	23.9	3,798,711	223,209	17.0
1976	4,792,006	199,937	24.0	3,700,472	217,313	17.0
1975	4,831,682	199,399	24.2	3,597,633	209,324	17.2
1974	4,873,037	195,581	24.9	3,499,654	200,426	17.5

Source: DES (1982c) *Statistical Bulletin*, p. 6. Reproduced with the permission of the Controller of Her Majesty's Stationery Office.

From the schools, however, the picture may look very different, even if they are in an LEA with no major financial worries. The LEA will have to decide when a school loses a form intake as its roll falls. The teachers may lose a colleague and in a small school this may require major reorganization or the dropping of a subject. It may also threaten complete closure. But even in a large secondary school, children do not disappear in neat groups of 25.

A few leave from many existing classes. The intake declines. A teacher is lost in line with the total loss of children but the number of classes remains the same. The 16–19 age-group may expand while there is an overall net loss. The threat to specialist staff becomes an increasing worry.

In time the problems multiply. Teachers do not retire or leave so that the balance of those left fits the curriculum. The consequence has often been that schools have lost their freedom to determine the curriculum. LEAs staff the schools to preserve a basic curriculum determined in county hall. At the centre the DES alters the balance of subjects of students in teacher training. But in the schools that balance may have gone awry. Movement between schools is a partial solution if new appointments to the authority are not to be made, and resistance to this has often been fierce.

Thus problems in a school may be very difficult given a national situation where teacher numbers have fallen at a slower rate than pupil numbers, giving improved pupil–teacher ratios. Nevertheless, it is easy to exaggerate the agony. In 1980 teachers received first between 17 and 25 percent through the Clegg award and then 13.5 percent as their annual rise. Within LEAs it has been a varied picture as successive governments have tried to hold back public sector spending. Between 1972 and 1977, Newham, a deprived London borough, produced stringent budgets in line with central government calls for economy (Tunley et al., 1979). But the Rate Support Grant worked to produce surpluses for the borough which were used to reduce rates and add to reserves, rather than to improve services. Part of the severity of government attempts to control overspending in the 1980s result from previous failures at both central and local government levels to align spending to levels appropriate in an ailing economy.

Behind the internal structure of finance for the education service lie political decisions about the allocation of resources to public and private sector and between the public services. There is continual adjustment of the balance of taxation and of the resources left for individuals to spend, or for public services to spend for them. The bargaining position of education has been weakened by falling school rolls while the number of elderly people increases. But it has also been weakened by the difficulty of sustaining claims that education has a direct economic and social pay-off. In 1962 the National Union of Teachers could produce a pamphlet entitled *Investment for National Survival* (1962). The experts who produced the report recommended 'a sustained and massive' recruitment programme for teachers. The programme would be expensive, but 'a higher rate of educational expenditure now will help that national income to grow faster in the future'.

The investment was made, but the economic benefits were not apparent. Twenty years later these claims seem unrealistic. In an economy that went downhill, not up, and in a society where educational and social inequality persisted, the claims for investment in education for national survival were muted. The problem was to establish a basis for investment that was less dependent on seeing education as a means to economic or social ends and as more of an end in itself.

CHAPTER 4

THE SUB-GOVERNMENT OF EDUCATION

The use of shorthand terms like 'state', 'bureaucracy' and 'policy' conceals much of the complexity and confusion that often marks decision-making in a complicated public service such as education. This chapter attempts to lift the curtain that often conceals the way policies are made and implemented. First, the simple model wherein the great and good decide where the service should go and how it should get there and leave the implementation to a hierarchical administration, is shown to be grossly oversimplified. Second, the influence of groups exerting pressure at all levels is spelled out.

Decision-making in educational organizations

Incremental, often messy and unpredictable decision-making within large organizations is not only a reflection of reality, but often a way to effectiveness (Weiss, 1980). The issue is not so much that 'he who must be obeyed' isn't, but rather one of the need to amend his directives to make them practicable. The usual picture of a decision being made by one or more persons at a particular time after considering probable consequences, followed by precise implementations, has been shown to have little relation to reality. Improvisation, accretion, negotiation, are as likely to produce the contributory decisions and their practical outcomes. The processes are diffused, incremental, not clear-cut and linear. Such a view of decision-making throws a new light on administration.

Three features allow for this often unplanned accretion of decisions and thus for the unintended outcomes of many policies. First, policies are made from information that flows up through the organization and are implemented as instructions flow down. But at each stage of both the up and down flows information is inserted laterally. Second, policies in a service such as education can never be so detailed or comprehensive that there is no need for interpretation at many levels. Third, the distance and time between a policy decision made at education committee and its impact in schools are both long. This provides opportunities for interest groups to exert pressure and for administrators to become aware of the attitudes of those affected. This pressure can be applied at all levels; chief education officers down to newly recruited clerks are all affected by numerous influences in their working day, through the media, and through personal involvement in educational issues.

These three features can be illustrated through the Alternative Use of Resources (AUR) method of resourcing schools adopted by the ILEA during the 1970s. This was the culmination of many moves by Dr Briault, the Education Officer, to ensure that the responsibility for allocating resources was placed where they were spent – in schools. Teachers were given a block of resources calculated on the basis of the school roll and the measured social deprivation faced. Teachers allocated these resources, within limits, to meet their own priorities. Rightly Briault saw this as important for professional development and as a cost-effective policy.

The AUR scheme was shaped over the years by decisions to allow schools virement in the allocation of earmarked resources. As the AUR scheme was polished into a policy, advice was given by teachers, divisional officers, administrators, inspectors, researchers and statisticians. Before the scheme was finally approved by the education committee, it had been affected by many sectors of the service. After the policy was approved, it was implemented through procedures planned on an annual basis. As these were worked out, officers at different levels again added their advice and adjusted procedures decided elsewhere. The scheme was Dr Briault's and it was universally welcomed as a major step towards putting responsibility for resources where they were spent. But it was a scheme that was adjusted before and after being made official policy, and these adjustments were seen as essential given changed circumstances, particularly falling school rolls.

The 200 secondary schools and 800 primary schools in ILEA are all unique institutions with differing resource needs. The AUR scheme did not fit all cases. There had to be discretion for inspectors, divisional officers and assistant education officers to meet special cases. Slowly exceptions became rules and the scheme was adapted in County Hall both as a bottom–up response to these local changes and as a top–down response to the switch from expansion to contraction, to the need to control the numbers of teachers appointed and to iron out any large fluctuations in resources received by schools year by year. Inevitably it was those schools which lost resources that applied pressure for a reconsideration of the rules, but over the years case laws were developed that supplemented the original rules and amended them.

In all the top–down and bottom–up flow of information there were opportunities for influence to be exerted. Headteachers, professional associations, advisory committees of teachers' unions and governing bodies pressed for changes or special treatment. Local councillors discussed cases with their colleagues on the education committee. This pressure group activity was applied at various levels. Political members, senior officers, divisional officers, district inspectors, the researchers who produced the data for the computer print-outs of resources, were meeting deputations and answering phone calls and memoranda.

At each stage in the annual procedure there were opportunities for interests to be pressed to produce minor changes in the allocation of resources. This incremental view of decision-making does not reduce the importance of the decision by Briault, as Education Officer, to design such a scheme or of the majority party to support it. Neither does it mean that there was a lax flexibility. Procedures were laid down and the fairness of the scheme depended on those involved resisting special pleading. This was not bureaucracy at work as defined in textbooks. Administering schools, colleges, teachers and lecturers is different from manufacturing nails or issuing television licences. There has to be flexibility in the procedures. But this does not replace bureaucracy with arbitrary judgement. Rules and procedures are the bulwark against competition and favouritism. They are adjusted at the margin to fit cases, but that adjustment must not extend to bending the rules. The danger in county halls or government departments is less one of negotiation and more one of coming to view the established procedures as the only ones possible. Above all, the existence of established procedures in large organizations binds those involved into a common perspective of the way things should be run.

Very similar features can be seen in decision-making in schools. Theorists used to model curriculum change as a linear process starting with the specification of aims and objectives, followed by the organization of teaching methods and content, and ending with feedback to secure continuous improvement. In practice the curriculum changed as a result of numerous small internal decisions, even where the school was involved in an externally directed project (Shipman et al., 1974). In the author's opinion curriculum decision-making was 'horse-trading' not rational management. Similarly, school organization can change without an identifiable and intentional decision. When there is such a decision, the outcome often surprises those who made it. Finally, the staff come to see their curriculum, their organization as the optimum way. It is, of course, but only because they have got into the routine they themselves established.

Insider and outsider pressure groups

Britain has been described as 'a paradise of pressure groups' (Sir E. Barker quoted in Wootton, 1978, p. 1). Whether viewed as the real stuff of democracy, as a way of getting at the back door what has not been voted for at the front, as the dynamic of social change, or as the cause of economic and practical stagnation as governments are stymied in the face of powerful yet conflicting interests, pressure groups are central to the political process. Because education is an expensive public service affecting the life chances of millions of children, numerous groups try to exert pressure on every policy. They range from a few irate parents temporarily pushing a common concern, to teachers' unions with a place in the 'sub-government'. The pressure groups in between these two extremes can range from visible and noisy protest on the pavements, to the discreet, quietly working, ear-bending at a gentile party. They can be 'insiders' known to each other, or 'outsiders' seeking allies among those who have a voice in decision-making. The groups range from the Society for the Protection of the Unborn Child, to the British Institute of Embalmers, stretching verily from beyond both cradle and grave.

Before decisions are made by the DES or by LEAs there will usually have been negotiations between the 'partners'. As policies are implemented more influence will be brought to bear. This will occur in central and local government, in schools and colleges, and will carry on indefinitely modifying the original policy and the procedures for implementing it. The negotiations can be both formal in committees and informal, eased by each party knowing whom to consult. The interests or political outlook of the different 'insider' groups may conflict, but these groups are often intimates when it comes to negotiating and making tricky decisions. Wootton (1978) identified 125 such organizations within the education service. Among these are a few powerful unions, local authority and consumer groups. Within each there are small groups who meet each other on committees, at conferences, at receptions, dinners and parties, in staffrooms, parent–teacher associations and on governing bodies. The conflict reported to the public can often conceal a mutual understanding that limits disruption. But from the top to the bottom of the service influence is being exerted.

'Outsider' groups can also get a foot in the door by obtaining access to key insiders. There are interlopers within the education service who are in regular contact with each other and with officials in government and union. The media consult them, report about them and consolidate their position. Access to insiders acts as a safety valve. That access is eased because pressure groups will tend to contain people with very different political views. Someone on the committee is likely to know someone who has the ear of somebody with leverage. But it can be arbitrary, unrepresentative and unfair. 'Who you know' penalizes the poor who tend to know each other and not those who feel at home in county halls, around politicians or in their dining rooms.

Pressure group access is eased by the distributed location of influence in the education service. Furthermore, even if your views are extreme, the absence of any tight centralized control increases the chance of finding some sympathy somewhere, because there is rarely a solid party or administrative line. The claques rooting for the survival of their favourite secondary school in North London in the late 1970s contained allies who on every other cause saw each other as bigots.

It is mistaken to view any political party, government, administration or union as monolithic. The state is an academic concept, consisting in practice of many, often conflicting organizations. Politicians from opposed parties meet often and can sort out many problems in private. Within the DES and within each county or town hall, there are many different views that have to be reconciled before action can be agreed upon. Local authorities differ in political control and this may not be the same as in central government. Shire counties and metropolitan areas may want to support different policies. Teachers' unions are often in conflict and within each union there will be a range of political views. At dinner in Islington or in a working man's club in Durham those who seem bitterly opposed in public are on first-name terms and work out ways forward. The education service is no different from all other services which are of pressing concern to individuals, and which as a consequence have become the focus of collective political action. Not everyone can have what he or she wants; claims have to be reconciled. But as Kogan (1978) has stressed, this political action is particularly intense in education because what people want always exceeds what they need. Education is of profound concern because it reflects parental aspirations and promotes anxieties. Inevitably it is the centre of political concern as power and influence are sought to further often conflicting interests.

The interest groups or pressure groups which try to influence policy in education range from established, well-organized associations, such as the National Union of Teachers (NUT), to short-lived local alliances of parents trying to stop the closure of a rural primary school or to introduce the teaching of Esperanto. Once again, it is misleading to think of such pressure groups as monolithic. Within the NUT will be Conservatives opposing its membership of the Trade Union Congress and members of Rank and File trying to introduce Socialist Workers' Party policies into what they see as a headmaster-dominated bureaucracy pursuing conservative and sexist policies. Groups representing minorities form, split and regroup frequently. All of them operate through the mass media, by lobbying MPs, or locally elected members, by meeting officials, governors and headteachers, by demonstrating, publicizing and ear-bending. In some cases they have gained a place in the institutional procedures for forming policy or determining procedures, and are consulted as a right. Others remain beyond the fringe. When the Inner London Education Authority decided to close its remaining grammar schools in 1975, 'save our school' leaflets were pressed on those entering County Hall. But the entrance was also jammed with supporters of the William Tyndale teachers, of the current strike by public service workers and by a noisy group protesting against immigrants jumping the housing queue.

The insider groups

The voluntary bodies   The voluntary bodies are so much a part of the education service that their presence can easily be overlooked. There are some 9000 voluntary schools, about 6000 of which are Church of England and about 2600 Roman Catholic. About 5000 of these, including all the Roman Catholic schools, have 'aided' status where the LEA meets the running costs, including the salaries of the teachers, but the voluntary body retains responsibility for maintaining the external fabric of the building and part of any cost of new building. In these schools the voluntary body appoints two-thirds of the governing body and has complete control over religious education. The remainder of the voluntary schools are 'controlled' and only one-third of the governing body and two periods of religious education are under the control of the voluntary body. But voluntary schools remain the property of the body that provided them. The DES and the LEAs have to work with the representatives of the churches when planning the service. This can be difficult. Catholic schools, for example, tend to be popular. During a period of falling rolls and teacher unemployment, these schools can take an increasing proportion of the available children, for they are not necessarily restricted to the denomination they serve. The local authority committee for voluntary schools can be lively when the diocesan authorities suspect that their freedom is being restricted.

The local authority organizations   The reorganization of local government in 1974 led to the formation of the Association of County Councils (ACC) and the Association of Metropolitan Authorities (AMA), which assumed the representative role previously played by the Association of Education Committees (AEC). The AEC had played an important and independent role in educational politics, particularly through its last general secretary, Sir William Alexander. The ACC, representing the 47 shire counties, will always tend to be Conservative. The AMA consists mainly of the metropolitan counties and the London boroughs and tends to be mainly Labour; hence the difficulty in merging into one association. The ACC and AMA have education committees with small secretariats. The members are usually chairmen of their education committees. Chief education officers act as their advisors. The two committees also established the Council of Local Education Authorities (CLEA) in 1974. This meets quarterly, provides members and officers for a number of national committees, for example on conditions of service for teachers, and acts as a meeting place for discussion between the two associations.

Because of their elected status, the local authority associations are probably the most important set of pressure groups in England (Isaac Henry, 1980). They act together or through CLEA to negotiate with the DES and with the teachers' unions. They are the formal channels through which the local authorities influence national policies. They are represented on some 50 bodies working in the education service (Brooksbank, 1980). As employers they form the management side of the Burnham Committee on teachers' pay. With responsibility for the everyday running of the service they are consulted formally and informally by the DES. The Consultative Committee on Local Government Finance negotiates with central government in the annual planning of public expenditure.

The local authority associations consist of politicians advised by chief education officers (CEOs). Political differences are therefore important when the associations are deciding on policies. Furthermore, because they are political associations, they guard their right to run education locally, according to the law. The administrators are important in giving advice and they can draw on the expertise of their departments. Central and local government administrators also meet regularly. But the political members, particularly the chairmen of education sub-committees, bring years of experience to bear. The accusation of amateurism is often raised against local politicians, but when local authority associations are negotiating with the teachers' unions or the DES, there is political as well as professional weight on both sides. The politicians bring a different, not an inferior or ill-informed view to bear.

Teachers' unions and professional associations   There is a difficulty in nomenclature over groups representing teachers. The National Union of Teachers (NUT) justifiably claims that, as the largest representative body of teachers, it should be consulted as one corner of the partnership that governs the education service. As a professional association the NUT comments on national reports and policies and produces important policy documents. But it is also a trade union which has belonged to the Trade Union Congress since 1970, and is involved in fighting for the standard of living of its members. This fight can include industrial action. The NUT has an honourable tradition stretching back over a century of struggle to establish teaching as a respected profession. The NUT insists on being represented on committees in line with its numbers as the largest teachers' union. At the other extreme is the Professional Association of Teachers, which is struggling to obtain recognition and representation. The importance of numbers in determining representation has led to bitter disputes between the NUT and the second largest teachers' union, the National Association of Schoolmasters/Union of Women Teachers (NAS/UWT). This applies not only to representation on the Burnham Committee for determining salaries and on committees organized by the DES and LEAs, but to their roles in the Trade Union Congress. In 1982 the NUT claimed 263,000 members, the NAS/UWT 156,000. The NAS/UWT has been rebuked by the General Secretary of the TUC for its criticism of political decisions made by the NUT. The Advisory Conciliation and Arbitration Service (ACAS) has been called in to resolve disputes. Both unions have opposed the right of the Professional Association of Teachers to a place at the bargaining table, despite its rapid rise to 23,000 members. Thus all the unions are active in applying pressure, but there is no unity. Indeed, the Assistant Masters and Mistresses Association (AMMA), with 89,000 members, is the voice of the independent sector. This is another example of the dangers of thinking of the government or sub-government of education as monolithic. Within each union there will be conflicting views. In the NUT, Rank and File on the left faces majorities who at times have opposed comprehensive schooling, the raising of the school-leaving age and the abolition of corporal punishment.

The NUT, the NAS/UWT, the AMMA and the National Association of Head Teachers will all send representatives to national as well as local authority advisory committees and will often supply the co-opted members on education committees. They are organized as pressure groups to ensure that teachers' viewpoint is heard in local and national issues. In 1972 there were 26 NUT members in the House of Commons. But it is misleading to overemphasize the committee work, the publications, the speeches of general secretaries, the legal advice for teachers, the parliamentary lobbying. The main work of the unions and professional associations is modest ongoing support for teachers backstage. These bodies are the creations of teachers and even though many are now powerful bureaucracies, their main work is in the engine room not on the bridge.

Coates (1972), in a study of teachers' unions and interest group politics, describes the changes that took place in the way the teachers' unions exerted influence in the 1960s. There were institutionalized contacts with the DES through membership of working parties and advisory committees. The general secretaries of the unions saw the regular informal contacts as even more important. The lobbying of Parliament, of local Members of Parliament and of local councillors, which Manzer (1970) describes as the exercise of the 'electoral' power of the unions, continued. The 'technical' power of the unions was also exercised with vigour in the 1960s. Manzer, for example, describes how the NUT pressed for the implementation of the recommendations of the Beloe Report in 1960 even though this reversed previous union opposition to any new external examinations. But as economic crises forced economies in public expenditure, the freedom of the DES to meet the demands of the teachers was restricted. The establishment of the Certificate of Secondary Education (CSE) was an example of successful pressure. But the campaign for a dependant's pension scheme on a 'shared-cost' basis in the early 1960s failed because of the financial implications such a scheme would have had within other public services. At a time when balance of payments crises, pay pauses and a low growth economy were forcing governments to look for ways of limiting public expenditure, generosity towards the teachers was too likely to lead to higher public expenditure through the action of other public service employees for the DES to be allowed much leeway in its negotiations by the Treasury.

The activities of the teachers' unions have been restricted by the tighter Treasury control over spending in the public sector and by corporate management in local government. This not only results from careful scrutiny of any increased cost for the largest block of white-collar public employees, but from the concern of the teachers' unions to protect employment, even at the cost of giving way on other issues such as movement between schools or accepting national monitoring of educational standards. For example, the NUT successfully opposed the introduction of a block grant from central government in 1957. But in 1980 it had no clout in similar opposition and such a grant was introduced. Some idea of the range of pressures exerted can be gauged from the autobiography of Ronald Gould, General Secretary of the NUT in the 1950s and 1960s (Gould, 1976). He remained a union official while there were 16 different Ministers of Education. Under Gould's leadership, for example, the NUT helped stop an attempt to delay the raising of the school-leaving age in 1947, and fought Durham County Council over the closed shop in 1951 by getting teachers to resign in the mass. These were only prominent examples. The struggle against cuts in teacher numbers has continued since the mid-1970s.

Alexander, the Secretary of the Association of Education Committees, and Gould at the NUT formed a powerful alliance capable of influencing successive ministers (Manzer, 1970). There were also annual battles over teachers' pay. Gould describes one such battle with Short, a Labour Minister of Education and an ex-primary school headmaster and NUT member. After a series of strikes the union invited the Minister to meet the teachers' panel of the Burnham Committee. Accidentally Gould had picked up a scribbled question put to the minister: 'What about £120 and staged restructuring from 1st Jan?' (Gould, 1976, p. 169). The Minister's adviser had replied: 'We *might* get this through if the teachers will *ask* for it'. Not surprisingly Mr Short soon took such a proposal to the management panel who reluctantly agreed. Roy Jenkins, the Chancellor, showed his displeasure and the LEA felt let down, but to Gould the settling of this dispute was Short's 'greatest achievement' as a minister (Gould, 1976, p. 168).

The teachers' unions are usually incorporated into the machinery of LEAs. There will usually be an advisory committee on which officers of the authority and representatives of the unions meet to discuss authority business. There may be another such committee where the teachers meet the elected members. The headteachers may be represented through another such committee. In ILEA, for example, there was a standing joint advisory committee, a consultative committee for educational matters and a central consultative committee, serving to give these three sets of links. But there are also other means of ensuring that the views of teachers and headteachers are known. The chief education officer is in contact with the secretaries of the teachers' unions and associations. They will come to see him if they are concerned about the direction of events. There may be regular meetings to anticipate and clear mutual problems.

It is the combination of formalized procedures and informal communication that enables central and local government to work. What goes on in a committee is the outcome of previous exchanges of view. It is rare for the parties involved to enter a committee meeting without knowledge of what will be acceptable to the other parties. They will ask for an adjournment in order to determine the union line if an unanticipated problem arises. Each party will have discussed its own line and will have tried to get the response of others to it in advance. The majority and minority parties on the education committee will have held a pre-meeting to sort out the line to be taken and who is to speak for it. This pre-meeting will have been preceded by the majority party discussing the agenda with officers. These officers will have consulted the teachers' unions.

This combination of formal and informal consultation may seem conspiratorial, even sinister. But if there is partnership, this is the way it works. If every policy was produced under wraps without prior consultation there would be recrimination and opposition. Business would be protracted. There are still numerous occasions when teachers are in dispute with a local authority, or when the teachers' unions refuse to cooperate with the DES. The parties push their own views and oppose those of others. But the service continues, despite the conflict, through numerous compromises and bargains. Where views are not reconcilable a clash is often avoided by talking it through before it becomes public.

Within the network of advisory committees, regularized communication and urgent or casual talk between politicians, administrators, inspectors, advisors, headteachers and teachers there are not only differences of view, but shared perspectives. The chief education officer, most of his senior administrators and the inspectorate or advisory service will share a professional view with the teachers, based on some earlier teaching experience. Sharing the teaching mystique does produce a sympathetic view of apparent teacher obstinacy and serves as a mutual defence. Politicians may abhor corporal punishment in schools and condemn teachers' representatives for their devious attitude towards its abolition, but an education officer will explain and defend the hesitation of the teachers in inner-city comprehensive schools in the 1980s. But this is only one basis for alliances. Politicians justifiably claim that they know the feelings of those who elect them, and the National Union of Public Employees can claim a very different constituency. Each party presses its case by reference to the interests it claims to represent.

The teachers' unions also campaign for more money for the education service as a whole, as well as for their own members. In 1963 all the teachers' unions participated in the Campaign for Education. The NUT conferences of 1961 and 1962 had pressed for a greater percentage of public expenditure to go to education. The initiative was taken by the NUT, but all the major teachers' associations and many other trade unions and voluntary organizations joined the campaign, which involved exhibitions, rallies, public meetings, booklets and films. At the end of the campaign, the Council for Educational Advance was established to carry on the fight for more resources.

The outsider groups

The interest in education ensures that all representative bodies will at some time try to influence the service. But there is also a wide range of pressure groups specific to the education service. They range from the National Confederation of Parent–Teacher Associations (NCPTA), which has representatives from all the major teachers' unions on its executive committee, is consulted by the DES and is itself represented on the Schools Council, to a group of parents trying to get a homosexual teacher removed from the local school. These groups often have acronyms for their title, such as the Campaign for the Retention of Eleven to Eighteen Schools in Manchester (CREEM) or the Campaign For A Uniform System of Education (CAUSE).

The NCPTA is a federation of groups concerned to press the case for cooperation between home and school. It includes the Home and Schools Council, the Parent–Staff Association and the Friends of the Schools. It presses for understanding between parents and teachers rather than parental influence over the curriculum, and this accounts for the support it receives from the teachers' unions. Other groups press more stridently for changes that may not be welcome to all teachers. For example, the Campaign for the Advancement of State Education (CASE) has, through local groups, sought to accelerate the move to comprehensive schooling, to abolish corporal punishment in schools and to increase parental participation in school government. Similar organizations are the Campaign for Comprehensive Education, the Programme for Reform in Secondary Education (PRISE) and the Council for Educational Advance. These and others press for more resources for education and for the completion of a system of comprehensive secondary schools. There are also groups such as the Campaign for Academic Standards and the National Council for Educational Standards who cry 'halt' to any further innovation in order to stop what they see as the accompanying decline of standards of attainment. Further on there is FEVER, the Friends of the Education Voucher Experiment.

The most remarkable example of successful activity is the Pre-School Playgroups Association. This started as a grassroots effort to provide playgroups until there were sufficient nursery places provided by LEAs. When the expansion of nursery schooling slowed down, the playgroups, which were started by mothers and supported by organizers from the Pre-School Playgroups Association, have filled the gap. Today they are seen as having a permanent place in the education service. This is a remarkable development as the movement has grown in the face of opposition from the NUT, who saw it as a threat to professionalism. There are other groups pressing the case for resources for gifted children, handicapped children, dyslexic children and numerous categories who need special facilities. The importance of these groups lies not only in keeping politicians, administrators and teachers aware of the need for attention to groups who require special resources, but in identifying problems for such attention. Pressure groups are an essential part of the democratic process. The position of the children of immigrants is a good example. There was not only a need to deflect resources to help such children in schools, but a need to bring home to those responsible that the communities were concerned and wanted to help.

It is not easy to affect change in education with half a million teachers claiming autonomy in the classroom and headteachers maintaining their freedom to run their schools in their own way. When MPs ask questions in the House of Commons about curricula, teaching methods or the way individual schools are run, they are told that this is not the business of the Secretary of State. When the Right to Learn or some other pressure group approaches an assistant education officer they are told that the running of schools is the concern of the staffs within them. The questions that most pressure groups ask are referred to the professionals. They claim autonomy and are sustained in this stance by the teachers' unions and professional associations. The Education Act might state that the Secretary of State should secure, or the LEA organize, efficient schooling, but actual practices and the informal agreements that reinforce them act as a barrier to those who press for change from the outside.

Here the difficulty of securing a democratic, parental or consumer interest in the service is most apparent. The Beveridge Report, and the legislation that founded the welfare state in the 1940s, omitted any direct public participation in the running of the new public services, on the assumption that this would not be necessary given the open, fraternal way in which they were to be run. Pressure groups may be only an inferior substitute. First, they usually represent those who least need help in getting the service they want. Second, the influence of groups tends to cancel out. Inaction in the face of pressure to support a Moslem voluntary school can always be justified by reference to other pressures for multi-ethnic schools. Finally, the rich informality of much of the negotiation involving 'insider' groups serves to exclude other groups. It is difficult to know where to lobby when meetings are not scheduled, or to look when there are no agendas, or to press when you don't know where the decisions were made. Justifiably, a frequent official response to a new pressure group is 'What is their constituency, how wide is their support?' But to those on the outside looking in, rejection can appear to be not only unfair, but sinister because the interests involved are concealed.

The influence of the corporate interests of the insider groups is discussed in Part Three. This description of interest groups has been necessary, not only to show the complexity of the sub-government of education, but to show how decisions can be influenced, accelerated or delayed. Interest groups bring a democratic dimension into government. But that can result in 'pluralistic stagnation' where the interests are not only influential, but conflicting and as a consequence inhibit action.

The actions of insider and outsider pressure groups feed grassroots views into decision-making. They make it difficult for government to act in unpopular ways. But the pressure also influences decision-making for if this is improvization and accretion, and not a top–down, linear procedure, influences can move up as well as down. Furthermore, they are influential at all levels. The ear of the Secretary of State may be a promising receiver for new ideas, but in a service with many decentralized centres of influence, access to a PTA or to an infant school teacher may also be effective.

PART THREE

THE EDUCATION SERVICE IN CONTEMPORARY SOCIETY

INTRODUCTION

In Part Three the working of the education service is placed in a wider contemporary social and economic context. Inevitably this contrasts with the conditions which prevailed when the education service and the welfare state were first organized. This is partly due to the expansion of the public sector. It is partly the result of the growth of large corporations through which employers and employees, in both the public and private sectors, have been involved in economic and social policy-making. The educational and welfare enterprise is a powerful force in economic and social affairs. It does not meet demands in a purely responsive fashion. It consists of powerful associations which have obtained important positions in the determination of policy. Those corporative, institutionalized positions are the subject of the two chapters that follow.

The close relation between the bureaucratic solutions to the problems of increased size covered in Chapter 5 and the professionalization of the teachers in Chapter 6 is at the heart of a major difficulty in delivering all public services. They develop a momentum generated from within. This is partly the result of investment determining the pattern of future delivery, and it is partly the consequence of the bargaining power of those employed. It is partly the claim by the public service professionals to determine the pattern of their own careers. Those who legislated in the 1940s could not have envisaged the strength of the arguments that were to be created, or the price that has to be paid, to reconcile the millions employed in the public services to policies proposed for development.

CHAPTER 5

EDUCATION IN THE CORPORATE SOCIETY

Richard Titmuss, who was a major post-1945 influence on thinking about social policy, acknowledged that welfare and economy were inseparable because '. . . the social services (however we define them) can no longer be considered as "things apart"; as phenomena of marginal interest, like looking out of the window on a train journey. They are part of the journey itself. They are an integral part of industrialization' (Titmuss, 1950). The problems of the welfare state by the end of the 1960s were largely the result of changes in the industrial structure of Britain.

The word 'corporate' is a crude way of describing the society which has developed since 1945 (see Schmitter, 1974). There has been neither the establishment of full socialism nor unfettered capitalism. Private ownership, private provision of welfare and private schooling flourish. There is government intervention, control, exhortation to reconcile public and private interests. To achieve this reconciliation governments negotiate with corporate interests such as trade unions, professional associations and employers' federations. There have been social contracts and social compacts. This is not the corporate state with a single political party, official trade unions and a fusion of business and government. It is a means of minimizing the conflict between powerful corporate groups in an economy vulnerable to pressure from both trade unions and big business and to the actions of public corporations. The involvement of those groups with government removes many decisions from Parliament and presents consumers, customers and clients with reduced choice over the product, its variety and its price. That corporate society is a long way from Beveridge's stress on individual responsibility in line with his status as a 'reluctant collectivist' (George and Wilding, 1976).

Three aspects of the trend towards large-scale organizations generating their own corporate procedures and interests, and hence influencing social and economic policy, will be considered in this chapter: first, their involvement with government; second, the tendency for governments to establish bodies with representative corporative interests that can act independently; and third, the bureaucratic organization that is used to secure the effective delivery of services. These aspects are neither necessarily invigorating nor debilitating. They are features of all advanced industrial societies, regardless of their political ideology. They may contrast with hopes at the end of the Second World War, but they are features to be analysed not condemned.

The corporate society

The transformation in the way people live and in their hopes for their children has been a triumph of organization. The modern state includes a large civil service, police and defence forces. The economy and society are dominated by large organizations, and government has itself been organized on a large scale. The potential for conflict between employees and organized employers has always been a threat to the smooth running of public services, as it is in private industry. But here too relations tend to be put on an orderly basis through routine negotiations between government, trade unions and employers' organizations. Professionals such as teachers are also involved in these national negotiations through their own associations. Through them the service offered is determined by the meeting of representatives, partners or agents. The success of large-scale organizations can be seen not only in the business corporation, the political party, the trade union and international agency, but in a service such as education, which is closely related to other services in the welfare state; but so too can the threat to the freedom of the individual to exercise influence over the services for which he pays. The Conservative government of 1979 was committed to removing this corporative apparatus. But the effect on the public services has been small.

To Beer (1982) the managed economy multiplied the power of those who ran the public services. Governments had to win their agreement. The consensus over the running of a service such as education deprived the public of choice. Each political party promised more than the economy could bear in order to win votes and cooperation. Those who worked in public services shared in a 'pay scramble' that was self-defeating because it forced up inflation, and in a 'subsidy scramble' to boost their service in competition with others.

Beer's analysis helps to pinpoint the worsening in the economic position that led to problems within education and other public services. This occurred before the oil crisis of 1973, in the wage–price explosion of the late 1960s, and it continued throughout the 1970s. Beer gives the actions of the National Union of Public Employees (NUPE) as an example. Membership of NUPE rose from 265,000 to 712,000 between 1968 and 1978. The union's policy was to maintain or increase public expenditure, hence its banner on the platform of the 1979 annual conference – 'Defend the Public Services'. In that year NUPE demanded a pay increase of 40 percent compared with the Labour government's figure of 5 percent. Before settling for 9 percent, NUPE caretakers closed many schools and the 'dirty strike' was probably an important factor in the Conservative election victory later that year.

While Beer describes this as a 'scramble' to protect the position of those who work in both public and private sectors, that protection is the prime purpose of trade unions. The NUT and NAS/UWT general secretaries now sit on the General Council of the TUC. Like other unions they exist to protect the standard of living of their members. That is difficult to reconcile with a claim to be a disinterested professional association. But it is realistic. Just as individuals welcome wage restraint and condemn tax avoidance, yet know that if they exercise restraint or refrain from fiddling, others will not be doing so and they will lose, so unions and employers, whether in the private or public sector, know that they cannot afford to be the altruistic ones while others use their muscle. Sir Ronald Gould wanted Ministers of Education to have 'brass elbows' so that they would win their way with the Treasury (Gould, 1976). But each union employs its own mailed fist. Buying them into a partnership can be expensive, and raising the price of cooperation is the job of union negotiations. Beer uses the response of Sid Weighell of the National Union of Railwaymen (NUR) to Alan Fisher of NUPE at the 1978 Labour Party conference as an example (Beer, 1982, p. 61): 'If you get 40 percent, Alan, in your world, I am going to get 40. And the difference between you and me: I have got some power to go with it.'

NUPE was only following the scramble of other public service and private sector unions, including those representing the teachers and local government officers. The important point is that this scramble took place at a time when successive governments, worried about the capacity of the economy to bear the weight of public expenditure, were involving unions and employers in key economic and social decisions. Realizing that key workers could paralyse the economy, governments adopted the corporate solution, binding employer and employee organizations into decision-making. The results have been described as 'institutional inertia' by Hayward (1976), and as the 'paralysis of public choice' by Beer (1982, p. 66).

The involvement of the organized teachers in corporatist arrangements can be seen in evidence presented by the NUT to the sub-committee of the House of Commons Expenditure Committee in January 1976. In a written memorandum the union stated that in their relations with the DES 'the main criticism of the DES's planning procedures must be that no attempt is made by the planners to involve the teaching profession . . .' (House of Commons Expenditure Committee, 1976, p. 134). Yet in evidence before the committee the union representatives refused to accept that they should be involved in ordering priorities. It was to reconcile the combination of professional association and trade union that Max Morris, an ex-President of the NUT, maintained that 'every improvement in teachers' conditions is inevitably an improvement in the education of the children in our schools. Equally every improvement in educational conditions within schools improves teachers' conditions. The two go together like that' (House of Commons Expenditure Committee, 1976, p. 141). The union's insistence on being consulted was coupled with an insistence that the service must be expanded, and that meant employing more teachers. A high price was being asked for partnership.

Corporatism is a move away from both the conservative, night-watchman role for the state and the socialist role as owner of the means of production, distribution and exchange. The House of Commons Expenditure Committee was discussing educational policy-making at a time when the economy was weak and governments were trying to get the cooperation of public and private sector employees and employers. By the mid-1970s Pahl and Winkler (1974) could argue that a new corporatist economic and social order was being organized. This was the era when CBI and TUC were called in to produce a 'solemn and binding' agreement with the government whenever an economic crisis occurred. Yet these decisions immediately affected other individuals through their wage packets or the prices in the shops, and they had no say in the negotiations. More important, the agreements were made behind closed doors and their consequences were to change the allocation of resources between public and private sectors and between the various public services.

It is easy to attack the tired corporatism of the 1970s, but economic and social problems in modern societies have to be solved. A strike can damage the whole economy, not just the company concerned. Large corporations could dominate a market to extort higher profits from the public. A balance has to be found between corporatism and open, democratic, publicly accountable organizations. In the public services the very provision of adequate services aggravates the administrative problem. Health, welfare, social security, personal social services, industrial training, housing and education take about one-third of the GNP in contemporary Britain. In these services it would be unfair if allocation was by payment, so that those who could pay received the goods. But once payment is rejected, how can services be allocated? The competition between public service unions, with those with muscle getting most, is a poor substitute. To Bell (1974) this is the major problem of post-industrial societies. There are no criteria for allocating welfare. It is unfair that the rich should be able to buy medical treatment that is not available to the poor. Moreover, treatment becomes increasingly expensive and we expect even the costliest treatment to be available in the Health Service. But how do you decide between X's arthritic hip and Y's erratic heart? Artificial joints and pacemakers are expensive. Elsewhere, how do you decide between a new brain scanner and a new nursery school in a deprived area, or between retraining for the middle-aged unemployed and courses in micro-technology for the young? That problem remains in the 1980s and corporatism persists because there is no easy solution. The alternative to consultation might disrupt some relations to a degree that would be politically unacceptable. It might also accelerate economic decline and thus make it harder still to fund public services.

The corporate solution to economic and social problems is backed by appeals to the organic, functional, interrelated structure of modern society. It is close to the appeal to fraternity in the 1940s. Conflict in one section of society soon affects the situation in another in a way that did not happen when industries and services were small scale and local. The interdependence and bargaining between corporations also ignore class, ethnic, gender and other differences. At one extreme interests can be assumed to be represented within the corporate interests by trade unions or employers' organizations. But in education and other services, as well as in economic life, assumptions by those with power that they can represent all the varied interests of those without it, can easily repress the conflict and leave the inequality intact. This is particularly dangerous in a service such as education, where the evidence of inequality is so strong and where the hopes of many parents for their children are bound to be frustrated.

The image of the education service being run by a 'partnership' of central and local government, and the teachers' unions, has a cosy reassurance about it. It suggests balance, consultation, a limit on the power of the state and the promise of agreement rather than conflict that could harm children. Most books on the English education system assume this partnership, including the official DES booklet *The Educational System of England and Wales* (1980c). There is no doubt that cooperation between the main parties involved gives the service a smooth ride. The inadequacies of the image arise partly out of differences within and between the partners. Unions rarely agree. The shire county LEAs oppose the metropolitan authorities. HMIs can adopt an independent line when detailing the harm done by sustained cuts in the education budget (DES, 1981b, 1982d). But there are defined partners and other interests have not been given partner status.

The main objection to the idea of a closed partnership is not just that other interests might be excluded, but that their right to be heard may be denied. The partners can assume that they answer for parents, for the deprived, for the minorities, for those wishing to educate their own children. Justifiably, pressure groups are challenged because they lack a constituency and a knowledge of how things really work. This week one group claims to represent a particular community, next week another group will arrive with contrasting views. Furthermore, many parents and groups are ignorant of the law on education, cannot understand the 1944 Act and do not realize how consultation occurs and committees work. There is no reason why they should, for only on the inside can the procedures be learned and used as other insiders anticipate. The 'language' of educational administration and the personnel within it become familiar not only at committees and briefings within the DES or town halls, but at conferences, receptions, dinners, over the phone or at the club. When an issue such as corporal punishment is in the air, unions, politicians, administrators and inspectors will have worked out their legal and procedural position. They would be culpable if they had not. But many interests may have been left on the sidelines while the partners have been horse-trading.

Quangos

Governments not only negotiate with corporations to bring stability to the economy and into social relations and cultural life; they also establish quasi-autonomous non-governmental organizations (quangos). The government uses these to avoid involvement in sensitive issues, to secure growth in areas where there are entrenched interests or to involve experts in allocating among themselves the resources they require.

The University Grants Committee receives money from the government and distributes it to the universities, thus preserving their independence. The Schools Council enabled the DES to promote the curriculum without controlling it. The Research Councils are funded by the DES but have independence in research funding. The Community Relations Commission, the Equal Opportunities Commission and the Commission for Racial Equality all enable the government to avoid direct involvement in sensitive racial and gender issues. Allocating contracts to private firms, universities or institutes can facilitate developments favoured by government while preserving the apparent freedom of those involved. In each case the organization is granted a degree of independence. Many decisions and developments made through quangos and contracts will affect the lives of many people unable to exert any influence, oversight or control.

In 1979 the Conservative government was committed to pruning the quangos as part of a general attack on corporatism. But the victims were few; more common was reorganization. The Schools Council, for example, while earmarked for cutbacks, was eventually split into two separate councils – one for curriculum development and one for examinations. Furthermore, just as economies in public expenditure were reversed by the money that had to be spent on unemployment benefit, so the Manpower Services Commission (MSC) became the biggest quango of all in the 1980s. Despite opposition from Shirley Williams, Labour's Secretary of State for Education, the MSC and programmes for the unemployed were placed with the Department of Employment. The Conservative government continued this arrangement and used the MSC to intervene in the education service.

There is a long history of attempts to nationalize industrial training in Britain. When unemployment among school leavers rose in the early 1970s, a fresh initiative was taken in the Employment and Training Act of 1973. This established the Manpower Services Commission with a Training Services Agency and an Employment Services Agency. The former took over the Vocational Training Scheme established 10 years earlier and renamed it Training Opportunities Schemes (TOPS), which was to become a major force in the next decade. Following the Holland Report *Young People at Work* (Holland Committee, 1977), the MSC was reorganized into three divisions, one of which, the Special Programmes Division, was given responsibility for the Youth Opportunities Programme. In 1983, there were

54 Area Manpower Boards to plan and promote the MSC's employment and training programmes.

The MSC has all the features of a quango. Its original governing body of nine included three representatives from employers, three from employee organizations, two from local authorities and one from the education service. The 1983 Area Manpower Boards consisted of five employer and five employee representatives, one from education and five or six others. The MSC was a public authority established outside government, and accountable to the Secretary of State for Employment who does not, however, carry direct responsibility for it to Parliament. The aims specified were vague, enabling the Commission to branch out into new ventures without challenge. Above all it works on an agency basis, unlike the education service which is run by elected local authorities. A quango is an organization with financial support and senior appointments from government but not controlled by it. The MSC has become a dominant force in the education of 14–19-year-olds in the 1980s. Over half a million young people were involved in the Youth Opportunities Programme by 1981, within four years of it being established.

By 1983 the MSC had moved into areas traditionally left to further education and secondary schools. Generously funded through the Department of Employment and not democratically accountable in the same way as LEAs, the Commission had launched two radical schemes – the Youth Training Scheme (YTS) and the Technical Vocational Education Initiative (TVEI). YTS guaranteed one year of full-time training to all unemployed 16-year-olds from September 1983. There were also to be expanded opportunities for the unemployed 17-year-olds. Much of this training was to be organized in further education. The rationale for the training was derived from an analysis of the economy, not from the educational requirements of the young people.

The TVEI extended the work of the MSC into secondary schools. It was announced in 1982 without consultation with the LEAs. Ten pilot programmes were to be set up in secondary schools and colleges for 14–18-year-olds at a cost of £40 million a year. The wording in the Prime Minister's statement announcing the TVEI includes: 'and, where possible, in association with the local education authorities'. The protests from the Association of County Councils were immediate (Times Educational Supplement, 19 November 1982) and included expressions about 'fundamental constitutional questions'.

The TVEI looked like a deliberate government action to use the MSC to intervene in the secondary school curriculum. It came after five years of DES publications on this subject. The constitutional position illustrated the threat of corporatism – the government was able to influence the curriculum without intervening directly. The department responsible was the DoE, not the DES. The initiative was never discussed by the LEA associations nor debated in Parliament. A well-funded development was being offered on a pilot basis to an education service strapped for funds, by a commission that was not accountable to the electorate nor in contact with parents. This initiative is, of course, a reflection on the failure of secondary schools to respond to rising youth unemployment. That point will be taken up later. The issue here is the way in which a quango can bypass democratic institutions and ignore the wishes of customers. This freedom can produce speedy action but at the cost of national and local democratic control.

The spread of bureaucracy

The education service is organized with a few painful hiccups. That efficiency is the result of procedures followed by administrators and professionals. It is customary to use the term 'bureaucracy' critically, yet it is the established procedures that secure the efficiency of the service. Furthermore, it has already been argued in Chapter 4 that innovations are made at all levels of organization and bureaucracies can often be adaptive and innovative. It is also usual to compare the bureaucrat following set routines with the professional exercising independent judgement, secure in his or her expertise. But in practice professionals flourish in bureaucracies. Furthermore, the established procedures are a defence manned by bureaucrat and professional alike against favouritism, nepotism and patronage. If there is to be equality of opportunity in a large organization such as the education service, it has to come by reducing favours, backhanders and special treatment.

The smoothness with which education is organized is typical of large public and private organizations. Ten million people use the service each year and it runs with only occasional disruption. This is a triumph of organization in two respects. First, the relations between the public services and government roll on regardless of changes of political complexion and policy. Second, each service keeps going smoothly so that the day-to-day running is rarely disturbed. There is a commitment and a skill among the administrators that is easily forgotten. This efficiency is only noticed when an adult evening class fails to run, or a grant arrives late. These two aspects –

the external relations and the internal working – secure a quality of service that can usually be assumed. The resulting order should not be under-valued. If public services did not work efficiently in a densely populated, urban society, life would be intolerable.

The capacity to organize a large public service and its relations with other, equally large and complicated services, has been developed through the selection and training of administrators and professionals to serve in predictable ways through established procedures. The jobs within the organizations are defined into routines. The files, the forms, the machines are designed to provide the information on which decisions are made in line with established norms. Citizens can rest easy about the opening times, the availability of staff, their ability to find answers, the adherence to the law, the absence of too many arbitrary and idiosyncratic decisions. Yet there is a point at which the cost of this orderly, routine response can get heavy. Services can work smoothly, but without response to the public that pays for them. Yet it is just the sources of efficiency in regulating the internal working of large organizations and the relations between them, that can reduce the choices open to individuals whom they are supposed to serve. The momentum of public services is their strength and weakness. Getting the trains to run on time is a boon; requiring official consent to purchase a radio set is not.

A public service such as education ensures basic standards of provision, some consistency across very different local authorities and a degree of equality of access to sectors that can lead to well-paid and prestigious jobs. Organizing such a service that is not too diverse and is reasonably fair in its dealings with the public took almost 100 years from 1870. As with all other such services, it involved the replacement of often arbitrary local arrange-ments by large-scale central and local government. That government has been organized without antagonizing the churches, which have played a major part in English education, and has yielded considerable local freedom to teachers to determine the curriculum. The 'national service locally administered' is a remarkable achievement, a triumph of organization.

However, allowing local freedom while ensuring consistency of provi-sion, providing predictable decisions in line with established procedures while catering for individual, local circumstances, and organizing a fair deal for all children of very different backgrounds while ensuring that very different talents could be given opportunity to flourish, takes highly rational organization. If such organization is multiplied across a developed welfare state, defence system and government economic activity, then the power of the state may threaten the liberal democracy that voted for its organization. The bureaucratic solution has been universally adopted in modern societies. This is not just a feature of capitalism. Indeed, the most rigid administrative hierarchies have been found in Soviet Russia and Nazi Germany. Djilas (1957) has argued that the bureaucracy enabled Communist Party officials to become the new ruling class, and Konrad and Szelenyi (1979) maintain that intellectuals now play a dominant part in it. In all countries, in public and private sectors, bureaucracies are organized to achieve effective, consistent administration. It is easy to use the term 'bureaucracy' as an insult. In practice, no modern state has found an alternative, and in the developing world the army often takes over government because it is the only approximation to a bureaucracy that is available to keep public services going. The triumph of bureaucrats lies in sewers, reservoirs, postal services, pensions and pay cheques.

Nevertheless, bureaucracies can pose a threat to democracies through the rigid application of rules, strict adherence to hierarchical line of authority, through centralization and an insistence on confidentiality and, above all, through the power exercised by the state over economic and social life. Administrators in a large organization are most secure when making decisions according to the rule book and referring awkward cases to their superiors. Confidentiality is often the price of being fair, for the information-seeker is often looking for evidence to support his case, and success for him may mean failure for someone else. But bureaucracies also reflect political conditions and it is easy to exaggerate their failings outside totalitarian states. Listening to a committee discussing the allocation of LEA grants to potential students, appeals by parents against placement in a particular secondary school or recommendations for qualified teacher status shows most cases being settled fairly by reference to the rules. For the few tricky cases the rules serve as the guidelines for a decision. There is rarely special pleading. If a case is known to someone involved in the decision, or that person has been approached, the interest is stated. In discussing the costs of bureaucracy the benefits have to be remembered. Playing by the book avoids personal favours. Furthermore, flexibility within bureaucracies has been described as normal in Chapter 4.

The long struggle for universal schooling in England has involved the establishment of administrative machinery within central and local government, of schools organized hierarchically, and of large, nationally organized teachers' unions. As the service was extended, its organizations became bureaucratized just as in any other large-scale public service. The demand for universality and consistency in popular schooling was secured by a series of Education Acts establishing the legal basis for centralized control to be exercised down to local levels through a hierarchy of offices. It brought order and predictability into administration and into negotiations. As in industry or the armed forces, effectiveness was secured through specified qualifications. A modern army is effective as long as orders flow through the hierarchy, in which each officer knows his responsibilities and the rules of procedure. The army, after the Crimean War débâcle, was bureaucratized at the same time as government. Bureaucracies are not conspiracies to subvert democracy but means of organizing industries, public services and other large-scale associations according to established rules.

The DES, LEAs, teachers' unions, examination boards, the Schools Council and so on keep the education service running year after year. However, for every strength gained from such a rational way of organizing a service there is a weakness. Centralization and hierarchical control at head-quarters can seem remote to those at the front, and inflexible to those with special cases to plead. The unusual case which does not fit the rules may receive arbitrary treatment. It may be possible to implement instructions from the top quickly and uniformly, but that places a lot of power in the hands of a minority. Above all, established routines may remove the arbitrariness of an aristocracy or the unfairness of patronage, but can still lead to inflexibility, rigidity and remoteness among officials.

It is easy to label the administration of education in England as bureaucratic and assume an organization hidebound in red tape. In practice, officials in Elizabeth House or in county or town halls are usually approachable and flexible. An assistant education officer for primary or secondary education in a county hall is likely to know the local headteachers, as well as being in contact with the relevant officers in the DES. However, from most positions in the administration it is difficult to see a way of organizing an education service other than by the existing procedures.

The predictability of bureaucratic procedures is, however, more than an effective way of running a large organization. If officials make arbitrary decisions, exercise patronage or make exceptions, someone will benefit unfairly. The rules and procedures of a bureaucracy ensure not only that student grants arrive on time but that eligibility for a grant is based on known rules, not on whom you know in the office or among politicians. The established procedures also secure predictability. Teachers can assume that capitation will be allocated, that they will be paid on time. Parents in turn can assume that schools will open on time and be reasonably clean and tidy.

If at every public examination there was anxiety over the arrival of the right papers at the right time and the right place, teachers would soon become neurotic. Even more important, the credibility of the examination results would be suspect.

Working to procedures does, however, make it difficult to conceive of alternative ways of doing things. It is easiest to assume that last year's budget will suffice once again, with a bit of trimming here and a few additions there. But changes outside the schools, such as rising youth unemployment, may require major changes within them and in the way the LEA allocates its resources. In practice procedures are always changing. Governments legislate and local authorities have to respond. The Health and Safety at Work legislation in the 1970s meant that a building programme had to be organized to bring schools up to the new safety levels. A new form is sent out from the DES and the education department and the headteachers have to adapt their routine to answer it. It is recommended that children with special difficulties should be integrated into ordinary schools and money has to be found for minor capital works and staff retraining.

The flow of memoranda and the passage of new legislation keep the demand for staff high in central and local government. The former create work for the latter and they complain that they are taking on staff not shedding. Within central and local government, administrators also keep each other busy. This usually comes from a genuine concern to improve the quality of the service, the effectiveness of the administration. More information is always needed; it improves the potential of the service. Down the line, executive and clerical staff learn a job with a restricted perspective and deal with routine matters by the book. Unusual cases are referred to seniors who will have had experience of ways of fitting them to the routine. Each will lack the perspective to answer the question 'Why do we always do it this way?', and each will be unlikely to ask it because every form on the desk, every piece of data on the visual display unit tends to confirm that the routine fits the cases. Furthermore, the information passing through the office binds the officers to the routines because each has expectations of the giver and the taker. The predictability reinforces the feeling that there is but one way.

The easiest way of confirming this reinforcement of existing procedures is to observe attempts to introduce computerization. Many offices have failed to benefit from the introduction of computers, to the frustration of efficiency experts and business management whiz-kids. They are easy meat for old hands who are convinced that the old ways are best and who are secure under the Employment Protection Act. But even in the top administration and among the professionals, change can look threatening. A Right to Learn group obtains an audience in county hall and presses for schools in deprived areas to stick to an academic curriculum so that the poor will not lose in the competition for jobs. This should be achieved by ensuring that all staff, however senior, do a share of the teaching. It is not an unreasonable request. But LEAs do not tell teachers how to organize their schools and the curriculum is settled by staff. Informal talks with the teachers' unions confirm that such suggestions are unwelcome. Even a modest proposal can look threatening; it can also look impossible if it is alien to routine – its legality will be looked at carefully. Under these circumstances, parents and others trying to initiate change will need political clout if they are to get any action.

It is customary to criticize bureaucracies. But as mentioned in Chapter 4, even at the humblest levels clerks can alter procedures. Indeed, if this were not the case, the automatized or computerized office would have arrived sooner. Discretion has to be used, for parents, children, teachers, schools, local authorities and government departments all have their individual characteristics. Policy-making and implementation are rarely top–down, straight-line procedures, because initiatives are taken at all levels. Bureaucracy is one of those handy catch-phrases; its textbook definition and actual practice may be poles apart.

The education service not only has to allocate huge resources, but has to meet competitive pressure from parents and others. The pressure to get a child into the school with the best reputation, to pass the most prestigious examinations or to enter university, is high. The education service, like other public services where there is similar high demand, was organized to control the competition. This is one important function of bureaucracy. The rules are impartial because that seems fair where many are competing and opportunities are scarce. The standards applied are universalistic, not adjusted for particular cases. This is a particularly difficult problem in the education service. Parents are naturally inclined to see their own children as possessing the qualities needed to achieve. The professionals and the administrators establish criteria for selection which will violate the hopes of many parents. Even with increased facilities, there will still be massive frustration. But the forms, the questions, the conditions and the criteria are not only the means of ensuring that all are treated alike, but that justice visibly appears to be done. The results are often unfair, but the reasons for that lie in the social conditions outside the bureaucracy, not in the procedures used in allocating benefits. However, once that wider perspective is adopted, the organization of the education service is open to question.

The first and most sensitive issue is that any procedures for exercising clout within any service can be utilized by those who need them least. Bureaucracy can minimize favouritism. But in education as elsewhere, getting the school of your choice, the attention and the interview is easiest for the articulate. In the best position of all are those who work in the service. The evidence on the success of the service class in using the expanded opportunities within education is striking (Halsey et al., 1980). Money helps because private schooling buys good public examination results. So does living in an area where the children of the service class set the tone of the schools. But everywhere it is possible to maximize opportunities for your own children by knowing which schools get good results.

In examining the problem of individual or communal choice in a large-scale public service, attention is inevitably focused on the articulate. But there may always be a larger, inarticulate, discontented section of the population below those who get the publicity. Thus it is fair to start with the 50 years of evidence that the education service has yet to raise the attainments of semi- and unskilled workers' children to anywhere near those of children from wealthier families. From there it is a short step to the increasingly articulate voice of the Black population and of women that they too consistently fail to benefit from the schooling offered, when compared with other groups. It is not due to lack of interest or information, for committees report regularly and the race relations industry has a productive research branch. Yet ways forward are constrained by the narrow range of options considered. Blacks may ask to be left alone by researchers, curriculum developers, psychologists wishing to test, and sociologists to survey. They may ask for support for their own schools and their own efforts. Indeed, the situation where teachers follow expert advice and organize Black studies and basketball in schools to raise self-image, while the Black parents use Saturday schools to enable their children to keep up with the basic skills is ludicrous (Stone, 1981). Maintained schooling in England is protected from radical innovation. Moslem parents might want to open their own voluntary school, but the partners in the education service do not see this as something to be encouraged.

Experiments in vouchers, in tax concessions, in money for communities to organize their own schools, which are popular in Canada and the USA, are seen as not practicable in England. Yet the law is not clear on the rights and duties of LEAs or parents. Section 36 of the 1944 Education Act says: 'It shall be the duty of the parent of every child of compulsory school age to cause him to receive efficient full-time education suitable to his age, ability and aptitude, either by regular attendance at school or otherwise.' Education Otherwise is an interest group pressing for the right to educate children at home. Yet many LEAs are reluctant to accept such a right and the matter often has to be decided by the courts. But parents in England could claim that some schools are not efficient and the 1944 Act seems to give parents the duty of ensuring that they are. There may be a duty on parents to remove their children from a school that they judge to be inefficient (Kitto, 1983). This is an embarrassing position for LEAs. In the end an attendance order will be made out and the parents taken to court.

If it was accepted that some parents could provide an efficient and an appropriate education at home this would only affect a few. They would be following the tradition of the English upper class who did not trust schools and used tutors. But it would open the way for communities to act to secure the education they wanted for their children. The definition of 'efficient' would pass from producer to consumer. This seems acceptable across the Atlantic, but it unites the 'partners' in opposition here. There is little choice for most parents. Few can afford private schooling. Few maintained schools offer a distinctive curriculum. Many parents have to accept places in schools with regimes that are abhorrent to them. Within the partnership it is easy to dismiss these demands as cranky. But Education Otherwise, Blacks, parents, women and those who speak for the poor share a criticism of the maintained sector of education that choice is restricted, and that parents and identifiable groups make little progress when they ask for alternatives that would suit them.

At the end of the 1970s central government pressed for schools to become more accountable. This is usually analysed as a conspiracy by the DES to strengthen its grip on the curriculum and teaching methods (Lawton, 1980). But it was a response to the proliferating pressure groups of the 1960s and 1970s, and to the Taylor Report on the government of schools (Taylor Committee, 1977). At this time the DES was recommending that there should be greater parental involvement in schools and that the latter should become more responsive to the communities they served. The Education Act 1980 implemented some of the recommendations of the Taylor Committee. All schools were to have their own governing body, and both teachers and parents should sit on it.

The other important and controversial part of the 1980 Act dealt with the release of information about schools. This was anticipated in the Green Paper (DES, 1977) which was published at the end of the Great Debate. The Act stated that LEAs and governors had to publish the rules about admission to the school, arrangements for parents to express a preference, the appeals procedure and the number of places available. If parents were to make a choice they had to know how to do so. But the Act left it to the Secretary of State to decide what other information should be published to help parents exercise their new statutory right to express a preference. The information was to include arrangements for visits to schools, details of the curriculum and teaching arrangements including homework, pastoral arrangements and the position over corporal punishment, extra-curricular activities, school uniform and examination results.

Most attention focused on the publication of examination results and the final form suggested was not unlike that already used by many schools. But there was uproar over this release of information. For example, Fiske, the Chief Education Officer for Manchester, described it as a 'time consuming irrelevance' (Fiske, 1980a). To him 'the most helpful information for parents is that which if published would run the risk of action under the libel laws'. Yet it is difficult to see how parents could exercise choice without information, even if they could not have the hot gossip about teachers X and Y. The publication of examination results could lead to very misleading comparisons being made between schools, and to schools being condemned for poor results when in practice they were really doing a first-class job (Shipman, 1978). But to deny parents the right to obtain information about the curriculum, homework and incidences of corporal punishment seems absurdly restrictive. Yet some schools were reluctant to give this information and it was most unfair on just those parents who needed the information most. Those who work in the service or in similar services know how to obtain information by a direct approach to head-teachers or the education office. A majority do not have this facility and there is sufficient evidence of blue-collar children failing while those of white-collar parents succeed for the Act to be seen to be doing something to equalize the information available to all groups. Yet it was greeted as a conspiracy to impose central government-defined league tables for parents to promote and demote schools at will as rolls fell.

The increased activity by central government to give parents and others rights within the education service has been part of a drive to reduce corporatism and its manifestation in quangos, contracts and understand-ings. The 1980 Act is one of many attempts to give consumers more say in the services for which they pay taxes. It is impossible to sort out how much of this political action to create an opportunity state is aimed at reducing the power of trade unions, professional associations and of government itself, and how much is a genuine attempt to increase choice in matters that are of personal concern to the public and over which corporations were increasingly making the important decisions. But central government can encourage corporatism or can discourage it. Not every move by the DES is an attempt to increase central government influence. Governments have the responsibility of translating into practice what they see as the majority electoral view. As corporate interests are not given up voluntarily such government action is often necessary. Indeed, just as governments use corporations to order economic and social life in modern society, so they have the power to reduce the strength of the arrangements between them. Government economic action usually seems to encourage the formation of monopolies, but there is also legislation aimed at stopping the monopolization of markets against the public interest. Similarly, it is convenient for government to use the educational partnership to secure the smooth running of the service, but there is also political sensitivity to the public feeling that not enough notice is taken of those who pay the piper but cannot call the tune.

The hopes behind the 1944 Education Act look strange in the 1980s. Corporatism and frustration at the insensitivity of officials are the opposite of the Beveridge principle that fraternity should be promoted not only by all sharing the social services, but by the humane relations between officials and the public. The rejection of stigma attaching to the receipt of free health care, social security or education required not only universal services provided by universal contributions, but fraternity in surgery, office and department. This was naive because it ignored not only the individualist drive to derive maximum benefit from services such as education, but the size of the organization that would be needed in the welfare state. It is difficult to see an alternative to bureaucracy if there is to be efficiency. But Beveridge also ignored the way power is unequally distributed. In 40 years a lot more power here as elsewhere, regardless of political complexion, has gone to the apparatchiks, the bureaucrats, because they provide the continuity through their capacity to organize on a large scale. In Britain we are far from the soul-destroying government machine of the USSR, but the demand for more open government in the 1970s was timely. Behind the continuity there was too much injustice for the critics to be muted.

CHAPTER 6

TEACHERS AS PUBLIC SERVICE PROFESSIONALS

In Part One we examined the place of education within the welfare state alongside other social services. That situation is now related to education as a large corporate enterprise. The professional role of teachers has both social welfare and bureaucratic, selective aspects. The range of activities carried out by teachers makes it difficult to treat teaching as a unified profession. At one end of the spectrum we have teachers as 'dirty' workers, taking on tasks that are similar to those of social workers, welfare and probation officers and policemen. They help clean up or cover up the mess created by breakdowns in responsibility outside the school. All teachers combine these control and pastoral roles with sorting, grading and differentiating between children to fit them into further and higher education and employment. At the 'clean' end of the spectrum are teachers who do not have to worry about discipline problems and are able to concentrate on maximizing attainment, understanding and enjoyment.

There is little in common between the extremes of 'clean' and 'dirty' teachers, yet discussions over professionality lump them together. There has always been an elementary school tradition that involved teachers in pastoral and control responsibilities, just as there has been a grammar school tradition. These differences persist within primary and comprehensive secondary schools.

There is an academic fascination with the position of teachers as professionals and with their status as middle or working class. The verdict on professional status usually reduces to judgements about the fit between lists of traits and the activities of teachers. The second often ends in daft discussions about whether teachers in independent schools are working class because they sell their labour to an employer and produce surplus value, while teachers in maintained schools are not productive workers because they do not work for capitalist employers (Open University, 1981).

The practical issue arises from the impact of the extraordinary growth in the number of professional employees in the public services. Public sector employment in the UK has risen since 1960, while in the private sector the 1980 level was below that of 1961. Professional and scientific employment rose from 2,124,000 to 2,989,000 in 1971 and to 3,717,000 in 1980 (Central Statistical Office, 1982). In 20 years from 1961 manual occupations as a share of total employment declined by over 10 percent. Non-manual occupations increased by over 10 percent (Manpower Services Commission, 1980). Between 1952 and 1977 the Clerical and Administrative Workers' Union was renamed the Association of Professional, Executive, Clerical and Computer Staff (APEX) and its membership rose from 40,000 to 150,000. In the same period membership of the National and Local Government Officers' Association (NALGO) rose from 222,258 to 709,000. The Association of Scientific, Technical and Managerial Staffs (ASTMS) became a major union with 441,000 members by 1977.

The growth in public service professionals has come through recruitment to existing groups such as lawyers and accountants and through the professionalization of other occupations. This latter trend had accelerated to a pitch where Halmos (1966) sees the professional service ethic as a new moral order in industrial societies. Certainly the public service professionals have become a major occupational group and the teachers form the biggest single section among them.

The claim to be treated as a profession rests on rather ill-defined criteria. Expertise in a non-manual job appears to be the common factor. Millerson (1964) extracted 23 elements that had been used by 21 authors to define 'a professional'. None of the authors agreed on any combination of elements, but three clusters are detectable and will be used to show that teachers take on such contrasting tasks that it is difficult to view teaching as a single profession. First, professionals give a disinterested, altruistic service based on established codes of conduct. Second, a professional career is mapped out on the basis of ensured competence. Third, there is training to give practical skill based on qualification. These three clusters of traits are not gates through which all groups have to pass to obtain recognition as professional. Indeed, the British Medical Association is hardly altruistic in bargaining over doctors' salaries, and the incompetence of some lawyers must worry the Law Society. They are rather the bases of the claim to be given independence of action. Although established when doctors and lawyers were in private practice, the criteria now have to apply to groups who mainly work in large private or public corporations. This is the common thread running through the first three sections of this chapter. Professionals have proliferated within the corporate society, serving large organizations. In the 1940s public services were organized into a welfare state when professionalization was a well-established stream. But it was soon to become a flood, with the education service as the floodgates. This expansion still left barriers to professional mobility, thus compartmentalizing the service. This is the subject of the final part of this chapter.

The growth in large private and public corporations employing administrators, professionals, scientific and technical staff has produced new, articulate and influential groups in industrial societies. The label 'service class' is usually used to describe those who use their expertise in, and on behalf of, corporate bodies. The rapid expansion of such bodies means that many staff have been newly recruited. Their appointment depends on educational qualification. They have been the beneficiaries of the investment in schools, colleges and universities. Teachers form a large part of this group and in this and the following chapter, their influence on social and educational policy is reviewed.

'Professional' is another of those slippery terms beloved in academia. Doctors and lawyers are professionals yet range from the royal family's gynaecologist to back-street abortionists and from the Master of the Rolls to legal eagles specializing in tax avoidance. In teaching, on the one hand there is the Professional Association of Teachers committed never to strike, and on the other there is the Workers' Action Teachers whose manifesto proclaims that 'History teaches us that the bourgeoisie will not give up its power without a fight, and the working class will only be able to resolve the situation by military, not economic means' (Workers' Action Teachers, 1977).

It is first necessary to recognize the compatibility between employment in government and in bureaucracies, with professional status. Bureaucratic organization seems to be a hostile environment for the professional. The independent and disinterested application of skills developed in higher education and through contacts with clients seems alien to organizations where hierarchy and routine dominate. But professionals in bureaucratic organizations can club together to claim special status, to resist subordination by administrators and to exercise the distinctive skills that can never be routinized. The spread of professions has accompanied the rise of bureaucracies.

Teachers, for example, have attained professional status through collective action as the education service has become big business within developing central and local government. Bureaucracy and professionalization have been developed in harness despite their apparently conflicting values; advanced industrial societies seem to be fertile ground for both.

In practice the activities of professionals such as teachers fit in well with large-scale organization. Thus the idea of autonomy in the classroom and the exercise of professional skills in dealing with children are easily reconcilable with a syllabus determined by a bureaucratic examination board. Similarly, a researcher in a bureaucracy can still exercise professional skills, but the scope of his work is constrained as the subject to be investigated and the style of report have to be geared to the requirements of the administrators who want the information. Much talk about being professional is meaningless. The free-wheeling professional minority are mainly found in the academic world, exercising an invaluable critical function. But they too are supposed to prepare students for externally examined tests of approved syllabuses. The majority of professionals draw their pay from large organizations yet exercise their skills within limits that are rarely restrictive. Both bureaucrat and professional are secure behind watertight contracts and inflation-proofed pensions.

The common factor linking bureaucrat and professional is that the steps in their careers are clearly laid out. The procedures that mark the bureaucracy also mark out orderly career patterns. The signs are the negotiated scales, the posts of responsibility, the increments, the sequence of promotions, the security of employment. Larson (1977) sees this as a privilege, and as the reason why professionalism and bureaucracy flourish together. The stability of the organization is the guarantee that the career will be secure. Regular increments, set proportions of senior posts, tenure and fixed criteria for promotion, make the future predictable. Professionals press for bureaucratization because it guarantees a secure future while not threatening their claim to be disinterested and altruistic. The consequence is to secure a mapped-out career pattern. There is also predictability at the recruitment stage. Private sector employers use a variety of recruitment strategies (Ashton and Maguire, 1980). Public sector recruitment is based on specified criteria including examination qualifications. The career can be planned well in advance.

Teachers in the public service

The connection between this close association of professionalism, bureaucracy and the expanding public services, such as education, lies in the universalism that was the major principle of the 1942 Beveridge proposals. This required the establishment of services in which everyone received benefits as rights, regardless of whether their contribution was direct or through taxation. Those benefits were to be predictable, based in legislation, and not determined at the whim of teachers or social workers or social security officials. Schools promise careers that are as predictable for pupils as for teachers and the prospect is similar to that of the man or woman approaching retirement or entering hospital for an operation. Security lies in predictability. The institutionalization is not a threat but a comfort to those involved. Universalism is a barrier against favouritism. It is also the principle behind the organizations that secure predictable benefits based on standard, public criteria. Public examinations are a good example.

An education service that is organized to produce and reward measured, examinable attainments has been provided since 1944. Whether the failure to increase the opportunities for the children of the poor is the result of adverse social conditions outside the schools or of the organization within, is still a matter of debate whenever evidence is produced. Reports such as those by Bennett (1976) and Rutter et al. (1979) suggesting that the organization of learning matters, have been followed by criticisms that they have underestimated the power of factors outside the school (see, for example, Gray and Satterley, 1976; Tizard et al., 1980). What is not in doubt is the way schooling has been organized to differentiate progressively between children as they go through primary and secondary schools. That differentiation is disinterested in the universalistic sense, in that opportunities are provided for all, even if that is hardly altruistic in the light of the evidence that the children of the poor lose while those of the service class succeed.

Below the debate about the professionalism of teachers lies a tragedy. Whatever the sense of vocation, studies of the aims of teachers suggest that they are committed to helping children become moral beings and good citizens, as well as knowledgeable persons (Ashton, 1975). But schooling takes in children at age five, and 11 years later they are sorted into groups going to university, maintained higher education, further education, apprenticeships, skilled, semi-skilled or unskilled employment, or unemployment. Schooling provides the qualifications and assessments that determine future prospects. Teachers prepare each new generation for the advanced division of labour in industrial society.

It is the relation between the categorization of children as part of normal classroom interaction and the sorting-out for future employment which produces the tragedy. There is overwhelming evidence that children from poor homes, girls and Blacks lose out in the race for qualifications and for high-prestige employment. Teachers who want to help children in far more than just learning skills witness, generation after generation, benefits going to the children of the service class and handicaps to the poor. It is genuinely tragic and particularly uncomfortable for the most concerned and egalitarian. This is well illustrated by a look at any review by Max Morris, an ex-President of the NUT, of a book on the sociology of education (Morris, 1980). Morris spent a lifetime supporting comprehensive schooling and fighting for the rights of poor children. Editors ask him to review sociology texts which repeat over and over again the message that all reforms seem to have failed to promote greater equality through education and that teachers play a part in the sorting-out that continues the unfairness. As anticipated by the editors he criticizes with the vigour and passion of the socialist idealist. But the evidence remains and recently has been reinforced by studies of the attainments of girls and of Black children. Teachers are in a tragic situation for as they act professionally they differentiate between children. That is their job. The net result is the reinforcement of the very injustice that most teachers abhor.

The key to this tragedy lies in the relation between the bureaucratic organization of the maintained sector catering for all children for a minimum of 11 years and the professionalism of the teachers. Teachers have a degree of independence, but children in both primary and secondary schools progress through a curriculum towards public examinations that are sufficiently rigid for central government to be relaxed about the possibility of excessive variety. For the teachers in schools serving wealthy areas with supportive parents, there need be little concern with discipline or caring for individual, personal problems. The teaching task is to keep up the momentum towards public examination success from an early age. The main task of teachers in many schools is to follow the predictable sequence of annual events. It is bureaucratic in following established procedures to cover examination syllabuses and ensure that children obtain the maximum possible qualifications. There is popular backing for this role; it is an important influence on all teachers. But in many schools it cannot be sustained. The alternative pastoral or policing role is considered later.

The compatibility between professional status and work in organizations such as schools is achieved through the security derived from the bureaucratic aspects of the education service. Teachers can concentrate on their work, whether this is primarily academic or pastoral, because the monthly pay cheque will arrive, because increments will come, because promotion ladders are visible, because syllabuses are prepared, because the examination boards are efficient in setting and marking papers and because higher education and employers use the examination results in a predictable way. However, no profession can relax and leave its rewards and conditions of service to the goodwill of employers, whether public or private. If professional disinterest also includes ignoring material rewards, no professional group has ever done much except make sure that they are not embarrassed by having to collect their fees direct from their clients. Teachers are only as concerned to keep up their standard of living as any other group. Their problem is that there are so many of them and their salary bill makes up such a large proportion of public spending that their annual pay claim attracts publicity and Treasury scrutiny.

The range of feeling in teachers' response to the cutbacks of the 1970s can be seen in the two extremes quoted earlier (p. 129). The Professional Association of Teachers (PAT) stated that: 'In order to provide employment for newly trained teachers and maintain satisfactory staffing ratios, members will be prepared to sacrifice £1 of the proposed £6 a week increase, due in April' (Professional Association of Teachers, 1976). Commenting after the same award, the Workers' Action Teachers wanted 'All qualified teachers to be employed' and 'Hiring of teachers to be done in the first instance from unemployed members of the union through local NUT branches . . .' (Workers' Action Teachers, 1977). These contrasting views among teachers reflect the breadth of interests in the profession. What was shared was a reluctance to use the only leverage available to obtain a bargaining position as any industrial action would harm the children. As public servants, teachers are visible because of their number, divided because the job can be so different and vulnerable because of the nature of their responsibility.

The regulation of competence

A profession can be seen as a way of controlling an occupation. Central to that is the guarantee that those involved will have at least a minimum level of knowledge and skill. This is secured partly by controlling intake by

insisting on specified qualifications. It is partly based on ensuring competence in post, which is not easy in teaching. The absence of self-government
and the difficulty in specifying and testing effective teaching will be discussed later. There are both control and technical problems. The two issues
have confused the debate over accountability since the mid-1970s.

The drive for a better qualified teaching force has been backed by the
teachers' unions for over a century. They have pressed for a graduate
profession, compulsory professional preparation and expanded in-service
training. The movement for the registration of teachers started in the 1860s
and merged into suggestions for a teachers' council a century later. But
there has been opposition to the setting up of a General Teaching Council
that would perform tasks similar to the Law Society or the General Medical
Council. Such a council for teachers was recommended by the government
in 1970. The council was to advise on the accreditation of new teachers and
to establish a code of conduct for those in post. But the teachers' unions in
England have been mainly divided, opposed or lukewarm in their attitude
towards it. The General Teaching Council established in Scotland has not
reduced this opposition because teachers do not sit on it as a right. Most
discussion in England founders on this issue of representation. The
organized teachers have shown no enthusiasm to have a body concerned
with a register of teachers and hence with the possibility of removal from
registration. Significantly the Scottish Council does not include consideration of professional competence in its terms of reference.

With public concern over education, and anxiety over the tendency for
contraction to centralize decision-making within the service, the inertia
over this management issue is unfortunate. An honourable exception has
been the College of Preceptors, which has pressed the case for a General
Teaching Council to 'establish teaching as a profession by constituting a
professional body applying and administering those standards of education,
training and conduct' (Phillips, 1981). Sayer (1980), an ex-President of the
Secondary Heads Association, after detailing the lack of management in the
preparation of teachers and in their pay and promotion structure, similarly
sees a solution in a General Teaching Council with wider terms of reference
than those usually discussed relating to professional standards and conditions of service. But unlike dentists, architects, surveyors, lawyers,
accountants, doctors and engineers, teachers are not chartered to admit or
exclude their colleagues.

The reluctance of the organized teachers to press for a council that would
have the power to judge teaching competence leaves a gap in professional

credibility. The NUT view is that there is no problem given the existing procedures for the inspection, assessment and, if necessary, dismissal of teachers. In response to the Taylor Committee's suggestion that governors should be involved in the career development of teachers, the NUT responded that 'Teachers are subject to conditions of tenure which make them fully accountable, and the Union regards the existing arrangements as entirely adequate. It does not accept that there is any need to open discussions on the subject between the Secretary of State, the local authorities and the teacher organisations' (NUT, 1978). Yet the Union is critical of standards achieved in teacher training institutions, stresses the inadequacies of the probationary year and acknowledges that every occupation 'contains people of varying abilities and standards of performance'.

Obviously no profession wants to advertise its incompetents. But out of half a million teachers there must be failures as well as successes. The former can be found in many schools and it would be extraordinary if this were not the case. It has been possible for graduates without any professional qualification to enter teaching in many years when there was an acute shortage of teachers. Failure rates on certificate and BEd courses have always been low. The probationary year is so meaningless that few new teachers realize they are on probation. There are areas of inner cities which never managed to recruit to strength during the 1970s. Inevitably many teachers were recruited and then turned out to be unsuitable. Given the heroic qualities sometimes required, this is not surprising. Yet there has been no way of identifying such teachers and removing them before they do more harm to children. The procedures for assessment and dismissal are cumbersome and authorities risk the possibility of the teachers' unions justifiably opposing dismissal by threatening industrial action. The costs of dismissing teachers can be gauged from the William Tyndale School inquiry. The tribunal heard 107 witnesses and examined over 600 prepared documents. There were 20 lawyers involved and the 12 sessions stretched over four months. Three politicians and a teacher member of the schools sub-committee attended all the sessions. The Inner London Education Authority provided the administrative, inspectorial and clerical back-up. Behind the scenes other officers prepared papers, advised lawyers, worked on statistics and negotiated at length with the teachers' unions. The report also led to major reorganization within the ILEA. Small wonder that such action is rarely taken in this formal way and that the acknowledgements made in the report begin: 'This inquiry has proved to be a much more onerous and lengthy task than anyone envisaged at the time when it was instituted' (Auld Report, 1976).

The viewpoint of the teachers' unions is understandable. They represent many members, senior and junior, good or bad. Yet the claim to be professional rests on the definition and maintenance by peers of standards of competence. Such regulation seems even more important when the clients are children not adults as with doctors or lawyers. Here the term 'professional' can easily become rhetorical. The reality is of a spectrum of teaching skills ranging from excellent to harmful. But there is no public acknowledgement of this even if there is much private, behind-the-scenes concern and cooperation to tackle the worst cases. Even when falling school rolls produce a surplus of teachers, the cutback is achieved through early retirement and ceasing to recruit even the best of the output from the teacher training institutions. The inadequate may stay in post with the rest and because of their deficiencies may stay put until retirement, despite efforts backstage. A lot of children can be affected by any one teacher across 40 years. The claim to be independent as a professional is difficult to reconcile with the absence of an established and visible procedure for controlling competence that has the public's confidence.

Academic views of professionalization tend to polarize. Some have seen the movement as the means of securing consistent standards with autonomy for teachers in their schools. But others see the rise of the expert as the way in which genuinely popular education, including that provided by family and community, has been undermined and then replaced by maintained schooling that secures a compliant workforce. Historically, teaching has been professionalized on the same basis as other occupations. First, recognition is gained that teachers provide identifiable skills not available among lay people. Second, those skills are built into training, and teaching is limited to those who have qualified after taking approved courses. Looked at this way, the fight for an all-graduate, professionally trained teaching force can be seen as a way of gaining control of the market, just as doctors or lawyers had done before. The amateur is excluded and the accredited can speak with authority to the lay public. The gains have been considerable. It is comforting to know that your doctor is not a quack and that your lawyer just looks Dickensian. Equally it is important that those in charge of children are morally and technically trustworthy and that there is some qualification attesting this. But separating the benefits for the professionals from those accruing to their clients is not easy, and there may be costs to the latter from the position of the former.

The theoretical basis of practical competence

The increase in the length of training for teaching and the raising of qualifications for achieving teacher status have been striking. Many teachers were trained on a one-year course in emergency training colleges after 1945. Others took a two-year certificate course. Graduates entered teaching direct or after a one-year postgraduate course. The one-year certificate courses were soon dropped and in 1960 a three-year certificate course was introduced. Today these certificate courses have been replaced by BEd degrees which increasingly last four years. Direct entry to teaching after graduation is being stopped and all graduates will have to obtain a professional qualification before teaching. An O-Level qualification in mathematics and English has also become a condition for entry. There is, therefore, graduate entry, compulsory professional training and minimum qualification in basic subjects. The teaching force is big, well qualified and increasingly professionally trained. The growth area in the 1980s is in-service education, which not only raises the level of professional skill, but enables those in post to raise their academic qualifications.

This insistence on professional training does not necessarily result from the construction of courses providing adequate preparation for future teachers. Indeed, it is not even possible to define what makes an effective teacher. Much of the early research was pursued at the University of Wisconsin. Between 1920 and 1960 there were 83 investigations into teacher effectiveness. They produced 183 measures, but a summary of this effort from within the University's School of Education saw none as satisfactory and concluded that each investigation started afresh rather than building on the previous one (Wisconsin School of Education, 1961). The search has continued. Dunkin and Biddle (1974) looked forward to an education service guided by research on teaching. Bennett (1979), reviewing the available evidence, presents a model for effective teaching, but he concludes than an educational system based on research is still a 'pipe dream'. Wilson (1975), writing as a philosopher looking at professional preparation, described it as a 'mess'. The British Journal of Teacher Education and the British Journal of In-Service Education are not for the nervous. Neither is there any consistency in the advice given to teachers. Her Majesty's Inspectors, who pressed a multi-disciplinary or integrated approach for primary teachers in training at the time of the Plowden Report (1967), were pressing for subject specialists 10 years later. Those responsible face only one constant factor: there will always be contradictory advice available.

The perennial criticisms of teacher education reflect the dilemma in trying to combine academic and professional training. Students are critical of the lack of time spent in the classroom while under training, of the gap between the experience and views of staff in college and practices in schools, and the limited value of professional courses (National Union of Students, 1971; Taylor, 1978). Teachers tend to voice similar criticisms (NUT, 1971b). HMI found one in four newly qualified teachers not good enough to teach (DES, 1982c). But the one-year postgraduate course is too crowded to permit much time in school. The BEd courses have to satisfy the academic criteria of universities or the Council for National Academic Awards (CNAA). The CNAA view is clear (Kerr, 1976); CNAA Director Edwin Kerr put it this way: 'The Council's not going to change its academic judgements, it cannot, it has got the chartered responsibility to make these academic judgements and if it makes an academic judgement of that sort and the proposing college cannot fill that judgement, then in the Council's opinion that course cannot start until that particular condition has been fulfilled' (Kerr, 1976). This is also the view of universities who would support Kerr's view that '. . . I don't think the Council is in business to lower standards'. Raising the academic level of courses is important, particularly as the qualifications of the intake rise. But the academic–professional balance remains a problem. Beneath it lies the very different needs of teachers destined for the clean and dirty ends of the teaching spectrum.

The major influence on the education of teachers has been the numbers required. This is under the direct control of the DES, and it has fluctuated wildly. The number in training colleges was increased to 114,000 in 1972. New buildings were still going up in colleges when they were closed in the 1970s once school rolls began to fall. In 1977 the output was planned to fall to 17,000 a year. Another 1200 places were cut off the intake in 1982. The colleges were the tap which was turned on and off as the demand for teachers changed. The expansion and the contraction of colleges also served as a means of expanding or contracting higher education.

Hencke (1976) has described how reorganization that started from considerations of educational matters became first political and then administrative. The James Committee (1972) consisted mainly of academics concerned with academic matters. It proposed that colleges should be linked to universities in an open partnership and that there should be regional associations of all institutions concerned with the professional training of teachers. But then teacher education became part of the problem of planning the non-university sector. The falling demand for teachers, the geographical distribution of colleges and the need for financial savings became the key factors in planning, not the quality of the professional preparation.

Working in Inner London at the start of the 1970s, where primary school intakes were already falling and where the birthrate had been rapidly falling for more than five years, it was obvious that there was a choice between cutting training places and producing a very large surplus of teachers. The cutback that started in 1973 led to the closure of 13 colleges and a halving of teachers undergoing training from the 114,000 in 1972. Output was cut after a decade of rapid expansion. By 1981 it was clear that not even this cut was sufficient to avoid excessive teacher unemployment and the planned output was to be 15,500 a year in the early 1990s (Advisory Committee on the Supply and Education of Teachers, 1981). There is no doubt that there was general concern about the role of the DES in these plans. This concern about the lack of consultation was expressed by witnesses to the House of Commons Expenditure Committee when it was looking into DES planning procedures in 1975–1976. But the tragedy was not that there was an arbitrary cutback, but that it came suddenly because it was delayed. A service with half a million teachers in schools with rolls that were due to fall rapidly, could hardly be fed for very long by over 100,000 teachers under training in an ailing economy.

The problem was the lack of time to consider and possibly implement the proposals of the James Committee. To stay in business, many colleges moved in the liberal arts college direction suggested in the James Report (1972). This was a long and difficult process however, for courses had to be organized and validated by the CNAA or the universities, as teacher training was cut back. It was the time when colleges were organizing their BEd degrees. Edwin Kerr, the Director of the CNAA, has pointed out that college staff were not appointed for the non-teaching courses that were proposed (Kerr, 1976). Libraries were not geared to academic courses. The success of these courses is a tribute to the work of the college staff. Monotechnic institutions have been rapidly diversified and within 10 years had become an important part of higher education. Teacher training survived, but was little changed, despite changes in the schools themselves.

The contraction of the teacher training institutions during the 1970s stopped the appointment of more than a handful of new staff. The time that had elapsed since they had taught in school lengthened (McNamara and Ross, 1982). Their tenure guaranteed that skills would become redundant.

But the 1970s were just the years when teaching was changing fast. In particular, the number of middle schools and comprehensive schools increased. There was also a change in the mix of pupils. Inner-city schools had often become multi-racial; the problems in these schools were met by new styles of teaching. Very few staff in the training institutions had experienced teaching in these new circumstances. There was no flow of new recruits to bring that experience. By the 1980s there was a further question mark over the legitimacy of teacher education.

This difficulty in maintaining the relevance of teacher education is only one illustration of the way contraction in the education service exposes the problems resulting from the separation of careers in schools, colleges, the advisory service, the inspectorate and the administration. Expansion enables recruitment and the launching of new initiatives to cater for new developments. The difficulties in lateral movement become visible when it is impossible to buy a way through to new solutions. Teacher education will become geriatric unless traditional patterns can be broken and new methods organized from existing resources. But, as in education generally, these resources are mainly personnel, and reorganization threatens the very predictability that makes a professional career so attractive. Institutional career patterns may become a barrier to the provision of an effective service.

Given the criticism of the content of teacher education and the major part played by discussions over quantity not quality, why is professional training given such emphasis? First, barring entry to teaching to the professionally unqualified at least excludes those not formally judged as competent. It aligns teaching to other professions by controlling intake. Second, it ensures that students experience teaching practice and have time to reconsider their initial decision to teach. Third, it makes entry to teaching unlikely before the age of 22 and ensures that problems and possibilities will have been met, discussed and assessed during training.

This time spent in training would be lavish if teaching was solely academic and all pupils were willing and enthusiastic pupils (see p. 127). The independent schools can safely recruit straight from graduation. But teaching has a social control, social welfare side. Whether this is seen as part of the ideological state apparatus for ensuring the cultural hegemony of the bourgeoisie, earlier known as 'gentling the masses', or as a contribution to producing a caring environment, or as a way of keeping children off the streets in some semblance of order, it is a stark contrast to the Mr Chips image. Teaching is often uncivilized, a struggle to maintain order in a confined space, outnumbered 30 to one by experienced disrupters.

Rainwater (1967) categorized American teachers, social workers and policemen as 'dirty' workers. They did the shameful work that nevertheless had to be done. Americans may have felt ashamed about the way Negroes were controlled, but the problem was best kept out of sight. Schools became custodial institutions in which less and less learning took place. The public is indifferent to the welfare of these 'dirty' workers. They have low prestige and low salaries. The public is also ignorant about what goes on in schools and social work, preferring not to know. The teachers in turn are reluctant to spell out the conditions under which they work as a bargaining ploy. They are squeezed between the indifference of the majority and the hostility of the minorities they try to control.

Many teachers are involved in 'dirty' work in this country. They face the same attitudes among the public of 'not wanting to know'. It is the range of work from 'clean' to 'dirty' that complicates the training of teachers. The differences between the heroic struggles of the committed inner-city teacher, doing her best to help children who seem to be doing their best to derange her, and the relative ease of her colleagues in suburbia, go deeply into their careers. If success is measured by parents and employers in academic terms, then the dice are clearly loaded. By public criteria those facing the longest odds are judged as losers. They will face the criticism because the outcomes from schooling are rarely related to inputs by the public, and it is difficult to take social backgrounds into account.

Typical examples of the criteria by which the public judge are public examination results in secondary schools and standardized test scores in primary schools. Comparing schools on O-Level or CSE results, or reading ages or mathematics test scores with national norms, ignores the contrast between pupils at intake. But even if the 'gain' from schooling could be obtained by comparing input and output for individual children, the different effects of their social background would still account for much of the difference. But parents will, quite reasonably, still try to avoid the school with poor results even through these might be miraculous given the disadvantages faced. The 'dirty' work teachers will feel the effects of falling rolls first and are liable to lose first just those motivated children who might help to establish an environment in which results could be achieved for all.

The consequence of this unfairness for teaching careers is that those at the 'clean' end of the spectrum will be doing the academic work, receiving the praise and will have the energy to obtain the further qualifications that will give them improved chances of promotion. The cleaner the work, the easier the upward path. Entry to lecturing in teacher education, movement into the advisory service or inspectorate, promotion to headship are eased by possession of a higher degree. Entry to masters courses requires a good honours degree. Teaching careers, like those of pupils, are dependent on formal qualifications. But once again, these are the means through which selection is made to posts for which competition is fierce, and during contraction gets fiercer.

These handicaps facing teachers in deprived areas are a pointer to the difficulty in getting agreement over the content of teacher education, whether pre- or in-service. Students are prepared for posts across the whole spectrum from clean to dirty. But the preparation required at one extreme has little in common with that at the other. One requires academic depth and pedagogy; the other requires a training in social work and in techniques of control. On teaching practice students may meet either extreme. The 'dirty' experience is likely to be new and disturbing for the majority who have come through the 'clean' avenue. The training institutions can do little to help students. Later, there is little planned induction into teaching and there may be little support in the probationary year. The only advice I received in my first post in Russell Lane Boys' School was from the headteacher who said: 'Just enter the room as if you expect them to behave and they will'. I did, they didn't. They rarely do.

Labelling teaching as a profession conceals the variety in the work done. None of the criteria fit; neither do they fit other occupations labelled as 'professional'. The term is a claim rather than a description. In public services such as education, the label 'professional' can cover up a range of work, at one end of which is teaching that has little relation to the expectations of students or the image of the public. It is heroic rather than academic, 'dirty' rather than respectable.

The institutionalization of teaching careers

The privilege of looking forward to a secure career in a public service such as education is clear during periods of economic expansion. Prospects improve as new posts are created. For teachers, this not only involves head and deputy headships, but movement into the advisory service, inspectorate and teacher education. Contraction brings a triple blow. First, the promotion prospects disappear. Second, those promoted during expansion form a barrier due to the age structure of a contracting workforce. Third, the procedures and pathways of the career, institutionalized in the good times, become a corset on hopes when opportunities for promotion disappear.

Teachers' salaries are tied to the size of schools and to administrative duties. In the 1950s, salaries and promotion were linked to the unit total system. Children were age weighted to calculate the unit total for each school. In 1971 consolidated scales replaced graded posts, but in each the number of posts above Scale 1 was determined by the unit total of the school. This benefited the secondary school teachers. The greater proportion of scaled posts in secondary schools was justified by the greater complexity of the administrative tasks when compared with the less fortunate primary schools. These tasks, rather than excellence in teaching, were rewarded (Saran, 1982).

The recurrence of size and numbers as the basis for decisions in careers as well as in planning generally, is another feature of large organization and dependence on universalistic principles. The national negotiations over teachers' salaries produced a unit total system that could be applied universally and to duties additional to, or as a substitute for, classroom teaching. Thus there was no need to get agreement on what counted as excellence in teaching. Yet Hilsum and Start (1974) have shown that teachers in both primary and secondary schools think that success in classroom teaching should be the main criterion for promotion. These problems arising from contraction came after two decades in which the rate of return on the investment made in becoming a teacher had fallen (Wilson, 1983).

By 1980 there had been a fall in the number of young teachers. But one-third of the teachers were under 30, while half were under 35. Their older peers tended to fill the scaled posts. There were nearly 100,000 teachers on Scale 1, 60 percent on Scales 1 and II, with little prospect of promotion. Furthermore, the opportunities to move out of teaching into the advisory service or teacher education had dried up. Contraction had exposed the lack of reward for effective teaching and by 1983 the teachers' unions were looking for ways of creating an improved career structure for rewarding teaching rather than administration. The Burnham Structure Working Party recommended an entry grade followed by a main professional grade which would reward duties and responsibilities. But movement onto and up the professional scale had to come through assessment of performance. With some justice the NAS/UWT objected to the method proposed by the DES in its White Paper *Teaching Quality* (DES, 1983), because this left assessment to headteachers, thus strengthening the dependence on judgement that could be local, arbitrary and less than objective (O'Kane, 1983).

These difficulties did not result from contraction; they were exposed by it. Improvements will not depend on marginal measures such as getting teacher educators back into the classroom as a refresher, but through a consideration of careers vertically up the teaching ladder and horizontally so that movement in and out of classroom teaching is not only expected, but made possible by unifying pay scales and pension rights across teaching, inspecting, advising, teacher education and administration. Entry to a university department of education with tenure secures the job until retirement and guarantees that experience of classroom will become increasingly distant. But it does in any other profession where movement is to different conditions of service.

It is easy to criticize teacher education because of available data (McNamara and Ross, 1982). It is fair because much of the criticism of teachers' competence has come from within teacher education. In 1980, out of a sample of 770 staff involved in teaching the BEd degree in colleges, polytechnics and universities, 77 percent were over the age of 40, 56 percent had been in the same institution for more than 10 years, 63 percent had been in teacher education for more than 10 years, 69 percent of those teaching infant school courses had never taught in an infant school, 49 percent of those teaching junior school courses had never taught in junior schools. A personal confession is called for here: I last taught in school over 20 years ago.

These figures are not an indictment of the quality of teacher education. Recent experience in school is not the most important criterion for preparing teachers. The figures indicate the perils of contraction, for in expanding times new staff come in every year. They are above all a symptom of a much broader problem. Classroom teaching is not rewarded in teachers' pay. Movement out of teaching is irrevocable. The lateral movement is one-way, draining the best away from children into the education industry where year by year, pay, pensions and conditions make a return or a further lateral move personally disadvantageous. The predictable, secure, professional career inside a bureaucratically organized service stops enrichment through mobility and devalues classroom teaching. The career structures are institutionalized, but they have their own separate ladders.

The institutionalization of teaching careers can be traced from entry into training. There is one coordinating body for initial training – the Advisory Committee for the Supply and Education of Teachers (ACSET). This body was reconstructed at the start of the 1980s, but did not sit during the reorganization of the colleges of education during the late 1970s. The NUT did not attend ACSET, arguing that they were underrepresented. However, even when the DES do use ACSET, its brief is to look at numbers and their allocation to various types of training rather than to the management of all the related phases through which teachers enter the profession. The relation between initial training, induction and in-service provision, and the organization of each, is not managed by either the DES or LEAs acting together. The DES grants qualified teacher status to those recommended by universities and colleges as fit to teach and also places a few miscreants on 'List 99', thus stopping them from teaching. But there is no council governing the teaching profession and planning careers.

The dilemma of initial teacher training can be seen in the progressive extension of the length of concurrent training to four years, while still leaving complaints about lack of preparation for the classroom. In reality, initial training can never do more than introduce students to the job and serve to identify those who are unsuitable for teaching. This was appreciated by the James Committee in the 1970s, as it was by the McNair Committee in the early 1940s and by a minority on the Departmental Enquiry into the Training of Teachers in 1925. These reports all stressed the overlap of initial training and induction. The White Paper, *A Framework for Expansion* (DES, 1972), confirmed the government's support for in-service training. However, agreement over the necessity for organizing pre-service, induction and in-service training has not been followed by sustained action. Pilot induction schemes were organized (Bolam and Baker, 1975). Some authorities started to release new teachers for courses in their first year. Experiments linked initial training and induction and there has been a build-up in in-service courses. But financial cuts stopped any major development, for released teachers have to be replaced in their classrooms and this is costly. Systematic implementation would also require synchronizing the three stages after planning the early career of teachers. This has never been attempted.

The organization of initial teacher education, induction and INSET at the start of the 1980s was chaotic. Initial training was spread between universities, polytechnics containing ex-colleges and technical colleges, and free-standing institutes of higher education and colleges. There were no longer area training organizations to synchronize activities. Qualified teacher status was given on the recommendation of these separate institutions. Apart from a few isolated experiments (Evans, 1978), there was no connection between the qualifying institutions and the LEA advisory services who judged that the probationary year had been completed successfully. INSET was organized by the DES, LEAs, schools and the training institutions with local discussions only to ensure minimum of overlap, and with the DES exercising discretion through the approval of courses for LEAs to obtain financial support to give grants to students.

To Sayer (1980) this was a symptom of the lack of management of the teaching profession. There was an absence of responsibility in decisions about the recruitment of teachers, their initial education, qualification, appointment and probation, pay and promotion, staffing levels and in-service training. Yet there was little disagreement over the importance of the training aspects in these career matters. The DES, LEAs and teachers' unions have all supported thorough probation and a coherent system of in-service training. The government is committed to a systematic one-year programme of induction involving a light timetable with in-service training (DES, 1972). In addition, 3 percent of the teaching force were to be released for INSET. In 1978 and 1979 the figure achieved was around 1 percent (DES, 1978d, 1980). This figure has probably declined since the 1979 survey as LEAs have tried to cut their education budgets. The unanimity among the partners has foundered on the drive to reduce the costs of the teaching force. The NUT position is that central and local government should cease the rhetoric about the need to expand programmes while withholding the necessary resources. The union also acknowledges the fragmented manner in which INSET is organized (NUT, 1981). All the partners see the need for collaborative planning, but all seem too exhausted or too poor to actually negotiate it. This is ironic as this is a rare example of unanimity, all agreeing with the DES that in-service education is '. . . a necessary investment in the future quality of the teaching force' (DES, 1978c).

In practice, unanimity over the need to further the professional development of teachers conceals a lot of disagreement over the purpose of the exercise. It is not just that each partner sees itself playing a major part, or that there is resistance among the academic institutions to running tailor-made practical courses for the partners. It revolves around the common issue of control of the curriculum and teaching methods. If training does influence the quality of teaching and affect curriculum development, then control of in-service courses is important politically. The NUT is cautious in case INSET is used to control the curriculum (Chambers, 1977). The LEAs see it as a way of ensuring that their policies are implemented in schools (Taylor, 1973). 'Whose INSET is it?' is an important question (Stammers, 1980).

There is then agreement over the need for the professional development of teachers to be planned, but little coherence in the way this is done. Looking laterally the scene is one of discrete activities. Viewed across the careers of teachers there is even more discontinuity. Justifiably the common motivation for attending award-bearing in-service courses or taking a further academic qualification is to ensure promotion (Hilsum and Start, 1974). Indeed, academic courses designed to promote intellectual enquiry may be contradicting the parallel efforts of LEAs or HMI to promote current practices, rather than to challenge them. This gap is increased as LEAs are forced to treat teachers as manpower to be deployed in order to solve staffing problems when recruitment has ceased and there is a need for retraining.

The lack of coordination between the agents responsible for the preparation, induction and in-service training of teachers, and the consequent weaknesses within each, is both a cause of the absence of a clear career pattern for teachers and a symptom of that absence. But behind this analysis of the organization of teaching careers is an assumption about the effectiveness of professional training. Central and local government, the teachers' unions and the training institutions assume that training pays off. However, the evidence for this should not be assumed. There is no doubt that it is useful to delay entry to teaching until students are mature and have experienced as adults the inside of a few schools. It is unquestionably valuable to give a new teacher a lighter timetable and support while domestic arrangements and the shock of a new job are sorted out. INSET enables teachers to find out what others are doing and to distance themselves from their own practices. But the effectiveness of professional training ultimately depends on knowing what makes a teacher effective in various teaching situations. Yet there is no evidence that defines the characteristics involved. There is a wealth of professional theory derived from the human sciences. There are various practical situations used as shallow or deep ends for dunking student teachers. But neither theory nor practice is based on evidence that is agreed to be reliable and valid.

It is rare for this question to be asked, because it is so obvious that a teaching career, from entering a course of professional training to promotion to senior positions, should involve continuing study and experience of learning and teaching. However, only at the end of the 1970s were graduates compelled to undertake professional training before entering the profession, and public schools have usually recruited direct from universities. Furthermore, students can teach any age-range in any school once qualified, even though their course may have been very specialized. There is no evidence confirming that success while under training results in success later in teaching (Crocker, 1974). There is a lot of evidence showing that practices learned on courses soon disappear once used in the classroom (Cope, 1971; Taylor and Dale, 1971; Hannam, 1976), and that future career prospects do not seem related to success on an initial course of training (Wiseman and Start, 1965).

Within the education industry there is little confidence in the research basis of professional training, regardless of its discipline. Few lecturers in psychology or sociology have many illusions about scientific status, given the attack on empiricism in these subjects. They remain worthwhile activities but the positivist optimism has gone. Yet theories and evidence are borrowed for courses in education with a disregard for the caution displayed by their producers. The Play Way and the Dalton Plan had their scientific basis years ago, just as competency-based and programmed learning have today. All these and others may have their use, but that is not justifiable by reference to child development or learning theories. It is useful to organize courses in the teaching of reading, but there is no agreement over how children learn to read, and existing beliefs are inexorably undermined as new evidence accumulates. The organization of teacher education has to be seen as professional development across a career and each stage viewed as problematic because of the status of the available evidence. There is no blueprint.

The weakness in career planning is apparent from admission to a course of initial teacher education through to retirement. The latter is still organized on a voluntary basis, with financial incentives to maximize the number retiring so that the teaching force is cut. But this can result in the best teachers going, and the inadequate ones staying. At each stage of the teaching career there is the same weakness. The probationary year remains a formality for most new teachers and plans for a genuine induction have collapsed. Increments come automatically. There is no routine check on competence. There is rarely any systematic preparation for promotion. The roles of head of department and deputy head remain ill-defined in many schools and posts of responsibility often carry the extra money but not the duties.

Perhaps the most remarkable gap in career planning concerns the appointment of headteachers. This is the key post in a school, and an inadequate head can soon allow a school to deteriorate, just as a good head can revive a depressed school. But there is rarely any preparation for the job. The House of Commons Expenditure Committee (1977) has not been alone in recommending limited tenure for headteachers to ensure that those who are not up to this job do not stay. But no action has been taken. Indeed, it is difficult to see where the action would be taken. The LEA has responsibility to appoint, but why should the headteachers' associations accept a probationary period when no other posts in teaching or administration carrying responsibility have limited tenure. Indeed, all teachers carry responsibility and there is a weakness throughout the career. There is little preparation, induction, in-service support or review of competence at any point, and appointments and tenure are confirmed after interview. To single out initial teacher training is also unfair. It can only be reformed as part of an overhaul of the arrangements for teaching careers from entry to departure.

But it is not enough to look at the teaching career alone. The key to an effective infrastructure for teaching lies in movement in and out of teaching, administration, training institution, whether it be college of education, polytechnic or university, and the advisory service or inspectorate. Without this mobility lecturers in initial training prepare teachers for schools of which they themselves have no experience. Advisors and inspectors, often with public or grammar school experience, work with teachers who have experienced a very different world. Researchers comment on schools from the comfort of senior common rooms. As contraction leads to schools closing or shrinking, promotion prospects decrease and discontent will rise among the recently recruited few who, because they were selected from among the many unemployed teachers, were exceptionally able. The movement from schools to colleges and university departments of education has also stopped and they too shrink. A one-way movement out of schools was bad enough in expanding times. With contraction all movement dries up and the need to take career planning seriously increases.

It is, however, easier to recommend career planning than to detail how it could be done. Here the 'distributed' location of power in English education is unhelpful. The teachers' unions support a coherent system of in-service education and staff development and want the teachers' associations to play an important role (NUT, 1981). But they have to look to the DES to provide the resources and justifiably want less talk about the importance of career development and more funds to make it possible. Yet a strong lead by the DES or LEAs to tighten up the probationary year, or to introduce limited tenure or routine tests of competency, would be resisted as an attack on professional independence. Everyone acknowledges the problems. But the organization of the service inhibits any speedy solution. The initiative for national measures has to come from the DES. The difficulty is that while such an initiative may only be recommended in a discussion document, it will be seen as another attack on the independence of the teaching profession, another attempt to control the curriculum and impose accountability. When resources are increasing, the partners are likely to be on friendly terms and innovations around the schools can be left to spread. When resources are contracting relations are likely to be sour. This is just the time when the only chance of innovation comes from central government because that is the only source of funds for it. The partnership works when the living is easy. But just when changes are needed as times get tough, the partners get distrustful. Career development has been an early casualty.

PART FOUR

AN EVALUATION OF THE EDUCATION SERVICE

INTRODUCTION

In this final part, an evaluation of education as a public service is attempted. The question asked in Chapter 1 was: 'Does the organization of the education service help or hinder the achievement of the ideals of those who framed the 1944 Education Act?' The principles behind the organization were that the service should be universalistic, serving general not sectional interests, it should be comprehensive so that ignorance did not remain to reduce the impact of the other services, and it should encourage individual and communal responsibility.

Looking across the past 40 years brings into focus an extension of education, a proliferation of examination successes, a spread of academic culture that has at least met part of Beveridge's demand for the conquest of ignorance. Behind this are two closely related developments. First, education expanded and its links to an increasingly differentiated division of labour were strengthened. That differentiation was most marked among white-collar professional occupations where expansion provided the scope for upward social mobility. Further and higher education, as well as schools, were more closely linked to employment through formal qualification. Second, that apparently objective arrangement whereby talent was assessed in schools to ensure that it went into appropriate occupations has not reduced sectional advantages and disadvantages. The expansion of opportunities in both education and employment has been universally beneficial. But inequality has persisted. Given the unequal resources available for education among different social classes in their homes, communities, incomes and attitudes it could not be otherwise. Furthermore, once the expansion slowed down, the prospects were for greater inequality. That is the main problem dealt with in this final part. It is, however, closely related to the capacity of the service to adapt and here its size and the institutionalization of procedures are shown to be barriers. Indeed, it is suggested that it is sometimes difficult to see whether the service is organized to benefit those who work in it, or those who depend on it.

Underlying this disappointment with education as with other universalistic public services, and providing the motive for political left and right to press for specific, earmarked action to get a better deal for the poor, is the quite natural drive to make one's own life as comfortable as possible and to ensure that this comfort is passed on to one's children. That motive results in nepotism in developing countries, 'new classes' of apparatchiks in communist states and inherited advantages in capitalism. The common motivation is to perpetuate advantages within the family. The balance between intervention to give a better deal for the poor and allowing the incentives derived from that human self-interest to run free is a major political question in the education service as elsewhere. Even rapid economic advance has not reduced the relative disadvantages of the poor generation after generation. Their lot may have improved with economic advance, but they and their children tend to remain poor. There has been a dissemination of culture and some social mobility, but the ability to benefit one's children through exercising determination, sacrifice and ingenuity has defeated political intention, professional concern and general goodwill. The loss is not only to individuals and to communities; it has wasted talent for many aspects of economic, social and cultural life.

CHAPTER 7

EDUCATION AND THE LABOUR MARKET

Six factors will be considered here as the principal obstacles to the achievement of the ideals that lay behind education in the post-1944 welfare state. First, schooling and higher education were further meshed into a progressively differentiated division of labour. Second, that connection to the labour market was made through public examinations that constrain the school curriculum. Third, the qualifications obtained steadily yielded less reward. Fourth, the opportunities for gaining high-prestige jobs through education were monopolized by the service class. Fifth, the independent schools were reorganized to take maximum advantage of the drive for qualification. Sixth, the direction of development in the education service was increasingly determined by its own internal momentum as its size increased, rather than through a response to demand.

However, before considering the constraints that account for the disappointments, the successes have to be listed. They include remarkable advances over 40 years, although the investment has been expensive. The numbers in the population who now share in the world of learning, through and into adulthood, who possess formal academic qualifications and who have taken up skilled white-collar or manual occupations form the context in which the shortcomings of the service have to be placed.

This examination of the spread of education is broader than the question usually asked about standards. The standards debate is complicated by technical difficulties. Even the most obvious indicator – public examination results – needs detailed controlling for intake characteristics and social background if schools are to be compared, and even then there are disputes about the results obtained (Plewis, 1981).

At national level there has been further dispute (Willmott, 1977). Repeated studies of reading showed apparent rises from a low base after 1945, but surveys in 1970 and 1971 suggested a levelling-off (Start and Wells, 1972). By 1976 they had risen again (DES, 1978b). But at all stages the test used made the results dubious. The Assessment of Performance Unit (APU), set up to monitor national standards, is still uncertain after years of academic squabbling whether the technique chosen to show trends is reliable (Bryce, 1981).

When the focus is on the spread of education the picture is clearest. In the most extensive study available, the dissemination of culture, not its confinement or reproduction, within social classes is stressed (Halsey et al., 1980). Of those born in the years 1913–1922, 1.8 percent went into higher education. This figure had risen to 8.4 percent for those born between 1943 and 1952. The proportion taking Ordinary School Certificate or 'O'-Level rose from 11.9 percent to 34 percent for the same two age-groups. The class differences remained the same across the period spanning these age-groups. This survey showed that there was still a great waste of talent among the working class. The key was expanded opportunities. Where places were scarce, as in university entry or entry to grammar school when bulge years were entering, the service class took the places. That leads to a pessimistic outlook for the egalitarian, but there is some comfort in the gains from earlier expansion.

The most obvious indicator, however crude, of this dissemination of culture is public examination entries and passes. Over 80 percent now leave school with some formal qualification. This figure has risen from around 50 percent 20 years ago. About 15 percent obtain one or more 'A'-Level passes. In 1979–1980, 121,000 in the UK obtained over two A-Levels or their Scottish equivalent (Central Statistical Office, 1983). In the age-group 25–29 in 1979–1980, 63 percent held some educational qualification. In the 65–69 age-group the figure was 24 percent (Halsey et al., 1980). Even more remarkable has been the rise in entries in public examinations. Between 1960 and 1980 the number of candidates for GCE O-Level tripled to over one million and the number of subject entries rose to three million. Over the same period candidates for CSE rose to 600,000 making three million subject entries. GCE A-Level entrants rose from under 100,000 to over 300,000.

Entry to further and higher education has also increased. In 1980 there were some 750,000 students in full- or part-time higher education and some four million in non-advanced further education. There are 6500 adult institutes. In all some 10 million persons are involved in education in any one year; over six million of these are adults. They are often involved in craft, aesthetic and sporting skill courses.

However, in comparison with other Western countries, the relative position is unsatisfactory. Compared with other Western European nations and the USA, British children tend to leave school earlier and enter full-time higher education less frequently. The evidence suggests that there has not been any significant reduction in class inequalities (Goldthorpe, 1980). There has been more room at the top due to changes in the division of labour, and the service class was recruited from all social groups. The inequalities rooted in the class structure remain. Nevertheless involvement in education at all ages spreads knowledge and helps overcome the ignorance that Beveridge condemned.

These crude indicators of the success of the post-1944 education service in overcoming ignorance and spreading culture, rather than merely reproducing its allocation, do not show the more profound, unmeasurable benefits. A democracy depends on the maximum participation by citizens in influencing decisions of government. Contemporary social, political, economic, defence and international problems are complicated. Education helps those affected to participate. Governments have to take note of pressure groups and protest movements. They also have to take note of the assumption that there will be welfare services, a decent standard of living, an effective education service. Before detailing the problems in the service this contribution to the democratic process should be acknowledged. A flavour of this intangible yet crucial benefit can be gauged from this letter from Clement Attlee, Prime Minister during the late 1940s, to Harold Laski (quoted in Field, 1956, p. 137): 'In my time I have seen a lot of useful legislation, but I count our progress much more by the extent to which what we cried in the wilderness five-and-thirty years ago has now become part of the assumptions of the ordinary man and woman.' Those assumptions are on the credit side of the education balance sheet.

Schooling and the labour market

The 1944 Act refers to individual attributes such as age, ability and aptitude, and to meeting the needs of communities. Yet education is geared to an advanced division of labour. This more than anything else determines what really goes on in schools, whether primary or secondary. Education may serve the economy. It may meet some communal needs. It is certainly highly stratified and affects the careers of both teachers and pupils. The pressure from the employment market comes through public examinations, entry requirements for jobs, and for further and higher education. It is the unintended consequences of this organization to differentiate between children that is at the heart of this chapter. The school curriculum, the tasks performed by teachers, the rewards that accrue to them and the anxieties of parents over the education received by their children are all affected. The process of differentiation is institutionalized, built into education. It is rarely spelled out in a frank way as sorting out, selecting, promoting, rejecting. Teachers and lecturers would not acknowledge that sorting-out is central to their work. Yet that is the reason for grading, for different curricula, teaching styles and lengths of schooling, for the variety in further and higher education and for the array of available qualifications.

The very different quality and quantity of schooling received by different groups of children is objectionable because it is unfair. Those who need the most support get the least. Because attainment is affected by outside factors, those blessed with financially well-off parents stay longer in school, college and university and leave with marketable qualifications. The children of the poor tend to leave as soon as it is legally permissible and have often absented themselves in spirit and in body before then. With high unemployment school has no reward for them. In all societies the young are prepared for adulthood and this includes formal training that is usually tested. Initiation ceremonies, rites of passage, public examinations, graduation have in common the confirmation of mastery bestowed by adults. To ignore this is to separate schooling from its rationale in the preparation of each generation by its seniors.

The identification, cultivation and accreditation of talent has been an objective in many modern industrial societies. In *The Rise of the Meritocracy* (1961) Young looked forward sceptically to a society where measured intelligence and effort were rewarded. Yet a meritocracy still seems a distant prospect as evidence appears at regular intervals showing that social background, and not intelligence or effort, determines a child's place in the adult division of labour.

The consequences for schools can be seen in the progressive differentiation that links the mixed-ability infant class to carefully selected, highly specialist graduate schools in universities. There are a number of identifiable key points, although the process of sorting out is continuous and starts when children are very young. The early grouping into readers and non-readers, on to fast- and slow-lane tasks, into sets and streams, will have provided clues for the children about their present ability and future status before transfer to secondary school. Their performance and future prospects will be recorded. Even with comprehensive secondary education, choice of school and placement into set, band or stream after entry will further differentiate.

The first three years of comprehensive secondary schooling will often have a common curriculum. But even in primary schools some children will have been sorted into groups requiring special help while others may be taking a foreign language as an extra subject. In the first three years in comprehensive schools there is a lot of setting, banding and streaming (Monks, 1970; Weston, 1970; Ball, 1981). When options are picked for the two-year run-up to O-Level or to CSE, the future managers and professionals are clearly distinguished from the future manual workers.

Schools offer options and prepare the third-formers and their parents with documents, talks and parents' evenings. But the available evidence suggests that the school has already selected the pupils for the different curriculum ahead, through placing them in different curriculum bands or streams at an early stage (Hurman, 1978; Ryrie, 1979). By the time choices have to be made in the third year of secondary school pupils have received the cues about their ability and advice from teachers that confirms them on the path on which they have been set earlier in their school career. By the time pupils come to choose, their choices have been restricted by the organization of their previous experience.

The process of differentiation is most visible in further and higher education. A university graduates its students at ordinary or honours level, the latter classified into third, lower and upper second or first. There is a clear break between upper second and first-class degrees and the rest; they are 'good' degrees, qualifying the holder for a research grant, registration for a higher degree or extra pay if he or she becomes a teacher. The higher degrees are themselves ranked through masters and doctorates. Across all higher education the qualifications ladder is twisted. Higher degrees committees looking over applicants have to sort out whether an ordinary degree plus an advanced diploma equal a good honours degree, or whether a three-year certificate in education plus a diploma is equivalent to an unclassified BEd. Such decisions matter, for teaching careers depend on qualifications as elsewhere. The apparent objectivity also conceals a lot of guesswork. As an external examiner it is often difficult to distinguish between one BEd long essay and another MEd dissertation. A BA in one polytechnic does not seem comparable with one in another college of higher education. One university produces masters dissertations that compare with doctoral theses at another; at a third you buy the masters for a small fee, at a fourth you work part-time for four years. The variety is staggering, but the purpose is identical. It is the last stage of the long process of differentiation. The first-class honours degree and the PhD categorize people for the future, just as leaving school without a qualification or with one CSE grade 5 does for the less fortunate several years earlier. The objectivity may be suspect at all levels, but the qualifications are made increasingly more fine.

This sorting-out through education would not go away if public examinations were abolished or the school curriculum converted to a mix of expressive arts and community studies, as recommended by Hargreaves (1982). Very different skills are required in employment and competition for entry would be on the basis of acquired competence. But while it may not be possible to get rid of the need to sort out the competent, this could be organized more efficiently and fairly. Such hopes lay behind the legislation in the late 1940s. It was in the tradition of Sydney Webb (see Chapter 1), a friend of Beveridge and a founder of the London School of Economics where Beveridge was Director from 1919 to 1936.

Universalism is a call for the elimination of sectional interests, of privilege, of the power of the purse from public policy. But the equality of opportunity in the 1950s and beyond was the chance to compete by receiving a secondary schooling and the chance of further or higher education. It was aimed at equality of resources for competing. It was meritocratic, but as with romantics who ignore the link between education and the division of labour in work, the sorting-out role was ignored. In practice, the advantages for the poor in education have come from the expansion of opportunities in work, rather than from a fairer or more meritocratic allocation of those educational opportunities. The failure to mobilize talent from all social groups remains a serious failure in the education service. It is aggravated when there is high unemployment, as Beveridge foresaw. Hope evaporates when there is no room at the top. The translation of the 1944 Act into selective secondary schooling is an example of this tendency to see differentiation as a natural feature of schooling. The post-1945 Labour education policy was to organize secondary schools on a tripartite basis so that those of high-measured ability were selected for grammar schools while the rest went to secondary moderns or to the few technical schools. The selection tests at the end of primary schooling were a watershed in the categorization process. The ending of selection 30 years later has only spread out the sequence of events. It may not be intended. It may be more convenient to ignore the universality of differentiation through schooling. Reforms change the procedures but they still route children along very different paths to a future career.

The advantage of this emphasis on the way pathways to adult occupation are organized is to avoid seeing the dominance of qualifications as more than a symptom. The underlying problem is in the dovetailing of education into the division of labour. This is not only a feature of a correspondence between capitalist industrial organization and education, but a universal relation between specialization and schooling. From the production of clerics in peasant societies to the contemporary sorting-out from unqualified school leavers at 16 to PhD 10 years later, schooling acts to qualify and disqualify, encourage and discourage, promote and demote. However humane, schools help to sort those apparently undifferentiated infants into categorized, graded entrants to the labour market.

In practice it is difficult to see why there is so much emphasis on accreditation, given the low predictive value of most assessment. Neither is there a universal demand by employers for applicants qualified by examinations. Indeed, Ashton and Maguire (1980), drawing on an investigation of over 100 employers, report strategies ranging from qualifications as the main criterion for selection, through their use as screening devices, to their use to disqualify applicants. The market for labour is complicated. The quest for qualifications is not, however, diminished by the tendency for skilled manual workers and operatives to be selected by non-academic criteria such as personality, physique, basic literacy, numeracy and evidence of work habits. Examination qualifications control entry to professions and their possession secures an appointment for most jobs.

It is in the professions and the public services that examined, certificated qualification tends to be most important. The service class is recruited through the application of carefully defined levels of minimum qualification. The rate of growth of the public services has stimulated the search for qualification in schools and colleges. A profession such as teaching has been an important avenue through which recruitment to the service class has been affected. Public services expand and the education service meets the demands for universalistic criteria for entry.

The diploma disease has occurred worldwide. Only the very rich can ignore this link between school and prestigious occupation. It has frustrated attempts to move away from an academic education in the developing countries. It is the entry ticket to the new class of apparatchiks in Eastern

Europe as it is of bureaucrats in the West. The instruments in the sorting-out process in Britain are public examinations. These are used because they are fairer to the poor than patronage and they are organized in an apparently detailed, objective way. The search for qualifications is realistic for individuals. The disease is not the examination but the part that schools and colleges were organized to play as occupations diversified.

The influence of public examinations

Public examinations offer the promise of identifying the most suited candidates for available occupations. Their public organization eliminates private influence and special pleading. They are set, marked and moderated by examination boards whose bureaucratic organization is a guarantee that all entrants will be assessed against known and universal criteria.

Public examinations proliferated as patronage and purchase were replaced in modern government, the armed forces and public and private corporations. As the division of labour in government, services and industry became more complex, public examinations were used to get squares into square holes. This process was utilitarian but also egalitarian. What you knew and were shown to know became as important as who you knew or who were your parents.

The expansion of public examinations as a way of demonstrating competence is well documented (Roach, 1971). By the middle of the nineteenth century the universities followed the professions in instituting formal entry requirements. From then on the universities set examinations for schools, and they have remained influential in organizing them ever since. In 1917 the Board of Education set up the Secondary Schools Examinations Council (SSEC) to advise it on examinations for the secondary schools, many of which were being established at this time, following the 1902 Education Act. This Council consisted of 11 representatives of the university examining bodies, five from the local education authorities and six teachers. The Council was to approve both the examinations and the university examining boards which would organize them. The Board of Education officially recognized the School Certificate to be taken at 16 and the Higher School Certificate to be taken at the end of the sixth form.

The SSEC was incorporated into the Schools Council for Curriculum and Examinations in 1964. During its life, the SSEC had succeeded in establishing the reputation of the School Certificate examinations as having national standards which were accepted by universities, the professions and employers generally. This recognition was extended to the General Certificate of Education (GCE). While this was a single subject examination at both O- and A-Level, the universities decided that a minimum of five passes would be required for entry, at least two of which should be at A-Level. This minimized the differences between the old School Certificate, which was achieved through passes in a group of subjects, and the new GCE examinations. It also confirmed the hold that university entrance requirements had over the examinations and, in time, on the secondary school curriculum. The representatives of the university examining boards had been removed from the SSEC in 1946 and the examining boards became more representative of LEAs and teachers. But by fixing entrance requirements and by asking for specific A-Level grades according to subject, the universities ensured that their influence persisted.

The universities are acting reasonably in insisting on minimum examination standards for entry, and on comparability between similar results on different GCE examinations. In this universities are supported by the professions and employers. All resist any move away from public examinations in the secondary schools and the substitution of reports or profiles on school leavers by teachers. If such examinations were abolished, the universities would, as in the mid-nineteenth century, set their own. These would immediately be the target for most secondary schools. The effect on the curriculum would remain and pupils in schools not accepting the new targets would be penalized. If the close relationship between public examinations and secondary school curriculum is to be broken, it will need central government action. But the political implications of that action might not be welcomed by those who are most vocal against the universities' insistence on standard qualifications. The poor would be likely to be further penalized and pressure to reduce the freedom of universities over their entry procedures would increase. This resistance by universities and employers in the public and private sectors is not just based on their blind acceptance of public examination results as the most reliable indicator of past performance and future promise. There is no alternative available and substitutes usually offer no universal standard. But there is also the trust established through the efficiency of the examination boards; they are an example of the effectiveness of bureaucracies.

Year after year examinations are organized with remarkably few hitches. The annual DES publication, *Statistics of Education, Volume 3*, gives an idea of the task facing the GCE boards. Each summer there are about two million subject entries. Most subjects will have two papers and many have practical tests and oral examining. The first examinations are sat in June and by the end of September all the results have to be available to candidates so that they can complete university entrance, confirm employment or decide on their sixth-form courses. All this is achieved by very small permanent staffs within the examination boards, and success depends on the cooperation of a large number of teachers to administer the examination procedures from entering pupils to posting in the completed papers.

Public examinations spread rapidly into secondary modern schools in the latter part of the 1950s. Only in 1955 did the Ministry of Education withdraw its opposition to these schools offering GCE. By 1960 many secondary modern schools had curricula modelled on the grammar schools. For those not taking GCE there was a variety of other examinations usually taken at the end of the fourth year and set by the Royal Society of Arts, the Unions of Educational Institutes and the City and Guilds. The SSEC appointed a committee under Beloe to advise on the possibility of a public examination other than GCE. They recommended a teacher-controlled regional examination designed for the 20 percent of pupils below the similar proportion that took GCE. The spread below this 40 percent for whom public examinations are designed continued. For example, in the years 1976–1980 in Inner London, 80 percent of the 15–16 age-group entered for public examinations (ILEA, 1981).

There is a long history of frustration concerning the hold of public examinations over schooling in England. The Beloe Committee, for example, condemned examinations at the age of 15 and intended the new examination replacing these to be for a minority only. But this was only one of a long line of regrets about the power of public examinations. The Taunton Commission of 1868 pointed to the danger of public examinations disrupting the work of the schools. The Board of Education repeated this warning in 1911 as it moved towards setting up the SSEC. The Spens (1938) and Norwood (1943) Committees also criticized the restrictive effect of the 'group' examinations in secondary schools. The Ministry of Education opposed external examinations in the secondary modern schools after 1946. In the late 1970s HMIs, reviewing secondary schooling that was largely comprehensive, criticized the hold of public examinations on the curriculum (DES, 1979b). This was not confined to the older children. The HMIs detected their influence in lower forms in the secondary schools. By the age of 14, and in many cases long before then, public examinations are the path along which over three-quarters of children are guided. Those who do not follow this path face a dismal future. Those who do are, for better or for worse, following a very limited curriculum that is certainly not the product of adventurous teaching autonomy.

The history of attempts to change the public examination system in England is the most telling commentary on their influence. It cannot be seen only as a plot by universities to stop curriculum innovation. The universities are saying that they require levels of qualification based on examinations that they recognize as reliable indicators. Employers, the professions and parents support the university-orientated GCE for the same reason. They may appear mistaken or misinformed, but their opposition to examination reform in the absence of support for strong central government action has produced a rate of reform that the *Times Educational Supplement* has justifiably described as 'glacial'. But all the warnings of the harm done by excessive attention to getting children to concentrate on passing examinations have not weakened the influence they exert over all sectors of education. In 1979, HMI reported that: 'Rightly or wrongly, examination results were commonly perceived by the school as the sole indicator of its success in the eyes of the community' (DES, 1979b).

In 1978 the Secretary of State for Education accepted the Schools Council's proposals for a common system of public examination at 16. There were to be different levels of papers for pupils expected to reach different standards but within the framework of one examination. This would ease the task of staff in comprehensive secondary schools in preparing increased numbers for public examinations. But it could consolidate rather than weaken the hold of these examinations on the curriculum. Furthermore, the combined boards which, by the early 1980s, were organizing the examinations, were bogged down in administrative problems. Establishing national criteria for the new examination to ensure common standards throughout the country was delayed. Britain will be the only European country still setting external examinations on a mass basis at 16. Interestingly the extension of secondary schooling and the older age at which children leave school, have been accompanied by a delay in the age at which selective external examinations are set. But in Britain there will be no relaxation of examining for a majority of children at 16 and the new examination could exclude much of the flexibility introduced with the CSE. The decentralization of British education and the autonomy enjoyed by teachers may rest on the constraint of these examinations. This is because they are a guarantee to the public and to the institutes of higher education that diversity between, and innovation within, schools will be limited. But the price paid is high, as the curriculum for the majority is determined by examination syllabuses for the minority.

The link of school organization and curriculum to the division of labour in society through public examinations, adds to the problems of those teaching children who are losers at an early age. When good examination results are the passport to employment, those with no hope have no incentive to work or behave well. Their teachers take on not only the consequent discipline problems but the effort to make schooling meaningful. This is 'dirty' work which the public prefers to ignore. It makes teacher education a nightmare for some student teachers. It can produce problems across the whole school, as behaviour at the 'dirty' end spills into the 'clean' (Woods, 1980). This is a worldwide problem as schooling everywhere is linked to labour markets with few high-status jobs. The difference in Britain is the early differentiation organized to secure good public examination results years later. That exacerbates the problems elsewhere.

Public services and individual satisfaction

The provision of education as a universal public service has been justified because it secures the chance for talent to be developed and rewarded wherever it occurs. Individual effort and ability are seen to be rewarded through qualification and by access to higher education and finally to prestigious and well-paid employment.

The major flaw in this assumption in education has been illuminated by writers such as Boudon (1974) and Dore (1976). It arises from the relationship between education and the stratified market for labour. Boudon, using data from France, has shown that behind the failure of investment in education to reduce social inequality and increase economic opportunity lie differences in rewards, prestige and power in different occupations. However egalitarian the schooling, selection occurs for occupations. More and more people enjoy extended schooling. But high-prestige occupations do not expand at the same rate as schooling. For the majority, qualification does not bring the upward mobility expected. They run faster to stand still. Dore, looking specifically at the spread of public examinations, reaches similar conclusions: obtaining a job requires ever-increasing levels of qualification. Dore also argues that the diploma disease devalues education as productive, creative, scholarly and replaces a love of learning with a quest for qualification. The problem is not just that expanded schooling raises the level required to obtain a good job, but that the competition involved distorts education itself.

The clue to this paradox also lies in the nature of the qualifications which often bestow prestige, yet seem to have little obvious utility for the economy or for promoting welfare. A classics degree from Oxford or Cambridge may still be a more promising ticket for employment than one in computer science from the Manchester Institute of Science and Technology. The perversity of rewarding those who acquire the least relevant qualification can be explained by their scarcity value. Restricted access leads to exclusive qualifications. When few received a full schooling, any qualification sufficed to mark out the educated. The literate were given benefit of clergy because they were too valuable to be executed, even if they were criminals. This benefit only ceased finally in the nineteenth century. Classics retained its power to distinguish the educated gentleman, as schooling became universal and popular. For the ambitious, the choice as education expands is to strive for increasingly higher qualifications to rise above the mass, or to look for a minority subject that retains traditional prestige. Any honest sociologist over the age of 50 will confirm that being one of a few leads to rapid promotion. But the market is soon flooded as sociologists under 30 will attest.

The problem is that goods that secure prestige and position for their owner do not increase in the same way as material goods increase with industrial efficiency. Hirsch (1977) described this as the 'social limits to growth' in his book of the same title. The demand for television sets, motor cars and houses can be met through economic growth. But goods that distinguish one person from another are limited by social factors. As increased numbers satisfy some wants, the cost of obtaining further satisfaction rises fast. Indeed, increasing production and availability reduces the value of these goods as donors of prestige to individuals. High-status jobs, the house of distinction, the holiday that is away from the masses, the space to be exclusive, a fast car on an open road, the qualification that is revered, the subject that sounds exotic, are more difficult to acquire when more and more people are qualified, affluent, mobile and aware of the possibilities of being individually distinctive. A graduate was distinguished in the 1950s; the same degree of distinction requires a master's degree in the 1980s. The PhD is the certificate of the plumber's mate of the twenty-first century. Professors receive little reverence when there are many of them.

This situation frustrates the majority. Much of the good life is available to only a few. If private enterprise or government manages to spread car ownership, or paid holidays, or higher education, roads get cluttered, that little secluded haven becomes a caravan site and graduates find that their degree bestows little advantage. The investment designed to increase individual welfare changes the characteristics of the opportunities provided and reduces their attraction. In a world of scarce resources and opportunities, many advantages are only open to a minority. This can be seen in the consequences of expanding higher education. The 'Robbins' principle that places should be available for all those qualified, promoted the expansion in the 1970s. The expansion was justified on social and economic grounds. Yet in the cold economic climate during the expansion, more for the elite meant less for the majority. In 1980 the annual per capita cost in universities was £3070 compared with £420 in primary schools and £600 in secondary schools. When resources were scarce it was difficult to defend the universities and higher education against cuts. The expansion had not visibly increased social justice or even educational opportunity and the economy declined as universities expanded. Those who went to university found that a degree was no longer a ticket to high-status employment or even a mark of prestige.

The economy, the civil service, the schools, the welfare services and the professions all require an intake of well-qualified entrants. A democracy is kept on its toes by social scientists. Life is enriched through scholarship in the arts. Research is increasingly the prerequisite of high technology industry. Scholarship is an end in itself. But a very small university sector could provide the scholarship, the research and the social criticism. In practice most activity in higher education is concerned with the quality of life of those involved, not investment in industry or criticism of social arrangements. It is a pleasant three or more years for students and a rewarding life for staff. The injustice is that these rewards go to such a limited range of the population and not necessarily to all the most talented. But for all, the return from the investment fell as supply outstripped demand in the market for graduate employment.

More and more children stay on at school to take a traditional, and in England, highly specialized set of public examinations. This might have benefited the economy by increasing the general level of skill available. However, the increasing numbers taking examinations served mainly to increase the level of qualification demanded for entry to the same job. The examination successes were used by employers as screening devices. Their content was of little concern. The qualifications ensured that the potential employer was only interviewing the most promising candidates. The 1970s and 1980s resounded with attacks on the grip that public examinations maintained over the secondary schools, even after the successful introduction of the Certificate of Secondary Education. Yet even minor reforms in examination structure were delayed. If they were screening devices for employers or for higher education it did seem wasteful to screw down the secondary school curriculum to produce credentials for a few. But it also disappointed the children concerned. They had run further and faster to obtain a qualification that left them just as badly off as their parents had been when leaving school without formal qualifications. The emphasis on the utility of education may have also devalued its intrinsic value. Certainly it ensured that non-examinees and early leavers had little motive to go on trying. Once education loses its intrinsic, scholarly rewards, it is a product at the mercy of a market.

Why then does the demand for qualifications remain high? The answer lies in the fear of being left behind. This is an international phenomenon, as rife in socialist as in capitalist states. Parents strive to give their children a headstart. The competition raises the stakes. In principle, comprehensive schooling was widely accepted as fair. In practice many of its supporters sustained the relative advantage of their own children within comprehensive systems, or by using the selective residues within and around it. Behind policies for education lies a deep intransigent human urge to benefit one's own offspring. The service class parents maintain the advantages of their children under many forms of capitalism and socialism. When access to prestigious occupations is limited and increasing numbers are eligible to compete for them through the expansion of schools, the gap between the public expression of equality and selfish private behaviour is likely to widen. The universities opposed cutbacks in 1981 by pointing to the adverse effect of contraction on the chances of the poor. But it had been the intransigence of the universities over the reform of the A-Level examinations and their own entry requirements that had ensured that independent schools and the children of the service class would continue to dominate university entrance. Fred Hirsch's 'hole in the affluent society' contained double standards (Hirsch, 1977). Those up the ladder cried out for more to come up, but they made sure their own children climbed up first. They simultaneously restricted access at the bottom and added more rungs at the top.

The success of the service class

The service class to which teachers belong has been formed from most social classes during expansion. The Oxford Mobility Group report on over

10,000 males aged 20–64 in 1972 showed that those in professional, higher-technical, administrative and managerial occupations that form the service class, came from diverse origins (Goldthorpe, 1980). Among the youngest group, born between 1928 and 1937, 68 percent came from service-class origins. Among the oldest group, born between 1908 and 1917, 55 percent had fathers in the same social class. Goldthorpe (1980) describes this shift as follows: 'Thus, we may conclude, while there can be little doubt that over recent decades the service class has been recruited from increasingly diverse social origins, there is no sign of any falling off in the capacity of its members to transmit social advantage to their offspring' (pp. 255–256). Indeed, while the service class was still expanding, those within it were making sure that their children stayed in the same fortunate position.

The transmission of social advantage has been achieved through education, partly through using the independent schools and partly through maximizing the benefits of maintained schools. Teachers as parents, in particular, are in a favourable position to select schools that are geared to obtaining good academic results. They appreciate the importance of qualification and even in 1977 (*TES*, 1977a) a majority of teachers still opposed the ending of selection and the phasing-out of the grammar schools. There is often a gap between the teaching role adopted for other people's children and that sought for one's own children.

We can only guess at the gap between personal ambition and practice. But the public services are run from the top by civil servants whose education has usually been in the independent sector. The proportion of service class offspring among direct entrants to the administrative civil service rose from 64 percent to 85 percent during the 1950s. In the mid-1960s the Fulton Committee (1968) found that 73 percent were Oxbridge graduates and 63 percent were from public schools. But the post-Fulton reorganization of recruitment only further strengthened the hold of the service class. The annual reports of the Civil Service Commission still show the dominance of Oxbridge. The administration of the public services, including education, tends to be by those who can afford to see them as an extension of private provision.

The professionals in the public services are also in a position to use a mix of private and public provision. Doctors support private medical practice. Social security administrators use the tax-efficient private insurance. Their unions are organized to support them. Local authority housing managers live in private housing. Teachers use the maintained schools to the maximum advantage for their children, reinforce these schools by their own efforts at home and use the independent sector just as other service-class groups. These efforts secure higher education for children, thus maximizing the benefits and the investment from taxation drawn from poor and rich alike.

This is not a criticism of teachers or other public servants. Teachers belong to the service class; they value education. In 1977, a survey confirmed earlier evidence in 1974 that teachers are mainly conservative and, if not rich, comfortable (*TES*, 1974, 1977a). For example, 77 percent owned their own homes, 81 percent their own car and 93 percent had a bank account; in each case these figures are well above the national average. Most intended to vote Conservative; in 1979 and in 1983 they did so. Even after four years of cuts only 26 percent intended voting Labour in 1983 (*TES*, 1983). In 1977, when most secondary schools were comprehensive, a majority still supported grammar schools and corporal punishment. This picture is unsurprising. The service class is a stabilizing, conservative force. Because they are recruited from higher education and work on the same staff teachers are often married to each other and their work makes double salaries a possibility. They are concerned for their children as much as any other group, but know more about ways of maximizing the opportunities.

The size of the service class, its members' concern for and knowledge of education, their comfortable if not wealthy financial position, make them important customers for maintained and independent schools. They tend to live in the more leafy towns and suburbs outside the metropolitan areas. They use maintained schools in these areas which are attractive to academically ambitious teachers because they contain motivated children and supportive parents. Parents select among the primary schools to obtain the best. They pick the secondary school with the good academic results. Some idea of the difference in results can be obtained from the many surveys by the Assessment of Performance Unit. The results for language (reading), mathematics and science for the 15-year-olds in 1980 used free school meals as an indicator of poor children. In reading and writing, the 13 mathematics categories and the 10 science categories, a consistent pattern was presented showing higher performance with lower proportions taking free meals. Similarly, non-metropolitan children scored consistently higher than those in metropolitan areas and, where presented, prosperous suburban children outshone the rest (APU, 1982a, b, 1983).

If the maintained sector looks unpromising, service-class parents will make sacrifices in order to use the independent schools. The 109 direct-grant grammar schools that became independent when the grant was discontinued after 1974, knew the strength of the demand and have flourished. The service class tends to be self-recruiting. With tax-efficient mortgages and inflation-proofed pensions, grandparents are a source of finance for paying school fees. The financial pages of the *Sunday Telegraph, Sunday Times* or *Observer* always contain ways of funding fees out of taxes.

The service class is, therefore, a powerful influence on maintained and independent schooling. Regardless of which type of school these parents use, their children are more likely to get into the sixth forms and higher education. In 1979, children of the service class, who comprised one-quarter of the population, took two-thirds of all university places. Unskilled workers contributed 1 percent of undergraduates. These are the expensive parts of the education service. The costs are borne by poor and rich alike. Education to a first degree or a higher degree is not only a way of improving the prospects of high-prestige employment. It is a way of getting the maximum value out of the service.

This success by the expanded service class within education is only one aspect of the benefits they have derived from social services and tax arrangements for supporting them. A family with both husband and wife in service-class occupations can look forward to an inflation-proofed retirement. They will have received tax relief on a mortgage in buying a house that will have appreciated in value. They will be insured to gain more tax relief. Their children are likely to have been successful in school and higher education and are likely to be themselves in service-class occupations. They will inherit a sizeable sum from their parents' house sale, insurance policies and savings. Much of this will have been protected from capital gains tax. They will be in a position to carry the advantage to their own children. There are some very rich families. The growth of the service class has produced an expanded second layer of people who are comfortably off and in a position to secure advantages for their children.

The growth of a service class in professional, scientific and administrative occupations has been a major but neglected factor in the development of the education service. First, it is this group which has pressed for, staffed and benefited from extended maintained education. The service class is recruited on the basis of public examination results and professional credentials. It is promoted on the basis of qualification and seniority. These establish an exclusive claim to expertise. Lawyers and doctors have long claimed the right to exclude the unqualified and the new professions have followed the same path. Entry to teaching, for example, has been progressively closed to the professionally unqualified after a long campaign by the teachers' unions that was similar to that pursued by dentists and midwives, and doctors before them. The law enforces these restrictions on entry, thus consolidating the position of those within. Service-class parents then ensure that their children obtain the credentials that in turn secure their status. This is not a capitalist phenomenon; it is a feature of socialist states too (Nove, 1975).

The success of the service class in securing the future of their children is made possible by their comfortable financial position, the security of home ownership and inflation-proofed pensions as well as their concern with, and knowledge of how best to obtain, educational qualification. The welfare state and the public service have not only been major sources of employment. They have provided the financial security and the educational opportunities for passing advantages on to children. But this is not only an important influence on maintained schooling and higher education. It is the reason why independent schooling has flourished. The rhetoric of abolition may be strong, but the fastest growing social class has ensured that reform remains in the manifesto.

Independent schools in the market for qualification

The demands made by the service class on independent schools have had two neglected but very important effects. First, they enabled many direct-grant and county grammar schools to become independent in the 1970s, secure in the anticipation that the service class would find the fees for a day schooling that carried on the academic tradition. Second, they reinforced the efforts of the remaining independent schools to obtain the A-level results in the high-prestige subjects that would secure entry to the universities.

There are over 2000 independent schools in England and Wales. They range from backrooms for very young children to high-prestige public schools. They contain about 400,000 children. In the past 30 years the number of such schools has decreased. However, the larger, more academic independent schools have flourished; they were strengthened in 1975 when the direct-grant arrangements were ended. This affected over 100 grammar schools which, unlike the majority of maintained schools, had received money direct from the government. All bar one or two of these schools decided to become independent, and they were joined by some of the older maintained grammar schools which were in a position to raise money to bargain their way out of the maintained sector by coming to an arrangement with their LEA.

The constraint exercised by the independent schools is both direct and indirect. They are competitors with the maintained schools. They offer an apparently very successful conservative model of education. They claim to educate an elite and the statistics confirm that they are successful in this. In Home's Cabinet of 1963, 91 percent of the members were from public schools. In 1971, there were 65 old Etonians in Parliament. Winchester has provided many Labour ministers, including Gaitskell and Crossman. Wilson's Labour Cabinet of 1967 contained 42 percent from public schools. This dominance of public life by the public schools has been repeatedly documented. The Public Schools Commission Report (1968) is a mine of factual information. Guttsman (1963) and Boyd (1973) both confirm that those in a position to make decisions affecting public policy are largely drawn from a narrow range of families and have been through the public schools. Indeed, Boyd argues that the educational route through public school to Oxbridge has become more important in attaining an elite position, and Halsey and Crewe (1967) have confirmed this for recruitment to the administrative civil service before and after the Second World War.

As academic qualifications became the key to more and more occupations, the independent schools preserved their position in the production of elites by securing more than their anticipated share of the degrees and diplomas, and in the subject areas where there is most demand. This can be seen in percentage participation rates. In 1981, those in or from English independent schools formed 4.9 percent of school children aged 5–18, 17.5 percent of school pupils aged 16–18, 25.1 percent of leavers with 2 or more A-Levels, 21.4 percent of applicants to universities, 28.4 percent of those accepted and 47.7 percent of those admitted to Oxford or Cambridge. When the universities raised their A-Level requirements as they cut intakes while the number of qualified school leavers rose, the influence of the independent schools was likely to increase further.

These figures do not merely indicate the success of the independent schools in maintaining their competitive position in the examination race. They show the effects of curricular reform. When the universities ignored science, the public schools turned out classicists. When university departments of science and engineering expanded and were short of well-qualified applicants, the independent schools were producing more than their share of A-Level science courses. Perhaps the most striking curriculum development since 1945 has been this switch to science in the independent schools.

The Industrial Fund for the Advancement of Science in Schools was set up in 1955 by industrial firms for the independent schools. Initially £3 million was provided, a far greater sum at 1955 prices than the funding of any curriculum development for the maintained sector. Classics shrunk in importance in the schools as in universities. The independent schools responded to the market. New mathematics and Nuffield science were pioneered in public schools and by the 1970s engineering and then science were the most popular careers among public school leavers. The image of public schools as antique yet influential relics is misleading. It ignores the real base of their influence: this is the ability to monopolize the entrances to prestigious occupations through qualifying their pupils in the subjects required for entry to the professions and to university.

The position that the independent schools now hold in relation to mathematics and science has been reinforced by the decision of the ex-direct-grant grammar schools to become fee-paying. Manchester Grammar, King Edward's Birmingham, Hampton, Bradford, Latymer Upper and many others have reputations as powerful academic institutions. The girls' schools among them have large A-Level groups in mathematics and science. A single-sex selective school, such as Godolphin and Latymer, retained a far higher proportion of girls in these subjects than was found in mixed, or smaller grammar schools. Independent girls' schools had not been eligible for grants under the Industrial Fund, but some found the money and built the laboratories and workshops in the 1950s. Partly because they were single-sex, but more particularly because of the need to ensure that the service class kept sending their children because they were providing entrance to scarcity subjects such as science, mathematics and modern languages, the girls' independent schools were as likely to prosper as those for boys. Boys' and girls' independent schools alike were responding to a demand, largely by the service class, for an intensive, academic and if possible day schooling that would secure success for their children in a competitive labour market.

These independent schools are influential beyond their provision for about 5 percent of the population. There are very many private schools with very low standards of attainment. But the image of these schools, and usually the reality, is of achievement. For those who cannot, as well as for those who can, afford the fees, this provides a model against which to judge the maintained schools, however unfair that comparison is given the resources available to each. But below the examination results, the university entrance figures and the promise of enhanced opportunities at work, lies a profound difference between the independent day schools and many maintained schools. From entry to preparatory school at age nine, or when work starts for the 11- or 13-year-old entry to independent secondary schools, the pupils in the independent schools are on course for the public examinations to be taken five or seven years later. There is no relaxed introduction to secondary schooling. Newcomers are already tested and then sorted out into streams for a clear run up to GCE. The homework is piled on. This settling into the O-Level groove tends to be delayed in maintained secondary comprehensive schools. There is often one year or two of mixed-ability grouping, with a gentle introduction to new subjects and to homework. It is an anomalous situation. The children who need it least get the longest and most pressurized run-up to public examinations. The children who need the boost most must wait until the privileged minority has a couple of years' headstart.

If unemployment remains high and if there is a continuing emphasis on high-level qualifications for a shrinking number of high-prestige jobs, the social inequality created by the existence of an independent sector will be likely to increase. The difficulty for the maintained schools is obvious. Many serve communities where the parental support for children makes an academic curriculum impractical. They have to concentrate on control and pastoral care. But there is a further problem. If maintained schools modelled themselves on the independents, they would have to allow for more starkly defined failures as well as more pupils achieving high academic success. What can be achieved for a minority may be unavailable to a majority, if education is seen as a means to improved adult prospects rather than as an end in itself. Universities are highly selective and high-prestige jobs are few. If more gain qualifications, the entry requirements are raised. It is a game with continually receding goalposts.

It would be a mistake to see this dilemma of independent schooling meeting some parents' wishes while diminishing the relative opportunities of the majority, as an English concern only. Private schools are flourishing in most advanced industrial societies in the 1980s. Furthermore, evidence from the USA (Coleman et al., 1982) and from Australia (Australian Council for Educational Research, 1981) suggests that parents using private schools in increasing numbers are attracted by the carrot of high standards as well as being pushed by doubts about the capacity of maintained schools to provide their children with the qualifications needed in the increasingly competitive job market. In these and many other countries there was political pressure to bow to this parental demand and to the difficulty of finding and funding a place in private schools. The proposals were to give tax credits or vouchers to individuals, or funds to groups or communities to establish their own voluntary schools.

The responsiveness of education as a public service

The size of the education service, its financial inertia, the difficulty of finding levers to shift it and the corporate nature of the interests involved have created a heavy weight of previous investment. This has established a speed and direction of change that are difficult to deflect. The momentum is largely generated within the service by decisions taken over a period of time, in many centres of influence. During contraction any except the most marginal changes require either political action from the centre, that would be opposed by the partners, or massive injections of resources requiring unacceptable levels of taxation. The response to the rapid rise in youth unemployment is a good example. The obvious solution – raising the school-leaving age and radically revising the curriculum – has never even been seriously discussed as a possibility. The response has been organized outside the service through the MSC, which is responsible to the Secretary of State for Employment.

It would be one-sided to see this inertia as all loss. Schools, even in inner-city areas which have experienced unrest in the streets, retain the confidence of parents (Johnson and Ransom, 1980; Tomlinson, 1980). The indicators that are available, such as public examination results, Assessment of Performance Unit reports and the now published HMI inspections, suggest that there is a lot of solid academic work being done. Even in an area such as Toxteth in Liverpool, where unrest in the streets spilled into the schools, HMI found schools to be normally calm and orderly despite facing severe social deprivation and a lack of leadership from the LEA (DES, 1982a).

The education service could proceed without disturbance if there were no research or development. It would not collapse if there were no professional training of new teachers or retraining of those in post. Indeed, the high-prestige public schools are proud of medieval buildings, traditional curricula and graduates appointed straight from universities. There is also a residue of ideas and practices that persists. A teacher resurrected from the nineteenth century would have no great difficulty in some contemporary secondary school classrooms. Indeed, he might find it far easier than his own experience with classes of over 100 children. I was taught that the atom was indivisible long after the physicists had split it. My children used the same mathematics textbook as myself, 40 years on.

This inertia is neither necessarily good nor bad. The continuity brings security. The simultaneous launch of curriculum development projects in the 1960s with secondary reorganization and a rapid turnover among teachers probably created a bustle that did disturb many schools. Continuity in organization and administration is an advantage. In deciding on next year's budget, it is difficult to do more than carry on as last year with marginal redistribution of resources given the resources tied to the salaries of teachers. From the schools, predictable administration and resources are helpful. A minor change in the index of deprivation, which played a small part in the allocation of resources between schools, in the Inner London Education Authority in the 1970s would be followed by storms of protest from headteachers, claiming that marginal changes had made it impossible to organize next year's work. This was not just pressure to regain lost funds, although the complaints only came from the losers. It was a symptom of the inertia that enables schools to ensure continuity for children. Cultural revolutions were attractive to Maoists, but the Chinese found them intolerable. Education suffered most. Few teachers are willing to sacrifice their children to secure radical change, and that is comforting for parents.

Keeping the enterprise going and, if possible, expanding it, is an important aim of those involved in private and public corporations. Indeed, smooth operation and preferably expansion are measures of managerial success. Contraction is liable to be taken as a sign of failure. There is also a built-in and understandable tendency to expand enterprises such as public services. A director of social services is in a position to see unmet needs all round. A hospital administrator sees waiting lists and patients who cannot be given artificial hips or a heart pacemaker. A director of education is pressed by teachers and governors for extra facilities to meet genuine needs. Within a service industry the possibilities for expansion to meet fresh needs are unlimited. This pressure to expand is increased by central government legislation which forces local government or private industry to take on new staff to meet new standards.

The mass of legislation and administrative procedures of the modern state is handled through bureaucracies. Their expansion has been the most noticeable trend in manpower over the past 40 years. As they do their job, gaps in the information they rely on, or in the control they exercise, or in accounting and forecasting, are noticed. To improve effectiveness there is expansion to set up the necessary offices. With around 10 million clients a year and nearly one million full- and part-time employees, the education service is prone to these expansive tendencies. As with all expensive public services, the tendency to expand has to be audited by the question: 'How much of the expenditure on staffing and running the service benefits the clients and how much benefits those employed?' Inevitably there comes a point where the extra funds might be seen to be more productively spent elsewhere. That point was reached by the public services in Britain in the late 1960s, and the pressure to monitor the cost of services has increased since that time.

In schools and educational administration alike, expansion and smooth running are seen as the criteria of successful management. Thus teachers evaluate their schools as working well if there are no crises (Becher et al., 1981). In county halls the priority tends to be first to maintain the share of available resources for education and then to engineer public acceptance of policies (Bacon, 1978). Gould's Minister of Education with brass elbows (Gould, 1976) is the central government champion of the service.

There are occasions when those who run the service act to preserve their own jobs, power and influence, rather than to respond to some public interest. Teachers would not be expected to support the closure of their school nor clerical staff to welcome their redundancy through the introduction of computerization. The opposition to the implementation of the Taylor Committee's recommendations on school government and to the release of information detailed in the 1980 Education Act is only understandable if the organization of the service is looked at from the perspective of both insiders and outsiders. Those inside the service are not only used to established procedures, but appreciate the disturbance that even small changes can make to the whole enterprise. They have organized the flow of information. As it appears on their desks and in agendas, it confirms and reinforces their view of organization. Outsiders have only limited access to that information and see the organization of the DES, LEA or school from a very different angle. This may yield a narrow and biased view but, however ill-informed, it is concerned with ends to be achieved rather than with the existing procedures which are often of most concern to administrators and professionals.

Looking at education as a public service brings the issue of insider–outsider control sharply into focus. Insiders do have more information. They organize it and see the service accordingly. The current organization of education seems logical, natural to those involved in it. But they and their predecessors have organized it that way. There is nothing sacred about it.

Suggestions for changes from outside might be inconvenient, but are often based on a knowledge of the rapidly changing context of schools. It was only after the Great Debate that school self-assessment became popular and, with the Education Act of 1980, became a way of giving parents more information. The legislation to get information released might not have been necessary if the professionals had been more open with their public before the media and the politicians felt that public discontent was in the air.

The tendency for public services to be run for the benefit of those who work in them is a feature of corporate societies. It occurs in fascist, communist, liberal, undeveloped and developed countries. Industrial societies are dominated by large private and public corporations. The former respond to the market, or manipulate it. The latter are only rarely the subject of national and local elections. Their mass and momentum make it very difficult to secure responsiveness to the public they serve.

The difficulty in avoiding organizational inertia can be clearly seen in teacher education, where both imposed expansion and contraction have been rapid. The age structure of staff and their time in a training institution since leaving teaching (see Chapter 6) show an increasingly unsatisfactory situation. Tenure in university, polytechnic or college guarantees that the skills of staff will become progressively more distant from the experience to which professional training refers. Meanwhile able and well-qualified younger teachers have few opportunities to join the trainers.

The White Paper, *Teaching Quality* (DES, 1983), reviewing the education of teachers, recommended the appointment of teacher-tutors and the periodical return of staff to the classroom, as well as the dismissal of the small minority of incompetent classroom teachers, once in-service support has failed to benefit them. This modest set of proposals skates along the surface of the underlying institutional problem. Teaching, training teachers, administering, advising, inspecting, working in research, development and support services are all part of the same education industry. Whether in schools, universities, polytechnics or colleges, in research, curriculum development projects or teachers' centres, in the DES, town or county hall, the personnel are part of the same enterprise. Lateral movement would benefit all of them. Career prospects would be enriched if the barriers of pay scales, pension rights and conditions of service were removed. But from within each sector the reasons for retaining tenure and distinguishing conditions of service seem overwhelming. Insiders and outsiders define situations differently. Each group has its union or its professional association to defend the boundaries. That is the way of institutionalization. It is the other face of the predictable career of the professional. That security depends on maintaining established personnel and procedures through accreditation, distinguishing conditions of service and marks of prestige such as qualifications, titles and offices. It is less the insolence than the insulation of office that inhibits adaptation. As professionals we jealously guard the organization of learning against lay interference. But within the service that organization is itself compartmentalized, and careers are secured within compartments. But the security is defensive and is based on a sectional view. The service was organized with assumptions about fraternity and universality. Public servants have every right to fight their corner. But the defence of interests by sections of the service can produce stagnation, redundancy and sectional interests. The size and strength of public sector unions and professional associations were not foreseen when the welfare state was created on assumptions of fraternal feelings in administration and the professions.

The close relationship between education and the labour market confuses evaluation. The 1944 Education Act outlined a service where parents had the duty to ensure that a child received 'efficient full-time education suitable to his age, ability and aptitude'. LEAs were given the duty of ensuring that education met communal needs. There was little attention to the constraints on the demand side of the service. Exercised by parents, employers and higher education these were, through public examinations, to be the major formative influence. On the supply side there was no consideration of the inertia built up in large-scale service industries, particularly from the establishment of insulated and secure careers.

It is the unconsidered and unintentional consequences of legislation that are often important in the long term. Part of the criticism of the DES in the 1970s was that its planning did not go beyond resource provision to laying down objectives related to social and economic conditions. In the 1950s and 1960s evidence had accumulated that sectional rather than universal interests were being served. The rich were not only using independent schooling to continue their monopoly of higher education but had managed to retain their grip on the grammar schools once secondary schooling became universal after 1944.

There has not been time to gauge the effect of comprehensive schooling, but figures show that there has been no increase in the proportion of working-class children entering university. Indeed, as universities protect their position by keeping their A-Level intake grades as high as possible, in order to give the impression of strength, the chances of a working-class child from the poor inner-city school may decline further. Many universities will become finishing schools for the independent sector. Neither does the evidence on comprehensive school organization quoted earlier suggest that the ending of selection has altered the progressive differentiation exercised through the curriculum. Indeed, the emphasis on the part that the service should play in preparing for occupation increases the pressure on teachers to sort out the fast and slow learners at an early age, in order to prepare children for specialized roles later. A service organized to suit different abilities and aptitudes will be differentiated. That may now have been delayed for many children. But, coupled to an advanced division of labour through public examinations, it is a recipe for competition and selection, and not for the promotion of community or fraternity. On the demand side the poor have not benefited beyond taking opportunities created by the proliferation of white-collar jobs. Their position relative to the children of the rich has not improved. On the supply side, nearly 40 years of investment have created a service with a momentum that is difficult to shift. That accounts for the lack of any sustained innovation to boost the chances of the poor. Even adaptations to acute problems such as unemployment have not been possible. The chronic problems of failure to reward talent wherever it occurs demand even more radical change, yet this seems as far away as ever.

CHAPTER 8

THE CONDITIONS FOR REFORM IN EDUCATION

In this final chapter the review of education as a public service will be used to present a context within which proposals for reform can be formulated. From preceding chapters the restrictions can be appreciated. The links with a stratified market for jobs mean that parents seek to optimize the education of their own children and hence limit both the opportunities of those with fewer resources and the scope for the identification and promotion of talent wherever it occurs. The service is unfair, being neither egalitarian nor meritocratic. Reformers have the option of either ignoring the restraining context, or of acting modestly within it. The former is dishonest, the latter frustrating.

It is this frustration that accounts for the tendency to ignore both internal and external constraints and to launch into free-floating recommendations that so often have unintended consequences and harm those who are supposed to be helped. The radical critics of education who look to the economic and political structure as the source for change are being more honest. If the capitalist class structure could be destroyed, or competing interests reconciled under a totalitarian regime, education could be reformed radically. But as most find the cost of this unacceptable, liberal modesty remains the most honest if frustrating stance for reform.

It is not possible to avoid being polemical in such a review. At the heart of the subject matter is the political question that has recurred in previous chapters. How far can collective provision through the state be reconciled with freedom of individual choice? That question reflects the liberal bias that has already permeated discussions of government and the corporate society. That was the reason for evaluating the service by reference to its origins with Beveridge and Butler. Education has been judged according to whether it promoted individual responsibility, for at the heart of our democracy is a faith not only in the worth of freedom, but in the ability of people to act responsibly and produce changes. L. T. Hobhouse, when Professor of Sociology at the London School of Economics before the First World War, expressed this in the following way: 'The heart of liberalism is the understanding that progress is not a matter of mechanical contrivance, but of the liberation of living spiritual energy' (Hobhouse, 1912). Hobhouse, like Beveridge, was in the tradition of reluctant collectivists; both realized the need for collective action. For example, both Hobhouse in 1912 and Beveridge in 1942 saw that employment had to be sustained by the state because individual action could not find or create jobs once industries declined. This explains why full employment was seen as a condition for the success of the welfare services, including education. It was why Butler included compulsory part-time education in the 1944 Act (Butler, 1971, pp. 123–124). It has taken almost 40 years and high unemployment for the truth of this to be appreciated and the action is now taking place outside the education service, in the form of training for employment.

If we accept the liberal view that collective action through the state should maintain the conditions within which individuals act responsibly to secure their own welfare, then the fundamental problem for education is that the persisting inequality of performance between social classes is a product of that individual initiative, whether through the selective use of maintained schooling or of the independent sector. But the poor also want a fair share of the good life and the failure of education as a public service is that they have not been given it. The rest of this concluding chapter shows the conditions under which a solution to this problem has to be found.

The constraints on reform

In any evaluation of education, the changed context is important. We have been looking at a service organized during a world war. A flavour of this difference can be gauged from this passage from *Educational Reconstruction* (Board of Education, 1943), which was written when the outcome of the war was still undecided:

> The war has revealed afresh the resources and character of the British people – an enduring possession that will survive all the material losses inevitable in the present struggle. In the youth of the nation we have our greatest national asset. Even on the basis of mere expediency, we cannot afford not to develop this asset to the greatest advantage.

R. A. Butler, moving the second reading of the Education Bill a year later, described it as the first of the government's measures of social reform:

> An educational system by itself, cannot fashion the whole future structure of a country, but it can make better citizens. Plato said 'the principle which our laws have in view is to make the citizens as happy and harmonious as possible'. Such is the modest aim of this bill which provides a new framework for promoting the natural growth policy itself towards education in the years to come.
>
> (*Hansard*, 19 January 1944, quoted in Gosden, 1966)

It is difficult to appreciate these hopes at such a distance, but they lay behind the organization of the service as it remains today.

Three themes have run through this book. First, education is affected by the same economic and political pressures that constrain the remaining public services. Beveridge's freedom from ignorance was wrapped in the same package as freedom from want, disease, squalor and idleness (Beveridge, 1942). But the achievement of those freedoms is not measurable against fixed standards. The investment to relieve the most pressing symptoms of ill health, squalor or poverty did not satisfy demand, it created higher hopes. The National Health Service Act (1946), the Housing Acts (1946 and 1948) and the National Insurance Act (1946) were the cornerstones of the welfare state. They were the means through which more and more people experienced a healthier, more secure life and came to hope that the improvement would continue. The Education Act 1944 built up similar hopes, raised even higher because they were for children with a potentially brighter future.

The discontent with the welfare state which was apparent by the end of the 1960s was partly a result of its success. Hopes had been raised and continued to rise. Supply stimulated demand and costs rocketed. There was no easy way of deciding priorities. By the end of the 1960s there was doubt about the continuation of increased investment in social services on an 'all contribute, all benefit' basis. This was not just a cry from the wealthy who wanted to buy medical care, private pension rights and independent schooling. The investment had not universally benefited all sections of the population. Positive discrimination for the poor, and opting out by the rich were both symptoms of weaknesses in the welfare state after 20 years of rising hopes which were not always met. The education service ran into the flak with the rest.

The difficulty in determining the level of spending on social services and of allocating resources between them was exacerbated by continuing economic problems. It is easy to see these in the post-oil crisis period of the 1970s and 1980s. But the Acts that created the welfare state in 1946 were followed by crisis after crisis. They did not cease with the post-war 'age of austerity'. The Korean War at the start of the 1950s created another crisis that led to Bevan and Wilson resigning from the Labour government over the introduction of NHS charges. In the late 1950s there were resignations from the Conservative government over the high level of government spending. Poor economic performance has forced successive Labour and Conservative governments to limit or cut spending on social services. One side split because the services were cut, the other because they were threatening investment in the productive industry that could provide the necessary resources. But in all cases during those 40 years, something had to give.

The pressure on available resources within and between the public services ultimately depends on the wealth created in the economy. In a mixed economy private and public sectors compete for funds for invest- ment. The level of taxation, of interest rates, of private and public affluence or squalor, rests on the health of the economy. Particularly in a country like Britain, which depends on trade to pay for food and manufactured goods, the level at which demand for services and standards of living can be satisfied is determined by political decisions about the investment of avail- able resources. Public services compete with demands from nationalized and private industry for scarce resources.

The second theme of this book has been that while the education service is meshed into the remaining public services and competes with them for funds, it is organized so that there is little room for manoeuvre. Most of the money goes to paying teachers. In expanding times extra staff are employed to reduce class sizes, introduce new subjects, improve pastoral care, link schools with their communities, develop curricula, help children with learning difficulties or to administer, inspect or advise on educational developments. But at times of level funding as well as contraction, a crisis centred on the numbers of teachers employed is inevitable. The annual increases in teacher employment between 1945 and 1975 became a powerful force for inertia in the contracting 1980s.

The combination of pressure for change to meet developments outside the schools and the effects of contraction on the location of power in the service is likely to produce more central direction. Schools which could innovate when receiving extra funds each year have to ask the LEA to help solve problems when there are reduced resources. Staffing to protect a curriculum is only possible from county or town hall. The DES publishes suggestions for a common curriculum. The authorities find they cannot meet legal or moral obligations as central government grants are cut and legislation is necessary to help them cut back. Much of the activity within the DES, which is often seen as a conspiracy to increase central influence over professional concerns such as curriculum or teachers' conditions of service, is the consequence of the way education is organized. In the good times innovation and adaptation can be organized by individual teachers in the schools. During contraction decisions are forced towards the centre, to headteachers, to advisors, to LEAs and from there to central government.

This relocation of power to the centre during contraction is neither inexorable nor disembodied. Archer (1979) introduces her book, *Social Origins of Educational Systems*, with this warning that change comes from calculating humans, that it 'occurs because new educational goals are pursued by those who have power to modify previous practices'. That power was given to central government in the 1944 Education Act. It was in line with the positive central government role which was seen as essential as the welfare state was organized. Criticisms of the DES from the OECD (1975) and the Expenditure Committee of the House of Commons (1975–1976) were that it did not adopt a sufficiently positive planning position. The latter recommended that: 'Broad educational objectives should be kept under review as regularly as are their resource implications' (para. 49). The DES agreed to strengthen its Departmental Planning Organization (DES, 1976). But there are few signs of sustained, synchronized central action. HMI remains visibly independent, particularly over the effects of spending cuts (DES, 1981b, 1982d). It is hard to see coordination and certainly not conspiracy in developments such as the Great Debate, the creation of the Assessment of Performance Unit or the splitting of the Schools Council into two separate bodies. The sustained threat is not a conspiracy in Elizabeth House, but financial constraint exercised by the Treasury and the activities of the Department of Employment through the MSC.

The centralizing forces within the education service are unlikely to diminish. Demands on the service are likely to increase its cost as they will probably be at the costly end of the service catering for older students. Competition from other public services in an ageing population with high unemployment will strain the economy. Scarce resources are liable to sustain the pressures to pass decisions back to central government. But that drying-up of innovation in the schools and in LEAs is not only the result of economies. The size of the service and its bureaucratization have been shown to be forces for inertia. Growth builds up momentum at the cost of flexibility. Alternative ways of organizing schools, colleges, universities, LEAs and the DES seem impractical to those involved. They have an investment in established procedures. Their professional status, mapped out as a secure career, is defined within the existing organization. The established procedures are the security of those involved.

The third recurrent theme of this book has been that it is difficult to reconcile the many claims made on education. Those made by parents, employers and the young people involved conflict with the positions adopted by those who work in the service. The claims are often irreconcilable. This is not just a result of poor communication or a neglect of public relations. What you want education to be and what you want to get out of it depend on the position from which you view it.

It is possible to explain the discontent that is consequent on differing expectations from the political left (Rubinstein, 1979) or right (O'Keefe, 1981). The reality will always be discontent because education is closely linked to the future prospects of children. Even if there were agreement over what should be taught, parents would still press a personal view that would clash with teachers' responsibilities for many children. Education has to be selective as long as school leavers have to be sorted out and prepared for an advanced, stratified division of labour. That selection is a tragedy for the majority. But only in a utopia without any specialization at work or in government would there be equality. We are not born or bred equal and teachers are forever bringing that truth home to children and their parents. If selection was not carried out by teachers it would be done at entry to employment. It is no consolation that employers often ignore educational qualifications (Ashton and Maguire, 1980). When they do so it is for work that few relish.

Teachers are, therefore, involved in the unfairness of life. No political arrangements can eliminate the individual differences that enable children to benefit differently from schooling. Even the most egalitarian regimes have failed to stop parents with influence getting superior education for their children to reinforce advantages at home. The professionalism discussed in Chapter 6 is often a defence against taking these tragedies personally. No doctor could survive if every tragedy in his consulting room was taken to heart. No lawyer can accept the blame for every case lost. Similarly, teachers can insulate themselves from individual tragedies through their responsibility to act in a detached, expert way when differentiating between groups of children.

This sounds callous. But the insulation from personal tragedies is part of the rationality of bureaucracies such as schools or LEAs or teachers' unions. To be involved with individual cases can lead to favours being exercised. The essence of bureaucracy is that judgements are made according to rules. Similarly, the professional is expected to transcend personal feelings in assessment and guidance. The moment an administrator favours one school or one applicant, he will be betraying others. When a teacher reluctantly gives in to a pleading parent, he or she is giving an advantage to one child, but not to others who may have equally good cases. Behind the drama there have been many political decisions about the way resources should be allocated and children sorted out for employment or higher education. Those decisions account for the procedures that professionals and bureaucrats are expected to follow. With conflicting claims on the education service anchored deep in different personal and professional positions, there are difficult choices to be made.

Below this tragedy lies the link between education and the labour market. The latter is highly differentiated; selection is made on the basis of sex and race, despite legislation. Entry is also partly determined by qualification. Public examinations provide the credentials; in addition they determine the school curriculum. But if they did not, some other arrangements would. Examination reform is not an answer to inequality in education. That is a consequence of the link between schooling and employment. On top of differentiated employment sit stratified social classes. The link between education and employment is used by parents to secure the future of their children. Education, whether maintained or independent, is one important way of using influence or wealth as an investment in your children. If it wasn't schooling it would be nepotism, patronage, direct inheritance or some form of education outside school that formed the basis for differentiation. It might be easier to even up the competition than to try to destroy the link of schools to employment, for that might weaken both.

This is not just an economic debate, but a bread-and-butter issue of how to allocate resources. Should sixth-form classes be much smaller than those for younger pupils? Should money go to the Youth Training Scheme or to sixth-form colleges or further education colleges? Is it best to lose classics or technical drawing if staff have to be lost? Is it fairer to stream or teach in mixed-ability groups? Should a teacher attend more to the least or most able, or share attention equally between all the children in a class? From legislation about subsidizing places in independent schools, to decisions about how to organize a reception class, this dilemma over justice is being resolved in the classroom, town hall and Cabinet.

The source of this fundamental dilemma lies outside the schools. Because we are neither born nor bred equal, occupations carry very different rewards, and because schooling is a process of differentiation that links these two conditions, this dilemma for teachers cannot be removed through legislation. The essential point is that those concerned with decisions about education, whether in central or local government, or in schools or colleges, should realize that a choice is being made. There is no accepted, necessarily acceptable basis for allocating resources or organizing learning. The conventions are problematic. Routine procedures incorporate political judgements. Radical critics of the education service may be trying to replace one balance between excellence and opportunity for all with another, but they are also pointing to the political nature of the decisions that have produced the present balance. Other countries, for better or worse, avoid streaming, early specialization, and public examinations at age 16, and have greater proportions entering higher education. The contemporary solutions have come from political decisions about the way children should be sorted out in preparation for their adult positions. There is nothing necessarily sacred or even rational about these arrangements. They are man-made and can be changed.

From Gray and Moshinsky (1938) to Halsey et al. (1980) evidence has accumulated on the close relationship between attainment in school and various measures of the home life of children. The explanations keep changing, but whether they are seen to lie in the material conditions, the culture or the support of the home, in the ways schools are organized to produce different rates of attainment, or in the class-based definition of the knowledge that is valued and assessed in school, the problem persists. Schools do not seem to be very effective in overcoming disadvantages rooted outside them. Even studies such as the one by Rutter et al. (1979), which do show differences in effectiveness among schools, are cautious over the extent to which environmental factors and attainment at intake are overcome by the efforts of teachers. Critics of *Fifteen Thousand Hours* (Rutter et al., 1979) have also been cautious. Thus Heath and Clifford (1980) have concentrated on 'the seventy thousand hours that Rutter left out'. The power of educative forces outside the school frustrates efforts within it.

This problem concerns every teacher, administrator and politician in the service. It accounts for positive discrimination, compensatory education, intervention projects, social priority allowances for teachers and extra points for schools in deprived areas. It is tackled by community education, home–school links and pastoral care. Teachers organize caring communities or hard-driving, no-nonsense regimes, to try to overcome it. In the classroom, some try mixed-ability grouping, while others stream in the hope that disadvantages can be overcome. It has been quite an effort, yet the problem persists, confirming the strength of the social background factors. Once again, teachers have to live with the problem, responding in diverse ways but never able to escape. If you assume that all children are equal you find that the result is inequality. To give the penalized a chance, you have to give them a boost. In order to be fair you have to treat children unequally.

In practice, despite the efforts at compensation, the organization of schooling serves mainly to further penalize the poor. The rich either buy or find a school with a traditional curriculum geared from the start to public examinations. Most innovations in the maintained sector have been to broaden or to integrate curricula, and to delay working on examination syllabuses. Those with the greatest need for a quick start, a straight run and a boost are given a more gentler, more relaxed regime and then zig-zag towards their target, while their more fortunate peers start on their GCE courses early and are directed straight at the target. Having reached it, they then obtain the places in higher education which guarantee them financial support from taxes raised from poor and rich alike (Shipman, 1980). Once again this is a genuinely tragic situation for teachers. Their idealism is tested against the failure of those they want to help. There has been considerable achievement in rewarding merit in the past 20 years (Halsey et al., 1980). But the odds are still against the able poor. Teachers still have to live with the knowledge that they contribute to a process that most of them abhor.

The conditions for reform

The education service is the handy panacea for most social ills. Analysts of racial tensions, lack of respect for the old, riots, crime, the state of the economy, a lack of national pride, illegitimate babies and low church attendance, tend to place the burden for improvement on the schools. Those in the education service must take some of the blame for this insanity. In the 1950s and 1960s, economists stressed the profit from investment in the education service, and sociologists pressed for expansion to promote social mobility and justice. Professional associations demanded more resources because education was the guarantee of prosperity and justice. Scholarship, enjoyment, education as an end in itself were seconded to claims that it was the means to the good life. The claims for investment in education were not only inflated but misplaced, tending to increase the level of competition.

The disillusionment of the late 1970s and the early 1980s was all the deeper for the excesses of the earlier decades. With falling numbers of children and rising numbers of very old people, the press and pull factors swung violently away from education as a profitable source for investment. But below the national competition for resources there is also a mismatch between expectation and delivery. Musgrove (1971) summed this up simply: '. . . schools are underpowered in relation to the goals they try to attain'. The evidence on school effectiveness suggests that they are very limited organizations for influencing attainment or behaviour. The same lack of power to deliver applies across the education service through both internal and external constraints.

In the classroom with older secondary school children, the weakness of the teacher's position is obvious. There are few sanctions that can be applied to those not working for public examinations. Even if corporal punishment is allowed, most teachers are reluctant to use it, even if they are physically powerful enough to do so with fourth- or fifth-formers. One teacher and an often resentful group of up to 30 adolescents are confined in a classroom built to house willing children scribbling in books or listening to a teacher. Classroom design has changed little since the days of elementary schools and when children left at 13 years. Life for the teacher can become un-civilized. Efforts to maintain order, industry, quiet and civility can be exhausting. The exhortations from media, government, church and industry are unreal for many harassed teachers. To load teachers at the 'dirty' end of the profession with high-flown ideals is a mockery, for survival is a triumph. Just as decisions that are marginal at Cabinet level can be a disaster for a small school which loses a teacher through cuts, so it is easy for academia to recommend reforms that will look like mockery to the teacher as hero or heroine in an inner-city school in a deprived area.

The constraints resulting from the place of education within the public services, from its labour-intensive organization and from its place in the stratification of society, hinder attempts to resolve problems. Husen (1979), a leading international writer on education, sees four overriding problems of formal schooling in modern society: (1) it is isolated from society by bureaucratization, unionization and the prolongation of school life; (2) it frustrates young people because success in school no longer guarantees an attractive job; (3) schools are confused over their aims in relation to family, media and other educating agencies; (4) schools are divorced from a rapidly changing world of work. The need for change has been stressed nearer home. There have been manifestos from the great and good suggesting a general need for reform. There have been attacks on the secondary school curriculum from the Society of Education Officers and the local authority associations (Lister, 1981). To Fiske (1980b), the LEAs are left with their responsibilities, but have lost the power to meet them. Individual LEAs have put pressure on schools. Given the meaningless experience of schooling for many children and the unrelieved corset of public examinations, there is every reason to press for change. Yet that pressure needs to be in context to have a chance of success, unless the intention is revolutionary.

A flavour of the breadth of this reformist zeal can be obtained from this selection of reforms suggested in the *Times Educational Supplement* in 1982: public examinations should be scrapped (16 July), extended to the whole year group (21 May) or replaced by profiles (18 June); schools should be in the hands of the local community (16 April), or the boundaries between school and community should be removed (25 June); schools should be places for worthwhile leisure (5 March), or should concentrate on preparation for work (28 May); they should be experienced-based or skill-based (4 June); there should be no place for academic subjects (23 July).

The most influential book in this reformist vein is *The Challenge for the Comprehensive School* (Hargreaves, 1982). First, Hargreaves shows how the comprehensive schools, with a curriculum concentrating on cognitive–intellectual knowledge, bear and lose the majority of pupils because they lack the cultural and intellectual resources to succeed. The school is organized to assault pupils' dignity. Hargreaves then recommends a curriculum more likely to interest this majority. Yet the parents of these youngsters could tell him why they do not want any dilution of the academic curriculum and their children would take care of the teachers who tried such a dilution. Such a reform would remove even the small chance they have of getting their share of the cake through education. They would queue up at any school which remained traditional even if elbowed out by the service class. They would all be in line for a spoonful of the gravy. The poor as much as the rich want the best for their children.

Thus the reforms often seem designed to penalize those children whom reformers are trying to help. The chances of the poor in employment and in access to higher education have not been improved during secondary reorganization. Identifiable minority groups continue to be disadvantaged. It is not far-fetched to suggest that reforms have usually harmed the poor and made it easy for the rich and the informed to continue using schools to maintain the advantages of their children. For example, children at the top of the social strata are five times more likely to go to university than those at the bottom.

The reason for this injustice lies in the natural wish of parents to obtain a bright future for their offspring and in their ability to secure it. The poor are not in that happy position. They lack the resources, the knowledge and the contacts. Because reformers are reluctant to think of the power and the influence that determine how the resources for education are actually used, they rarely think through the very different consequences of their recommendations for different social groups. Parents with the resources or the knowledge of how to get the schooling they want, exploit the new as they did the old, within maintained as well as independent schools. The reasons why this is possible can be spelled out in a few brutal, over-simplified features of the education service and its relation to the labour market.

1   Entry to higher education and to the labour market is competitive and during economic contraction the competition gets fiercer.

2   Across the years in school, children acquire very different skills with which to compete on leaving.

3   Much of the learning that enhances a child's competitive position is picked up in the home, giving an advantage to the knowing.

4   Public examinations serve as the main criterion for selection in higher education and for employment.

5   Rich parents can use the independent schools to buy an academic education tightly geared to achieving public examination results.

6   Knowing parents make optimal use of the maintained primary and secondary schools to secure the best prospects of eventual examination success for their children.

7   Teachers in maintained schools serving poor areas have the most difficulty in motivating children and have most incentive to adopt innovations that deflect attention from academic work leading to public examinations. That enables them to survive doing the 'dirty' work that most of us prefer to keep under cover in order to preserve our own comfort.

8   Academics, administrators, advisors and inspectors, for the best of motives, press reforms which are differentially adopted. This reinforces the tendency for the children of the rich and the knowing to continue to get a long and intense preparation for public examinations, while the children of the poor are given a later start on academic work and a more leisurely, diversified programme.

9   It costs about seven times more to keep a student in higher education for one year than a pupil in a primary school.

10   The taxes paid by the poor help pay for the children of the rich to enjoy a heavily subsidized higher education.

Those at the soft centre of the educational establishment, who contribute the suggestions for reform, tend to ignore the different impact of these suggestions on rich and poor. The radical critics come from both left and right. The former focus on the advantages accruing to the rich from the economic and political structure of capitalism. Unfortunately it is difficult to change this from within the DES, the LEAs or the schools. But they have kept the injustice in the spotlight. The hard right has concentrated on protecting the academic curriculum. This offers little hope to the harassed teacher in an inner-city school, but it has defended the remaining prospects of the able poor.

For those who hold the liberal centre for education it has been difficult to balance increasing government intervention to effect increased equality of opportunity, with the protection of individual freedom of choice. Because there is no clear model of the way the service works, there is no readily available lever for reformers to operate. The model selected in the Introduction suggests two approaches to reform. The first starts from the political axis and the impact within schools will be mediated by teachers. But the outcome of the interaction will be unpredictable. Such reforms carry a high risk. The second sources of pressure for reform lie on the professional axis with teachers, advisors, inspectors, curriculum developers and so on. These are often conceived out of context but soon run up against political, financial, legal reality. This is the low-risk approach. The educational developments are spelled out in advance. Their implementation may often contain unintended elements, but the contextual factors tend to limit the impact on the service, hence limiting the risks involved.

High-risk reforms

The first high-risk development is already the nightmare of many writers. It is to acknowledge the legal position of central government to 'control and direct' the education service and to allow the central arm of the partnership to exercise more power. At present the difficulties in coping with youth unemployment by changing the secondary school curriculum and examinations, with or without raising the school-leaving age, have left the initiative with the government through the Department of Employment. With continued cuts in resources the LEAs are likely to be even more constrained in their freedom of action. Teachers will also find their scope for innovation severely restricted. Centralization is likely to be the consequence of contraction.

There is also a clear political element in recent central government activity in the education service. It has come from both major political parties. From Prime Minister to local councillor there has been support for a more accountable and responsive service. The teachers' unions saw the consequent action as a threat. The NUT commentary on the Taylor Committee's (1977) recommendation that governing bodies should give consideration to constructive suggestions from individuals or organizations concerned with the school's welfare was that 'Governors and parents have an interest in the curriculum, but the education of children should be protected from the intrusion of non-professionals who claim to have "a concern for the school's welfare" ' (NUT, 1978). Fred Jarvis, the NUT's General Secretary, more bluntly described the Taylor Report as 'a busybodies charter' (*TES*, 1977b). Similarly, the proposals in the 1980 Education Act for the release of information to parents on the curriculum of the school, have been met in the same defensive way. So have suggestions from the DES about a common curriculum. Where the curriculum is in focus the unions stoutly maintain the right of teachers to retain control. The priority motion at the NUT conference at Eastbourne in 1977 stated that: '. . . teachers must retain the right to exercise their professional judgement in identifying the needs of the young and in determining teaching methods and the content of the curriculum. The Union will resist the imposition of an externally determined curriculum and of universal testing of children at particular stages of education, either at local education authority level or nationally'.

Yet not only were the proposals for parental involvement, monitoring and a common curriculum suggested by central government mild, but most had already been adopted within LEAs and by individual schools. One indicator of the lessening resistance to parental involvement has been the spread of parent–teacher associations. In 1967 the Plowden Committee found 17 percent of primary schools with PTAs (Plowden Committee, 1967). In 1977 the National Foundation for Educational Research found 35 percent (Cyster and Clift, 1980). Many LEAs have placed parents on governing bodies. Many schools welcome parents onto the premises. It would have been difficult to find a school without the items suggested for a common curriculum. Furthermore, teachers seem to support some central guidance over the curriculum provided it is not detailed control (Wicksteed and Hill, 1979). The government has been carrying out its historic role of promoting consistency by backing existing developments and, where necessary, legislating for minimum levels of service.

Most accounts of the shifting balance of power in education have concentrated on the DES or the teachers' unions. But it is in county or town halls, or in the schools that changes in the partnership have been organized, and it is at this level too that the cuts have been felt most severely. Participation by the public has been encouraged, albeit tentatively. Central government action has followed as well as anticipated changes organized by those working within the service. With contraction, power has shifted to the centre and to the taxpayer. Central government has taken action to broaden the partnership, but so have LEAs and teachers. To ignore these grassroots movements is to undervalue the political sensitivity and the awareness of the relation between attainment and home and work among those in daily contact with adverse changes in social conditions in the past decade. The advantage of a 'distributed' balance of influence in the service is that half a million teachers are not just an important political force at the ballot box, but have their own constituencies of parents and employers. A top–down view of the education service emphasizes the big political switch, but it can miss the continuing fine tuning that often anticipates it.

Thus the panic over central government strength can be exaggerated. The legal position in education is clear, so is the need for the DES or the DoE to take positive action over unemployment. There are gross differences in the level of service within different LEAs. The bottom 40 percent of pupils remain unmotivated and inequality persists. Furthermore, the three-cornered partnership excluded other legitimate public interests, particularly parents, and it is central government, through the 1980 Act, that has pressed for an extension of information and influence to the lay public. The publication of HMI Reports on schools opens another corner. Of course there is a fear that an authoritarian government could attempt to control the curriculum, select teachers and censor textbooks. The outcry against what looked like the first tentative steps to examine the curriculum in the late 1970s was a healthy warning. But many other democratic rights would have to be lost before a government could control the content of education in Britain. It is right to be vigilant, but it is also necessary to be balanced. Central government acts for democracy as well as being a possible threat to it. Some extended influence could be beneficial. Historically government has often acted to raise standards of provision and to secure some consistency and equality among local communities.

The high-risk reforms are political, altering the balance of power within the education service or between it and other services or institutions. This can be achieved by legislation, by altering the resources made available, by government action altering the balance of the partnership or by bringing others into it. Because these steps are political their impact on education tends to be unpredictable. The threat in the move from percentage grants for individual services to a block grant where education had to compete for central government money in competition with other local government services is one example. It was bitterly opposed by the National Union of Teachers and the Association of Education Committees in 1958 because its effects were seen to be unpredictable as well as threatening (Gould, 1976). Similarly, government efforts, in the form of the 1980 Education Act, to increase the information available to parents, were seen as a threat because of the difficulty of predicting the impact of even a small increase in parental activity at a time of falling school roles. The action of the MSC in launching the Youth Training Scheme is a similar contemporary concern. It alters the resource-base of education and its influence is difficult to predict.

The high-risk political approach becomes a possibility when there is discontent with the service. Those who get a poor deal, such as working-class families, minority groups and women, press for a say in the running of the service. Radicals on the political left press for more power to be given to the classroom teachers. On the political right, the call is for more control over teachers in order to raise standards. Some call for deschooling, others for a return to basics. There is pressure for the abolition of private schooling and for vouchers to increase choice in the maintained sector. All aim at specific but contrasting changes in the political balance around the service. The impact on education itself is less clear. The risk is high because greater justice is promised but through policies that are in bitter opposition.

There are three further high-risk moves which could alter the current momentum of the education service and make it more responsive to communities and, it is to be hoped, fairer to the poor. The most radical would be to give communities influence over local schools. For better or worse this would open the schools to political pressure as in the United States. At present in the UK parents have little say in determining the curriculum or the organization of schools. Except for the 1000 families in Education Otherwise and those who can pay for private schooling, the majority do not have much choice and never have had. The 1980 Education Act places parents on governing bodies, but it would be possible to strengthen this representation or to move to community schools where management was genuinely shared between teachers and the communities they serve. This would be in the spirit of fraternity built into the 1944 Education Act. But it would have unpredictable results. A return to selection for secondary schooling would be possible and competition might be increased without benefiting the poor. Schools run for, and by minority groups would be likely to enter the maintained sector.

The advantage of community control could be to increase parental interest and participation. But there is no guarantee of this. There could be reinforcement for teachers through the involvement of the community in cases where children were troublesome, but it is difficult to see this as an effective control in urban areas. Yet that support for teachers is essential. Another possibility would be a change in the law defining parental rights and duties. These are obscure at present and teachers have few sanctions available when parents allow or even encourage children to be disruptive.

Thus a third way forward, although at a high risk, would be a contract in which the rights and responsibilities of parents and teachers were spelled out and, in extreme cases, enforced by law (Shipman, 1980). This would not be necessary in most cases for the evidence now available suggests that a majority of parents do try to support the work of schools (Johnson et al., 1980; Becher et al., 1981). But a legal contract would define expectations and enable action to be taken in the small number of cases where the learning of the majority was being disrupted by the behaviour of a minority whose parents were not fulfilling their duties.

The Education Act of 1944 does not define parental responsibilities. In wartime fraternity of interest was assumed. The wording of the Act suggests that parents have a duty to judge the efficiency of the schooling received, rather than to support that schooling through their own efforts. But the meaning of Section 36 is still being sought in the courts. Neither does the Act spell out the duties of teachers towards children and their parents. National and LEA negotiations to define conditions of service and to produce a contract that would specify non-teaching duties such as lunchtime supervision, have not produced any agreement. A successful education is the product of the efforts of teachers and parents. These are left to the voluntary good sense of both parties, and in the majority of cases this works well (Becher et al., 1981). In many cases teachers actively help parents to help their children (Pugh, 1982). But the minority of uncaring parents and teachers can disturb many who do care. The caring majority deserve some definition of the duties expected.

A final, open-ended, high-risk way of initiating equitable changes in the service would be to guarantee some 15 years' full-time equivalent education free to everyone, to be taken at any time of life. The Youth Training Scheme will secure some universal education and training beyond school, but the unfairness of full-time higher education being largely confined to the children of the rich, yet subsidized by the poor, will remain. If the present selection at the ages of 16 and 18 was essential for the effectiveness of higher education and the numbers in universities and polytechnics were essential for economic survival or the maintenance of the culture, the present selectivity would be justifiable. But stressing the utility of higher education misses the point: this is paramount for only a few students. The experience of higher education mainly benefits individuals and it is scholarship not utility that is rightly prized. A few can provide that scholarship and the personal experience for the majority could be spread across all sections of society by allowing entry to tertiary education, on a full- or part-time basis, at any time of life. This is not to devalue the contribution made by higher education to the wealth of the country. It is to emphasize that the conventional entry after A-Level could be reduced without harm to the economy, cultural life or scholarship. The redistribution of opportunities to enjoy the world of learning would be just and might enrich higher education as well as the students. The three- or four-year degree course begun at 18 has become part of the cementing of careers into bureaucratic structures. It is increasingly seen as a right not a privilege, despite the cost to those who will share neither it nor the benefits it brings.

These four high-risk innovations could promote movement in the education service. But the high risk arises from the difficulty of predicting the impact on the schools. The problem is illustrated in voucher schemes and in moves to introduce private funding into the maintained sector. Education vouchers enabling parents to choose between maintained schools or to opt for an independent school might increase choice. But that choice might close unpopular schools which could be doing an excellent job in adverse circumstances. The main threat is the unpredictable outcomes. The National Union of Teachers expresses it this way: 'The potential for disturbance and uncertainty which a voucher system would create is frightening' (NUT, 1983). The union illustrates this by reference to accelerated movement, the threat to continuity and planning in schools, and overcrowding in some schools while others empty. It is seen as a 'lottery' with very few winners.

There is also unpredictability in the extension of private contributions to maintained schooling. Payments for swimming, textbooks, music tuition and minor capital works might increase the divide between schools for the rich and the poor. Yet it is difficult to deny the right of parents to contribute to improving the maintained schools of their children while others pay for independent education. The contributions might be small but they supplement the marginal resources left once existing commitments are funded and hence can be very important as 'free' money. Furthermore, the parental commitment would be a step towards more meaningful and sustained involvement.

The risk in such changes in the political balance surrounding education is also high for the professionals employed within the service. Reforms soon run up against the resistance of teachers and lecturers to increases in the influence of parents and others outside schools, colleges and universities. This is the spectre behind radical books such as *Unpopular Education* (Centre for Contemporary Cultural Studies, 1981). Making education popular in the political sense means reducing the power of the professionals. Yet they claim autonomy and their careers are mapped out in a service over which they can exert influence. Popular control in education is a threat not only to the right of teachers to control school organization and curriculum, but to the predictability of careers within the service. Teachers and lecturers are not unique in defending their security. They are acting with the remaining service-class professionals to secure their future. Separating that motive from their concern to benefit the learners is difficult. Public services are very often unpopular because democratic control is a threat not only to the universalism that secures fair dealing, but to the careers of those who need security in their work to be in a position to resist special pleading.

Low-risk reforms

Low-risk reforms tend to be produced from the professional axis of the forces affecting the education service. These can, however, ignore not only the meshing of education into the market for adult labour, but the inertia within the service. Administrators, advisors, HMI, researchers, academics and so on suggest very different reforms because each group defines the service differently from within distinctive career patterns. Thus administrators in the DES and LEAs see academic recommendations for reform as impractical or utopian while their own suggestions are dismissed by academia as fiddling around the edges. The problem is partially caused by the lack of lateral movement created by different structures. The unification of pay scales, pension schemes and promotion ladders would help create mobility and concentrate minds on issues defined with sufficient agreement for communication to be profitable and misunderstanding minimized.

The most prominent low-risk policy since the 1960s has been positive discrimination aimed at increasing the resources available to deprived areas, the schools serving them and their teachers. The policy was spelled out for education in the Plowden Report of 1967: 'The first step must be to raise the schools with low standards to the national average; the second, quite deliberately to make them better' (Plowden Committee, 1967, para. 151). But the constraints from previous investment and the marginal resources left for innovation (see Chapter 3), coupled with the persisting influence of deprived social conditions, minimized the impact of the positive discrimination that followed. However, the projects provided models for further action.

The second limit on the effects of positive discrimination is that it was never spelled out in terms that would have served to direct resources to achieve specific objectives. The money was distributed in penny packets to schools facing deprivation, or to projects that were often doomed to fail given the contrast between their ambitions and the resources made available. The Inner City Partnership, for example, produced £10,000 to support the teaching of Asian languages in London schools. The grant for the Educational Priority Area schemes was £200,000. But any gain was also likely to be cancelled out by losses caused by the tendency to reward failure rather than success. The criteria used for allocating funds were often measures such as low attainment, bad behaviour, low teacher morale (Cole and Shipman, 1975). Resources went to schools that failed to cope, while those that succeeded in similarly adverse conditions did not benefit (Shipman, 1980). Accompanying this tendency to compensate failure, resources went to building up compensatory education, race relations and equal opportunities industries. These have produced valuable pressure groups, but are often staffed by those who were previously on the job rather than administering others. Innovation too often consists of shifting around those involved to create the impression of change. Often it removes those doing the job into careers removed from the action.

From this experience with positive discrimination in the past, a strategy could be implemented to benefit the service in the future. First, the allocation of resources can be geared to supporting the majority who leave early rather than concentrated on the minority who stay in full-time education into their twenties. The Youth Training Scheme is a move in this direction by offering all school leavers a year of work experience with a minimum of three months' training and education off-the-job. The intention is that eventually the scheme will cover all under-18s who have left full-time education. Although funded by the Department of Employment, it can be seen as a massive switch in the resources available to education as well as training. That switch will increase resources for the early leavers and inevitably limit spending on conventional further and higher education. It will also affect the schooling that precedes it and could provide new entrants for further and higher education.

The second strategy to use positive discrimination to achieve the public service ideals of fraternity allied to efficiency would be to concentrate resources on successful developments achieving clearly identifiable benefits for obviously disadvantaged groups. The attempts to train unemployed school leavers have provided examples that add to those identified in the attempts to help children in deprived areas and children from minority groups. This usually means supporting local community-based or school-based efforts rather than those of government agencies. The lesson of the Inner City Partnerships, the last of a long line of efforts to revive the big city centres, is that bids for money made available are slow to come from local communities and from education. Yet only when those communities support the schools and the services will programmes be effective. The mobilization of communal enterprise is likely to be the key to achieving the ideals of the founders of the welfare state.

A third low-risk reform would be to create the conditions under which the poor could compete with the rich on more equal terms. If individual initiative is to be preserved alongside justice for those who lack the resources to exercise it for the benefit of their children, the competition within education has to be made more fair. At present the children of the rich have all the advantages. They have the material backing, the educated parents and the schools in the nicest areas. They are placed in schools, and streams within schools, that have an academic bent. They speak the same language as teachers and hear it in their homes. It is slanted towards examination success and higher education. The children of the poor are more liable to receive little backing, a less academic curriculum and the prospect of an education finishing at 16.

The competition could be made more fair if there was a campaign to raise the academic targets for the poor and to concentrate innovations in the

204 Education as a Public Service

wealthier schools. A meritocracy might be unpopular, but largely because it would threaten the dominance of the service class in education. It would mean reversing many moves to produce a learner-centred curriculum not geared to public examinations. It means concentrating on academic subjects from an early age. If there were to be innovations broadening the curriculum, they would be for those who could afford a more relaxed approach rather than the usual target group – the children who are expected to leave at the earliest opportunity. Of course this is reactionary. It would be vigorously opposed in primary as well as secondary schools. Yet it would be fair in evening up the chances of the poor. Stone (1981) has used such a tough-minded argument on behalf of Blacks, who can easily be given a relaxed education for the best of motives but with little profit. A meritocratic drive in schools could help all the poor. A move in that direction would be low risk, but could bring high dividends. But it is wise to be cautious. Low risk tends to go hand in hand with low rewards. Curriculum innovation tends to produce slow and often superficial change.

The tendency of low-risk curriculum development, changes in the organization of learning, teaching styles, in-service and initial training, management, evaluation and so on to have little impact is explicable, given the forces for inertia detailed in this book. Nevertheless change occurs, particularly when there is pressure from outside the service. The efforts of the MSC have already been extended into schools through pilot projects for the 14- to 18-year-olds, which in 1982 were allocated £40 million. There has been a build-up in pressure from minority groups trying to rectify the disadvantages faced by their children and pressure from feminists for more justice in the education of girls. All these developments are changing curricula directly or through affecting the attitudes of teachers.

Change is also steadily created by government pressure and by the actions of teachers in many schools, colleges and institutes as well as through bodies such as the Schools Council and the Further Education Unit. In a few years from the mid-1970s, the DES and HMI have changed the agenda for discussing the school curriculum and have given evaluation a prominent position. Primary school teachers abandoned streaming during the 1970s. Full-time higher education in the public sector broadened to offer new courses, planned and examined in a very systematic fashion through the Council for National Academic Awards.

The advantage of these low-risk initiatives is that good ideas can spread and centrally imposed curricula and standards do not become ceilings on performance by children, teachers or institutions. Such measures are modest and require no major reorganization. Redistributing resources to the poor would be just; giving more influence to parents would be democratic; reforming public examinations and even scrapping them at 16 would balance some of the increased competition that could result from increased parental concern. These measures might hurt some of those who now get most out of the service, but that is the price of greater equality when resources are scarce. It would be a test of the sincerity of those who work within the service. We may not like the way industrial societies are organized. We may deplore competition and the selfishness of parents when seeking advantages for their own children. We may detest the independent schools. But we should at least acknowledge that our reforming zeal has not so far helped the poor. Indeed, all the efforts seem to have conveniently sustained the position of service-class children whose parents staff the education service. There is something wrong when a public service which was organized to be universally beneficial, continues to serve sectional interests.

I would recommend three maxims for reformers of education; each would enhance it as a public service:

1 Assume that the poor would like their children to have a chance to be rich.
2 Remember that innovation here may improve the competitive position of children there.
3 Never do unto children of other people that which you would not have done to yours.

APPENDIX

MODELS OF THE EDUCATION SERVICE

The interpretations presented throughout this book rest on a perspective of a service in which action results from the resolution of conflict between interest groups. Those groups have conflicting objectives but interact according to unspecified but identifiable rules. Indeed, those rules are often the bases for the careers of those involved as well as defining the conventional ways forward for all.

This perspective emphasizing conflict within agreed procedures for reconciliation contrasts both with summary descriptions of the service in common use, and with models constructed either through analyses of the relation between education, the state and the economy or by viewing the service as a system of interacting parts.

Summary descriptions

It is common to describe the education service in England and Wales as 'decentralized'. The DES does not appoint teachers, determine the school curriculum or approve textbooks. Yet the Education Act of 1944 gives power to the Secretary of State while the day-to-day running of the education service is in the hands of 104 LEAs. Descriptions such as 'distributed' (Briault, 1976) or 'diffused' (Bognador, 1979) also suggest the sharing of decision-making between central and local government, the organized teachers and the staff in 30,000 institutions.

In the official booklet from the DES, *The Educational System of England and Wales* (1980c), the service is described first as '. . . a national system locally administered' and, second, as a 'partnership of central government,

LEAs and the teaching profession'. The first sums up the legal position in the Education Act of 1944 and the complicated shifting relations between central and local government. The second describes not only the contracts between the three partners to work out ways forward, but the expectation that there will be agreement between them.

The essence of this model of partnership is faith that somehow differences will be resolved and policies worked out to the satisfaction of all. Some flavour of this belief in the ability of the partners to keep the service working without disruption can be gauged from this evidence from Sir Toby Weaver to the Education, Arts and Home Office Sub-Committee of the House of Commons Expenditure Committee in the 1975–1976 session (House of Commons Expenditure Committee, 1976). Weaver described what would happen if a school behaved in a stupid way and the LEA did not have the power to act: '. . . it seems to me that the Secretary of State would find some legal way of intervening. I do not think he would get up in the House of Commons, if there were an established curricular scandal, if you can envisage such a thing, and say "Sorry, I have no power to deal with this". I do not believe that this would happen in real life. Similarly, although a local authority may have delegated full power to the governing body or the headmaster of a school, or the principal of a college, in a similar case it seems to me completely unlikely that the local authority would turn round and say "We wash our hands of this".'

These descriptions are realistic for anyone who has attended advisory or consultative committees or informal meetings to work out an agenda that will secure agreement between the partners. However, the cosy consensus view ignores the clash of interests over education and the exclusion of parents and other interested parties. The hypotheses drawn from models of partnership relate to cooperation, negotiation and mediation. Change is conceived as agreed, democratic and evolutionary. But other models suggest repression, and struggle between groups with conflicting interests.

Constructed models

The attraction of describing the education service as disseminated, decentralized or distributed is that it rings true because the readers fit their own experience to the image, selecting and defining for themselves the factors involved. To ensure that the explanations have some reliability, social scientists try to define the factors and specify the relation between them in advance. The model can then serve as a source of hypotheses to be examined against reality. It is, however, wise to be cautious. It is easy to jump from model to conclusion, using the data collected or reported as confirmation or illustration. The model tends to become the reality instead of a source for hypotheses about it.

In the following pages two groups of models are distinguished. First, there are those that focus on the balance of power within the education service. Their concern is with the relations between central government, LEAs, the organized teachers and the various interest groups. The models are close to the action, deal with short-term changes in the balance of influence and are rarely extended to the relation of education to wider political, social and economic factors. These factors are at the centre of the second, social system model. Here the focus is on the part that education plays in sustaining the structure of contemporary social and economic relations. Two versions are considered, one built on the relation of education to other large organizations and the other on its place in the capitalist economy. In both cases the model is abstracted, concerned with generalizations such as state, corporation and particularly the economy.

There is need for caution in the use of models to generate interpretations of the working of a complicated service such as education. In practice as distinct from theory, chaos rather than conspiracy, muddle rather than reason, may be common. Using a model always leads to a reasonable explanation. That explicable, rational shift in the balance of influence, or this move to support the economy through curriculum change, may actually be inexplicable. Not everything can be satisfactorily explained. But a model provides explanations. It is a source for understanding. Specific cases may not fit. Models rationalize, simplify, tidy up the often messy reality.

Balance of power, pluralist models

In all the models that follow the emphasis is political – on the distribution of power either within education, or between it and other institutions. In this first set, the concern is to model the service in order to understand the way power is distributed or being redistributed, to trace the consequences for the government of education and the effect on the schools. The aim is to explain changes that have taken place as the distribution of resources or political power changes. The models are pluralist in assuming that power is dispersed, not monopolized by one class or its agents.

Resource dependency theory   This model is based on power accruing to those who hold scarce resources. They can exact compliance from those who want the money, the skilled personnel, the information, the capital resources, the power they have monopolized. Archer (1981) has elaborated this exchange theory into a complex theoretical model. Here the political exchanges, the resources available within education, their ownership and the tactics employed in negotiations over their exchange are defined and interrelated. Hypotheses are then presented on the relation between these factors. Archer (1979) has also produced a major comparative study using this model.

This approach wherein resources are exchanged for power has been especially fruitful in examining the relationship between central and local government. Thus Rhodes (1981) has organized a review of evidence around the changing balance of influence between central and local government as their mutual dependence changes. With central government providing the major part of the funds spent by local government and the difficulty of raising local rates, the centre's capacity for securing compliance among LEAs is great, particularly in periods of financial stringency. Similarly, in a period of falling school rolls, the bargaining power of teachers is reduced as the demand for their skills decreases.

Rhodes starts with the view of the Layfield Committee (1976), expressed in their report on local government finance, that the question to be asked is about the ambiguity and confusion of central–local government relations, rather than about the assumption that central control has increased and is to be countered. To answer that question, Rhodes uses resource dependency theory. But the relation between the need to mobilize resources and the dependency this can bring, is placed within the context of political and economic organization.

The model is intuitively familiar to administrators, union officials and politicians. The implementation of policies requires resources. To obtain these, alliances are formed to mobilize funds and to ensure that support for the policy will be forthcoming. Rhodes gives five related propositions as a framework for analysing central–local government relations.

1   Any organization is dependent on others for resources.
2   To achieve goals, organizations have to exchange resources.
3   This need to exchange constrains each organization, but a dominant coalition can retain some freedom of action.
4   Dominant coalitions of organizations operate within established procedures.
5   Variations in the balance of power between organizations depend on

their goals, their relative power and therefore the availability of resources to them.

These five points leave the central–local balance open to analysis at any one time. They do not assume a partnership or a dominant agent. Furthermore, this perspective is placed within the context of the trend for the state to minimize conflict in order to achieve stability in an economic order which lies somewhere between capitalism and socialism. As stability is secured by the government negotiating with organized employees and employers in the private and public sectors, the 'rules of the game' wherein bargaining for resources takes place, are changed. Discussions of these corporatist trends follow. Their importance for central–local relations can be seen in the annual round of public sector pay settlements. Every year the money on the table, the bargaining positions, the alliances and the stresses change as governments implement new policies. Central and local government, public corporations and trade unions, negotiate to try to reach agreements. The rules of the game are changed, often by the Treasury or the Department of the Environment as it works out the annual grant for local government. The bargaining over resources continues, but new procedures may have to be worked out annually.

The shifting balance in the partnership   The spotlight on education since the early 1970s, and the shock of reduced resources and falling school rolls, produced many explanations of the new balance of power. Thus Fowler (1979) sees the contraction of resources forcing the location of power to shift to the centre. Similarly, Archer, drawing on her analytical model of educational politics, sees increased dependence on central government for resources and diminished professional independence (Archer, 1981). This argument can, however, be carried further, to the point where the shortage of resources means that the DES also loses power as the Treasury leans on the big spending departments. But the emphasis on resources can give a partial explanation only. The most remarkable development has been the expansion of the Manpower Services Commission, responsible to the Department of Employment, providing new educational services while those promoted by the DES are contracting. The reason for channelling resources that way rather than through LEAs has to be explained in political terms not directly related to the total resources available.

The most comprehensive attempt to plot the factors in recent educational change has come from Salter and Tapper (1981). They seek to explain the increasing centralization of educational power in England and Wales and in particular the role of the DES administration. This explanation is not, of course, everybody's favourite. Fowler (1979) agrees on the centralization, but sees this as the consequence of financial stringency. Archer (1979) stresses the limits on central government domination from the long tradition of decentralized authority. Kogan (1982) has stressed the strength of central and local government politicians in the last decade rather than of the administrators. Indeed, anyone working in educational administration since the mid-1970s would have felt the pressure from political masters rather than opportunities to press for mastery themselves. Salter and Tapper (1981) argue that educational change is politically controlled and that the exercise of power is directed towards economic recovery. The 'state bureaucratic apparatus' takes on the task of defining the needs of the economy and of changes in schooling that are needed to help. Education, however, does not merely legitimize the social class domination of capitalist societies, which is the Marxist view described later (p. 215). At any one time, teachers, politicians, administrators and so on are actively changing the service. But recently the bureaucrats have been setting the pace.

The sequence of events for Salter and Tapper (1981) is first, the articulation of the policies seen as needed, then negotiation between often conflicting parties, then the legitimation of those policies. Much of the effort required is put into getting the policies approved and judged as appropriate. Only then are they pressed home. The story is told in terms of active groups pressing their case, not through references to economic or political forces without flesh. Most convincing is Salter and Tapper's account of the way the bureaucrats in the DES have fixed the agenda for the debate about education from the mid-1970s and mobilized support for changes that will link education to their perception of the needs of the economy. The service is managed, but support has to be obtained from the distributed and varied partners, before action can be taken with a chance of success.

This analysis presented by Salter and Tapper is convincing. Yet it is difficult to see how the 'state bureaucratic apparatus' relates to the work of DES officials. Indeed, this illustrates the strengths and weaknesses of modelling. Salter and Tapper interpret recent events through hypotheses derived from their model of educational change. But while this opens up interpretations, it also excludes others and can lead to gross oversimplifications. Orchestrating the Great Debate on education, attacking the Schools Council and launching the Assessment of Performance Unit, were all important features of the 1970s. But muddling on would be equally convincing as an explanation. Even more convincing would be a deliberate political act from successive Labour and Conservative leaders in local as well as central government.

Social systems models

Modelling societies as social systems has been a profitable if perilous way of generating hypotheses about the way they cohere, survive and adapt. The model is of interacting parts wherein change here produces compensatory changes there. From being the dominant model in sociology, through such works as *The Social System* (Parsons, 1951), such essentially biological, functional models have been rejected. But the attempts to link education to other social institutions, particularly the economy, survive. They are based on assumptions about the concentration of power in large organizations or about the primacy of economic relations. They are at a high level of abstraction, facilitating generalization which is distant from everyday experience.

Education and corporation   The state in contemporary Britain neither holds the ring within which there is a free market economy, nor acts as socialist owner of the means of production, distribution and exchange. It acts to secure order and stability. In the economy it acts to reduce conflict between management and labour by arranging for these interests to be represented in national planning. In social welfare it acts to relieve the more pressing problems that could lead to unrest. These efforts are centred on the mediation of potentially conflicting interests. Schmitter (1974) has described these liberal arrangements as 'societal corporation', to be distinguished from imposed authoritarian state corporation whereby fascist governments stopped the spread of socialism.

The involvement of the education service in the corporate society is described in Chapter 5. State intervention can be seen in the welfare state and in the government's role in controlling the economy. Organized groups such as teachers' unions are directly involved in decision-making with government, and bargain to avoid conflict. This bargaining means that policies are often determined outside Parliament or the market-place, denying parents, employers and other 'consumers' a democratic say in the decisions that may profoundly affect them. The size of business, professional, government service and labour organizations makes it easier to organize ways of reducing conflict. Governments increasingly rely on the corporate representation that secures co-operation and minimizes clashes of interest.

There are numerous versions of the corporate society. There is also scepticism about its usefulness as a model in a society where many issues in areas such as education revolve around social class differences. Yet social contracts and compacts, standing committees and conferences, institutionalized consultations, working parties and the lobbying and persuasion of pressure groups do play a major part in the government of modern Britain. The operation of these corporative activities is often beyond the public eye or the ballot box. An important example for the education service is the Manpower Services Commission established in 1974. This has representation on its governing body from the TUC, the CBI and educational interests. It has been used to bypass local government to get quick action over increased unemployment and increasingly has become a power in education without being responsible to elected education committees locally or to the Secretary of State for Education.

The most sustained and subtle analysis of corporation is by Offe (1981), who sees the state apparatus in advanced capitalist societies as expanded to secure social welfare and economic stability. Yet that expansion is itself the source of further tensions which aggravate the original problem. The cure may be worse than the disease. According to Offe, state power is used to solve a fundamental problem of advanced capitalist democracies. Governments depend on success in elections. Yet they also depend on taxes drawn from profits. These profits accrue from production that is built on inequality. That should be electorally a disaster for any political party supporting capitalism. To Offe the solution has been for the state to ensure that all citizens are put in a position where they are available in the market as commodities. Most have the promise of employment and a comfortable life. Education is used to ensure that new generations are valuable to employers. Training schemes reinforce the market value of labour. Welfare services enable people to compete for work knowing they are fit and housed. This is not the production of specific technical skills to secure correspondence between the demands of employers and the supply of labour coming on to the market. It is the provision of services to allow employees and employers to enter into capitalist productive relationships.

State intervention to regulate the economy is, however, seen as self-defeating. To pay for the state services, taxes have to be high and this reduces the profits from capitalist investment. Furthermore, the sectors of the economy to expand fastest are not in the private, but in the public sector. Civil servants, teachers, health service employees, who work to prepare a suitably skilled and amenable workforce for a market economy, themselves become major groups removed from that market. They expand to secure the capitalist market for labour, but their expansion diminishes it and the profits out of which they are paid. One crisis is replaced by another.

The second approach, based upon the interventionist, corporatist state, comes from Beer (1982). Beer takes the concept of pluralist stagnation, the tendency for a proliferation of pressure groups to make it impossible to obtain radical change or even adaptation to deepening economic crisis as they bargain and balance each other. To Beer, successive British governments have intervened in the economy in order to boost exports, or control inflation or restrain incomes. Similarly, they have increased the scope of social services in order to increase equality of opportunity, or rebuild inner cities or raise the school-leaving age. To raise the taxes and obtain the cooperation of trade unions, professional groups and employers' associations, governments have had to buy consent. The result is a scramble for benefits, for pay, for subsidies, that has been ruinous for the economy and morally degrading.

In *Modern British Politics*, Beer (1965) praised the success of British political parties in reconciling popular choice with strong government. This political system was seen as an example of effective democracy. By 1982, Beer saw successive governments as incapable of effective action and an economy ruined by the greed of interest groups exploiting the need of those in power to obtain their votes. The interrelatedness of institutions gives power to any that are willing to threaten the disruption of the rest. The welfare state produced groups of beneficiaries, none willing to be self-denying. By 1968, the annual increase in expenditure on public services was absorbing the entire increase in the GNP. It was to go on increasing as the GNP started to fall, hastening the economic collapse.

This escalation of bids for a larger share of the cake was not only an organized competition for benefits, whether in health, pensions, housing, social security or education. Consumers and producers, trade unions and employers, rich and poor, acted rationally by organizing to secure their bargaining position. As other groups ignored the national interest, nobody was willing to give their electoral support unless they were rewarded. Behind the apparent comfort of the 1960s, the consensus politics of Butskellism, of Crosland and Boyle as Secretaries of State for Education from different parties but with similar views, there were the seeds of economic and political stagnation.

Beer's analysis lays emphasis on the role of pressure groups grasping as much as possible from governments that bought cooperation. The part played by such groups in education is discussed in Chapter 4. But it is necessary to be cautious. Such groups often reflect deep divisions in society; in particular, they often represent class interests. It is difficult to see why the poor should put the national interest first, when the consequence is to sustain inequality. It is difficult to blame the old, the unemployed, the deprived, for getting together to try to improve their lot. The state may not serve the interest of any one class, but it is in the business of accommodating the fundamental differences between employers and labour. Marxists go beyond this to view the state not as neutral or securing the conditions for advanced capitalism, but as a means for the domination of one class by another. Education is involved in that state machinery for securing the acceptance of inequality.

Education in the capitalist state   It is not possible to do justice to the copious Marxist literature on the state and education. Yet it cannot be ignored, for it relates education not only to the capitalist economy, but to the political organization that secures the domination of one class by another. It is a rich mine for hypotheses about education. Much of the disagreement springs from the depth of the original insight. So the start is with Engel's introduction to the 1891 edition of Karl Marx's *Civil War in France*: 'The state is nothing more than a machine, for the oppression of one class by another'. Add to this the fact that education is part of the state, and you have the basic Marxist insight.

Elaboration of the Marxist view of the state, and education, as organized by capitalism to secure the domination of one class by another, can be found in Holloway and Picciotto (1978). Here education stands alongside the police, the army and the law courts as an arm of political and hence economic repression. The working class is not only exploited economically, but it is persuaded that there is a distinction between economic struggles for better living standards and political struggles for power. Education is used by the dominant class not only to secure a pliant workforce, but to ensure that the illusion of political democracy is maintained.

There are many variations on this hard version. Althusser's distinction between the 'repressive state apparatus' and 'ideological state apparatus' makes it possible to distinguish baton-wielding from chalk-and-talk (Althusser, 1977). But both are still within the capitalist state. Bowles and Gintis (1976) similarly concentrate on the way education prepares people for a place in unequal and unsatisfying work. Schools supply labour not only with suitable skills but with attitudes that ensure a subordinate, diligent and docile workforce. Sexual, class and ethnic differences are reinforced not diminished. A correspondence between the social relations of work and schooling is a necessity for a capitalist economy. Capitalism is a system of social relations that binds economy and politics. An unequal organization at work requires subservient attitudes among the workforce. Schools are organized to achieve this.

There are many objections to these theories and there is something objectionable in the assumption that teachers play a part, albeit unthinking or falsely conscious, in securing a subservient consciousness among children. Indeed, many classrooms seem designed to encourage rather than inhibit revolution. But there is no denying the insights derived from the application of various Marxist models to education. *Learning to Labour* (Willis, 1977) and *Schooling the Smash Street Kids* (Corrigan, 1979) are examples of observational studies inspired by this view, while Sarup (1982) and Sharp (1980) present theoretical perspectives on Marxism and education. To liberals who assume that the state is neutral, these analyses of education within capitalism as part of the state apparatus may appear absurd. But Corrigan's kids and Willis' lads are familiar to most secondary school teachers. Their behaviour and the inadequacy of the schooling they received have to be explained.

The dangers of using models to explain what is observed in schools, county or town halls, or in the DES, are well illustrated in the Marxist explanations of the behaviour observed among the unmotivated low achievers. Willis explains that behaviour by reference to the capitalist class structure. But the same observations of behaviour in school could be interpreted very differently if another model were used. Indeed Scharff (1976), observing similar working-class children in multi-ethnic, inner-city comprehensive schools in the same year as Willis, came up with an entirely different interpretation based not on the structure of capitalism but in psychiatry. Models are sources for explanation, but the disagreements in the latter show the frailty of the former. Scharff's school-leavers never use four-letter words, Willis hears little else; his lads loathed school and long to leave, Scharff's were so upset at leaving that they went into a state of mourning. The model determines the interpretation.

There are also objections to the position adopted by the authors of models that deny the objectivity of others. From academia, school teachers may seem to be agents of repression, supporting the capitalist class structure, but so then are university lecturers. To explain the misguided action of the well-meaning half a million professionals in schools and colleges in terms of false consciousness, while exempting yourself from this political rationalizing, takes a lot of faith in Marxism and very little respect for those doing the 'dirty' work. It also leaves unexplained how the Marxist intellectuals freed themselves from the effects of their class position while others remain locked in what is modelled as an inescapable class-based pressure on consciousness. Models should be seen as sources for hypotheses about reality and not mistaken for it. Those who design them should face the problem of claiming detachment from forces defined as universal. We are part of the world we model.

BIBLIOGRAPHY

Abel-Smith, B. and Townsend, P. (1965) *The Poor and the Poorest*. London: Bell.

Advisory Committee on the Supply and Education of Teachers (1981) *The Future of the Teacher Training System*. London: HMSO.

Althusser, L. (1977) Ideology and ideological state apparatus, in Cosin, B.R., *Education, Structure and Society*. Harmondsworth: Penguin.

Archer, M.S. (1979) *The Social Origins of Educational Systems*. London: Sage.

Archer, M.S. (1981) Educational politics: A model for their analysis, in Broadfoot, P. et al., *Politics and Educational Change*. London: Croom Helm.

Ashton, D. and Maguire, M. (1980) The function of academic and non-academic criteria in employers' selection strategies. *British Journal of Guidance and Counselling*, vol. 8, p. 2.

Ashton, P. (1975) *The Aims of Primary Education*. Basingstoke: Macmillan.

Assessment of Performance Unit (APU) (1982a) *Science in Schools Age 15, Report No. 1*. London: HMSO.

Assessment of Performance Unit (APU) (1982b) *Mathematical Development, Secondary Survey, Report No. 3*. London: HMSO.

Assessment of Performance Unit (APU) (1983) *Language Performance in Schools, Secondary Survey, Report No. 2*. London: HMSO.

Association of County Councils (ACC) (1982) *Rate Support Grant 1982/83*. Chichester County Hall.

Atkinson, A.B. (1969) *The Economics of Inequality*. Oxford: Clarendon Press.

Auld Committee (1976) *The William Tyndale Junior and Infants School*. London: Inner London Education Authority.

Australian Council for Educational Research (ACER) (1981) *School, Work and Careers*. Hawthorn: ACER.

Bacon, W. (1978) *Public Accountability and the Schooling System*. London: Harper & Row.

Ball, S.J. (1981) *Beachside Comprehensive*. Cambridge: Cambridge University Press.

Barker, R. (1972) *Education and Politics, 1900–1951*. Oxford: Clarendon Press.

Barnes, J.H. and Lucas, H. (1975) Positive discrimination in education: individuals, groups and institutions, in Barnes, J.H. (ed.) *Educational Priority, Vol. 3*. London: HMSO.

Becher, T., Eraut, M. and Knight, J. (1981) *Policies for Educational Accountability*. London: Heinemann.

Beer, S. (1965) *Modern British Politics*. London: Faber.

Beer, S. (1982) *Britain Against Itself. The Political Contradictions of Collectivism*. London: Faber.

Bell, D. (1974) *The Coming of Post-Industrial Society*. London: Heinemann.

Benn, C. and Simon, B. (1970) *Halfway There*. London: McGraw-Hill.

Bennett, S.N. (1976) *Teaching Styles and Pupil Progress*. London: Open Books.

Bennett, S.N. (1979) Recent research on teaching: a dream, a belief and a model, in Bennett, S.N. and McNamara, D., *Focus on Teaching*. London: Longman.

Bennett, S.N. et al. (1980) *Open Plan Schools*. Windsor: National Foundation for Educational Research.

Beveridge, W. (1942) *Social Insurance and Allied Services*, Cmnd 6404. London: HMSO.

Birley, D. (1970) *The Education Officer and His World*. London: Routledge & Kegan Paul.

Board of Education (1943) *Educational Reconstruction*. London: HMSO.

Bognador, V. (1979) Power and participation. *Oxford Review of Education*, vol. 5, no. 2, pp. 157–168.

Bolam, R. and Baker, K. (eds) (1975) *The Teacher Induction Pilot Schemes Project*. Bristol: Bristol University School of Education.

Boudon, R. (1974) *Education, Opportunity and Social Inequality*. London: Wiley.

Bowles, S. and Gintis, H. (1976) *Schooling in Capitalist America*. London: Routledge & Kegan Paul.

Boyd, D. (1973) *Elites and Their Education*. Slough: National Foundation for Educational Research.

Briault, E. (1976) A distributed system of educational administration: an international viewpoint. *International Review of Education*, vol. 22, no. 4, pp. 429–439.

Brighouse, T.P.R. (1979) LEA expenditure: needs for the long term and shifts for the short term. *Education Policy Bulletin*, vol. 7, no. 2, pp. 141–148.

Brighouse, T.P.R. and Hainsworth, G. (1983) Week by week. *Education*, 11 February, p. 99.

Brooksbank, K. (ed.) (1980) *Educational Administration*. London: Councils and Education Press.

Bryce, T.G.K. (1981) Rasch fitting. *British Educational Research Journal*, vol. 7, no. 2, pp. 137–153.

Burgess, T. (1982) Falling for the prayer book error. *Times Educational Supplement*, 17 December, p. 4.

Burgess, T. and Travers, T. (1980) *Ten Billion Pounds*. London: Grant McIntyre.

Burgin, K.H.L. (1978) *Trends in Education, Vol. 4*. London: HMSO, p. 32.

Bush, T. (1982) *Occasional Paper One*. London: Society of Education Officers.

Bush, T. and Kogan, M. (1982) *Directors of Education*. London: Allen & Unwin.

Butler, R.A. (1944) Moving the 2nd reading of the Education Bill, in Gosden, P.H.J., *Education in the Second World War*. London: Methuen, pp. 322–323.

Butler, R.A. (1971) *The Art of the Possible*. London: Hamish Hamilton.

Byrne, E. (1974) *Planning and Educational Inequality: A Study of the Rationale of Resource Allocation*. Slough: National Foundation for Educational Research.

Byrne, D.S., Williamson, W. and Fletcher, B.G. (1975) *The Poverty of Education: A Study in the Politics of Opportunity*. London: M. Robertson.

Central Statistical Office (1982) *Social Trends*. London: HMSO.
Central Statistical Office (1983) *Social Trends*. London: HMSO.
Centre for Contemporary Cultural Studies (1981) *Unpopular Education*. London: Hutchinson.
Chambers, J. (1977) In-service education: its rationale, organisation and finance. *British Journal of In-Service Education*, vol. 3, no. 2, pp. 93–97.
Chartered Institute of Public Finance and Accountancy (CIPFA) (1982) *LEA Estimates*. London: CIPFA.
Coates, R.D. (1972) *Teachers' Unions and Interest Group Politics*. Cambridge: Cambridge University Press.
Cole, H. and Shipman, M.D. (1975) Educational indicators in the allocation of resources. *Secondary Education*, vol. 5, no. 2, pp. 37–38.
Coleman, J., Hoffer, T. and Kilgore, S. (1982) *High School Achievement: Public, Catholic and other Private Schools Compared*. New York: Basic Books.
Cooke, G. (1980) Too tough at the top. *Times Educational Supplement*, 1 February, p. 4.
Cope, E. (1971) *School Experience in Teacher Education*. Bristol: Bristol University School of Education.
Corrigan, P. (1979) *Schooling the Smash Street Kids*. London: Macmillan.
Cox, C.B. and Boyson, R. (eds) (1975) *Black Paper 1975*. London: Dent.
Cox, C.B. and Boyson, R. (eds) (1977) *Black Paper 1977*. London: M. Temple-Smith.
Cox, C.B. and Dyson, A.E. (eds) (1969a) *A Black Paper*. London: The Critical Quarterly Society.
Cox, C.B. and Dyson, A.E. (eds) (1969b) *Black Paper Two*. London: The Critical Quarterly Society.
Cox, C.B. and Dyson, A.E. (eds) (1970) *Black Paper Three*. London: The Critical Quarterly Society.
Cox, C. and Marks, J. (1982) *The Right to Learn*. London: Centre for Policy Studies.
Crispin, A. (1980) The new block grant and education – central control or national direction? *Local Government Studies*, vol. 6, no. 6, pp. 25–37.
Crocker, A.C. (1974) *Predicting Teaching Success*. Slough: National Foundation for Educational Research.
Crossman, R. (1969) *Paying for the Social Services*. London: Fabian Society.
Crowther Committee (1959) *15–18*. Report of the Central Advisory Council for Education. London: HMSO.
Cuthbert, R. (1981) The neutrality of the Department of Education and Science. *Higher Education Review*, vol. 13, no. 2, pp. 8–21.
Cyster, R. and Clift, P. (1980) Parental involvement in primary schools: the NFER survey, in Craft, M., Raynor, J. and Cohen, L., *Linking Home and School*. London: Harper & Row.
Dent, A.C. (1944) *Education Act 1944*. London: University of London Press.
Dent, H.C. (1982) *Education in England and Wales*, 2nd ed. London: Hodder & Stoughton.
Department of Education and Science (1972) *Education: A Framework for Expansion*. London: HMSO.
Department of Education and Science (1976) *The Government's Reply to the Tenth*

Report from the Expenditure Committee Session 1975–76. London: HMSO.

Department of Education and Science (1977) *Education in Schools. A Consultative Document.* London: HMSO.

Department of Education and Science (1978a) *Report on Education: Assessing the Performance of Pupils.* London: HMSO.

Department of Education and Science (HMI) (1978b) *Primary Education in England and Wales.* London: HMSO.

Department of Education and Science (1978c) *Making INSET Work.* London: HMSO.

Department of Education and Science (1979a) *Local Authority Arrangements for the Curriculum – Report on the Circular 14/77 Review.* London: HMSO.

Department of Education and Science (HMI) (1979b) *Aspects of Secondary Education in England.* London: HMSO.

Department of Education and Science (1980a) *A Framework for the School Curriculum.* London: HMSO.

Department of Education and Science (HMI) (1980b) *A View of the Curriculum.* London: HMSO.

Department of Education and Science (1980c) *The Educational System of England and Wales.* London: HMSO.

Department of Education and Science (1980d) *Statistical Bulletin 9/80: Induction and In-Service Training of Teachers: 1979 Survey.* London: HMSO.

Department of Education and Science (1981a) *The School Curriculum.* London: HMSO.

Department of Education and Science (1981b) *Report by HMI on the Effects on the Education Service in England of Local Authority Expenditure Policies – Financial Year 1980–81.* London: HMSO.

Department of Education and Science (1982a) *Educational Provision by Liverpool Education Authority in the Toxteth Area.* London: HMSO.

Department of Education and Science (1982b) *The New Teacher in School.* London: HMSO.

Department of Education and Science (1982c) *Statistical Bulletin.* London: HMSO.

Department of Education and Science (1982d) *Report by HMI on the Effects on the Education Service in England of Local Authority Expenditure Policies – Financial Year 1981–82.* London: HMSO.

Department of Education and Science (1982e) *5 to 9: An illustrative survey of 80 first schools in England.* London: HMSO.

Department of Education and Science (1983) *Teaching Quality.* London: HMSO.

Djilas, M. (1957) *The New Class.* London: Unwin.

Dore, R. (1976) *The Diploma Disease.* London: Allen & Unwin.

Douglas, J.W.B. (1964) *The Home and the School.* London: McGibbon and Kee/ Allen & Unwin.

Dunkin, M.J. and Biddle, B.J. (1974) *The Study of Teaching.* New York: Holt, Rinehart and Winston.

Edwards, J. and Batley, R. (1978) *The Politics of Positive Discrimination.* London: Tavistock.

Evans, N. (1978) *Beginning Teaching in Professional Partnership.* London: Hodder & Stoughton.

Field, G.C. (1956) *Political Theory*. London: Methuen, p. 137.

Field, F. (1981) *Inequality in Britain: Freedom, Welfare and the State*. London: Fontana.

Fiske, D. (1980a) What the 1980 Act is really about. *Education*, 25 April, pp. 409–411.

Fiske, D. (1980b) Responsibilities, power and the LEA. *Local Government Studies*, vol. 6, no. 6, pp. 39–46.

Floud, J., Halsey, A.H. and Martin, F.M. (1956) *Social Class and Educational Opportunity*. London: Heinemann.

Fowler, G. (1974) Towards recurrent education in Britain, in Houghton, V. and Richardson, K. (eds) *Recurrent Education*. London: Ward Lock.

Fowler, G. (1979) The politics of education, in Bernbaum, G. (ed.) *Schooling in Decline*. Basingstoke: Macmillan.

Fulton Committee (1968) *Report of the Committee on the Civil Service*, Cmnd 3638. London: HMSO.

George, V. and Wilding, P. (1976) *Ideology and Social Welfare*. London: Routledge & Kegan Paul.

Goldthorpe, J.H.G. (1980) *Social Mobility and the Class Structure*. Oxford: Clarendon Press.

Gordon Walker, P. (1969) *The Cabinet*. London: Jonathan Cape.

Gosden, P.H. (1966) *The Development of Educational Administration in England and Wales*. Oxford: Blackwell.

Gould, R. (1976) *Chalk up the Memory*. Birmingham: George Philip Alexander.

Gray, J.L. and Moshinsky, P. (1938) Ability and opportunity in English education, in Hogben, L. (ed.) *Political Arithmetic*. London: Allen & Unwin.

Gray, J. and Satterley, D. (1976) A chapter of errors. *Educational Research*, vol. 19, pp. 45–56.

Guttsman, W.L. (1963) *The British Political Elite*. London: MacGibbon and Kee.

Halmos, P. (1966) *The Personal Service Society*. Inaugural Lecture. Cardiff: University College Cardiff.

Halsey, A.H. and Crewe, I. (1967) *Social Survey of the Civil Service*. Evidence to the Fulton Committee. See Fulton Committee, op. cit., vol. III (1). London: HMSO.

Halsey, A.H., Heath, A.F. and Ridge, J.M. (1980) *Origins and Destinations*. Oxford: Clarendon Press.

Hannam, C. (1976) *The First Years of Teaching*. London: Penguin.

Hargreaves, D.H. (1982) *The Challenge for the Comprehensive School*. London: Routledge & Kegan Paul.

Harris, R. and Seldon, A. (1979) *Overruled on Welfare*. London: Institute of Economic Affairs.

Hayward, J. (1976) Institutional inertia and political impetus in France and Britain. *European Journal of Political Research*, vol. 4, pp. 341–359.

Heath, A. and Clifford, P. (1980) The seventy thousand hours that Rutter left out. *Oxford Review of Education*, vol. 6, pp. 3–19.

Heclo, H. and Wildavsky, A. (1974) *The Private Government of Public Money: Community and Policy inside British Politics*. London: Macmillan.

Heidenheimer, H.J., Heclo, H. and Adams, C.T. (1975) *Comparative Public Policy*. London: Macmillan.

Hencke, D. (1976) The Government and college reorganization. *Higher Education Review*, Summer, pp. 7–18.

Hilsum, S. and Start, K.B. (1974) *Promotion and Careers in Teaching*. Windsor: National Foundation for Educational Research.

Hirsch, F. (1977) *Social Limits to Growth*. London: Routledge & Kegan Paul.

Hobhouse, L.T. (1912) *Liberalism*. London: Williams and Norgate.

Holland Committee (1977) *Young People and Work*. London: HMSO.

Holloway, J. and Picciotto, S. (eds) (1978) *State and Capital: A Marxist Debate*. London: E. Arnold.

Hough, J. (1981) *A Study of School Costs*. Slough: National Foundation for Educational Research/Nelson.

House of Commons Expenditure Committee (1976) *Policy Making in the Department of Education and Science*. London: HMSO.

House of Commons Expenditure Committee (1977) *Tenth Report: The Attainments of the School Leaver*. London: HMSO.

Hunter, C. (1983) Education and local government, in Ahier, J. and Flude, M., *Contemporary Educational Policy*. London: Croom Helm, pp.81–108.

Hurman, A. (1978) *A Charter for Choice*. Windsor: National Foundation for Educational Research.

Husen, T. (1979) *The School in Question*. Oxford: Oxford University Press.

Inner London Education Authority (ILEA) (1981) *Monitoring Examination Results within a Local Education Authority*. London: ILEA.

Inner London Education Authority (ILEA) (1983) *Capital and Revenue Estimates 1983–1984*. London: ILEA.

Isaac Henry, K. (1980) The English Local Authority Associations, in Jones, G.W., *New Approaches to the Study of Central–Local Government Relationships*. London: SSRC/Gower, pp. 40–58.

James, P.H. (1980) *The Reorganisation of Secondary Education*. Windsor: National Foundation for Educational Research.

James Committee (1972) *Teacher Education and Training*. London: HMSO.

Jennings, R.L. (1977) *Education and Politics*. London: Batsford.

Johnson, D. and Ransom, E. (1980) Parents' perceptions of secondary schools, in Craft, M., Raynor, J. and Cohen, L., *Linking Home and School*. London: Harper & Row, pp. 177–185.

Johnson, D. et al. (1980) *Secondary Schools and the Welfare Network*. London: Allen & Unwin.

Jones, K. (1983) *Beyond Progressive Education*. London: Macmillan.

Jordan, B. (1973) *Paupers: The Making of the New Claiming Class*. London: Routledge & Kegan Paul.

Kerr, E. (1976) Validation and development of curricula, in Further Education Staff College, *Phoenix from the Ashes, Prospects for Teacher Education*. Coombe Lodge, pp. 293–295.

Kirp, D. (1979) *Doing Good by Doing Little*. Berkeley, Calif.: University of California Press.

Kitto, D. (1983) *Whatever Happened to Ivan Illich?* Paper read at conference on Alternative Educational Futures, University of Birmingham, 21/22 April.

Kogan, M. (1971) *The Politics of Education*. London: Penguin.

Kogan, M. (1975) *Educational Policy-Making*. London: Allen & Unwin.

Kogan, M. (1978) *The Politics of Educational Change*. London: Fontana.

Kogan, M. (1982) Changes in perspective. *Times Educational Supplement*, 15 January, p. 4.

Kogan, M. and van der Eyken, W. (1973) *County Hall: The Role of the Chief Education Officer*. London: Penguin.

Konrad, G. and Szelenyi, I. (1979) *The Intellectuals on the Road to Class Power*. Brighton: Harvester Press.

Larson, M. (1977) *The Rise of Professionalism: A Sociological Analysis*. Berkeley, Calif., University of California Press.

Lawton, D. (1980) *The Politics of the School Curriculum*. London: Routledge & Kegan Paul.

Layfield Committee (1976) *Committee of Enquiry into Local Government Finance*, Cmnd 6453. London: HMSO.

Lister, D. (1981) CEOs press for change in curriculum. *Times Educational Supplement*, 15 May, p. 5.

Little, A.N. and Westergaard, J. (1964) The trend in class differentials in educational opportunity in England and Wales. *British Journal of Sociology*, December, pp. 301–316.

Lowndes, G.A.N. (1937) *The Silent Social Revolution*. Oxford: Oxford University Press.

Maclure, S. (1970) The control of education, in History of Education Society, *Studies in the Government and Control of Education since 1860*. London: Methuen.

McNamara, D.R. and Ross, A.M. (1982) *The B.Ed. Degree and its Future*. Lancaster: University of Lancaster.

Manpower Services Commission (MSC) (1980) *Manpower Review*. London: MSC.

Manzer, R.A. (1970) *Teachers and Politics*. Manchester: Manchester University Press.

Millerson, G. (1964) Dilemmas of professionalism. *New Society*, June 1964, p. 15.

Milner Holland Committee (1965) *Report of the Committee on Housing in Greater London*. London: HMSO.

Monks, T.G. (1970) *Comprehensive Education in Action*. Slough: National Foundation for Educational Research.

Morris, M. (1980) Review of Brown C.H., *Understanding Society* (London: J. Murray). *Education*, 7 March, p. 253.

Musgrove, F. (1971) *Patterns of Power and Authority in English Education*. London: Methuen.

National Children's Bureau (1972) *A Pattern of Disadvantage*. Windsor: National Foundation for Educational Research.

National Health Service (1968) *Twentieth Anniversary Conference*. London: HMSO.

National Union of Students (NUS) (1971) *The Education and Training of Teachers*. London: NUS.

National Union of Teachers (NUT) (1962) *Investment for National Survival*. London: NUT.

National Union of Teachers (NUT) (1971a) *The Reform of Teacher Education*. London: NUT.

National Union of Teachers (NUT) (1971b) *Teachers Talking*. London: NUT.

National Union of Teachers (NUT) (1978) *Partnership in Education*. London: NUT.

National Union of Teachers (NUT) (1981) *The Importance of In-Service Education in the Professional Development of Teachers*. London: NUT.

National Union of Teachers (NUT) (1983) *Our Children, Our Future. A Manifesto for Education*. London: NUT.

Newsom Committee (1963) *Half our Future* (Central Advisory Council for Education). London: HMSO.

Norwood Committee (1943) *Report of the Committee of the Secondary Schools Examination Council on Curriculum and Examinations in Secondary Schools*. London: HMSO.

Nove, A. (1975) Is there a ruling class in the USSR? *Soviet Studies*, vol. 27, no. 4, pp. 615–635.

Offe, C. (1981) Theses on the theory of the state, in Dale, R. et al., *Schooling and the National Interest*. Brighton: Falmer Press, pp. 77–84.

O'Kane, E. (1983) Whose move? Teacher promotion: the future. *Schoolmaster and Career Teacher*, June, pp. 10–11.

O'Keefe, D.J. (1981) Market capitalism and nationalized schooling. *Educational Analysis*, vol. 3, no. 1, pp. 23–36.

Open University (1981) *Society, Education and the State*. Block 6, see Policies of Schools and Teachers. Milton Keynes: Open University.

Organization for Economic Cooperation and Development (OECD) (1975) *Educational Development Strategy in England and Wales*. Paris: OECD.

Pahl, R. and Winkler, J. (1974) The coming corporatism. *New Society*, 10 October, pp. 72–76.

Parsons, T. (1951) *The Social System*. New York: Free Press.

Pattison, M. (1979) Intergovernmental relations and the limitations of central control: reconstructing the politics of comprehensive education. *Oxford Review of Education*, vol. 6, p. 1.

Peacock, A.T. and Wiseman, J. (1961) *The Growth of Public Expenditure in the United Kingdom*. London: Allen & Unwin.

Phillips, J.F. (1981) Obtaining a professional council. *Education Today*, vol. 31, no. 3, pp. 3–5.

Pile, W. (1979) *The Department of Education and Science*. London: Allen & Unwin.

Plewis, I. et al. (1981) *Publishing School Examination Results: A Discussion*. London: Bedford Way Papers.

Plowden Committee (1967) *Children and their Primary Schools* (Central Advisory Council for Education). London: HMSO.

Professional Association of Teachers (PAT) (1976) *Education Cuts*. London: PAT.

Public Schools Commission (1968) *First Report, Volumes 1 and 2*. London: HMSO.

Pugh, G. (1982) *Parents as Partners*. London: National Children's Bureau.

Rainwater, L. (1967) The revolt of the dirty workers. *Trans-action*, vol. 5, no. 2.

Ranson, S. (1981) Changing relations between centre and locality in education. *Local Government Studies*, vol. 5.

Rhodes, R.A.W. (1981) *Control and Power in Central-Local Government Relations*. London: Social Science Research Council/Gower.

Roach, J. (1971) *Public Examinations in England 1850–1900*. Cambridge: Cambridge University Press.

226   Education as a Public Service

Robbins Committee (1963) *Higher Education* (Committee on Higher Education). London: HMSO.

Rubinstein, D. (ed.) (1979) *Equality and Education*. London: Penguin.

Rutter, M. et al. (1979) *Fifteen Thousand Hours*. London: Open Books.

Ryrie, A.C. (1979) *Routes and Results*. London: Hodder & Stoughton.

Salter, B. and Tapper, T. (1981) *Education, Politics and the State*. London: Grant McIntyre.

Saran, R. (1982) Why quality must pay in the classroom. *Times Educational Supplement*, 22 October, p. 4.

Sarup, M. (1982) *Education, State and Crisis*. London: Routledge & Kegan Paul.

Sayer, J. (1980) Managing the teaching profession. *Local Government Studies*, vol. 6, no. 6, pp. 47–56.

Scharff, D.E. (1976) Aspects of the transition from school to work, in Hill, J.M.M. and Scharff, D.E., *Between Two Worlds*. London: Careers Consultants Ltd, pp. 66–332.

Schmitter, P.C. (1974) Still the century of corporatism?, in Pike, F.B. and Strich, T. (eds) *The New Corporatism*. New York: Notre Dame.

Seebowm Committee (1969) *Report of the Committee on Local Authority and Allied Personal Social Services*. London: HMSO.

Sharp, R. (1980) *Knowledge, Ideology and Schooling*. London: Routledge & Kegan Paul.

Shearman, H. (1944) *The New Education Act*. London: Workers Education Association.

Shipman, M.D. (1978) *In-School Evaluation*. London: Heinemann.

Shipman, M.D. (1980) The limits of positive discrimination, in Marland, M., *Education for the Inner City*. London: Heinemann.

Shipman, M.D., Bolam, D. and Jenkins, D. (1974) *Inside a Curriculum Project*. London: Methuen.

Silver, H. (1980) *Education and the Social Condition*. London: Methuen.

Spens Committee (1938) *Report of the Consultative Committee on Secondary Education*. London: HMSO.

Stammers, P. (1980) Whose INSET is it? *British Journal of In-Service Education*, vol. 6, no. 1, pp. 5–9.

Start, K.B. and Wells, B.K. (1972) *The Trend in Reading Standards*. Slough: National Foundation for Educational Research.

Stone, M. (1981) *The Education of the Black Child in Britain: The Myth of Multicultural Education*. London: Fontana.

Taylor, J. (1973) In-service provision, in Watkins, R. (ed.) *In-Service Training*. London: Ward Lock, pp. 33–40.

Taylor, W. (1978) *Research and Reform in Teacher Education*. Slough: National Foundation for Educational Research.

Taylor, G. and Ayres, N. (1969) *Born and Bred Unequal*. London: Longman.

Taylor, J.K. and Dale, I.R. (1971) *A Survey of Teachers in Their First Year of Service*. Bristol: University of Bristol School of Education.

Taylor Committee (1977) *A New Partnership for our Schools* (DES). London: HMSO.

Times Educational Supplement (1974) Survey of teachers' opinions, 4 October.

Times Educational Supplement (1976) Extracts from the Yellow Book, 15 October.
Times Educational Supplement (1977a) Survey of teachers' opinions, 2 September.
Times Educational Supplement (1977b) Report of a speech by General Secretary of the NUT, 23 September.
Times Educational Supplement (1982) The grim battle to win the numbers game, 24 September.
Times Educational Supplement (1983) Election '83, 27 May.
Titmuss, R.M. (1950) *Problems of Social Policy*. London: HMSO.
Titmuss, R.M. (1968) *Commitment to Welfare*. London: Allen & Unwin.
Tizard, B. et al. (eds.) (1980) *Fifteen Thousand Hours*. London: University of London Press.
Tomlinson, J. (1981) Time for the Empire to strike back. *Times Educational Supplement*, 3 April, p. 4.
Tomlinson, S. (1980) Ethnic minority parents and education, in Craft, M., Raynor, J. and Cohen, L., *Linking Home and School*. London: Harper & Row, pp. 200–214.
Tunley, P., Travers, T. and Pratt, J. (1979) *Depriving the Deprived*. London: Kogan Page.
Weiss, C.H. (1980) *Social Science Research and Decision-Making*. New York: Columbia University Press.
Weston, P. (1970) *Framework for the Curriculum*. Windsor: National Foundation for Educational Research.
Wicksteed, D. and Hill, M. (1979) 'Is this you?' – A survey of primary teachers' attitudes to issues raised in the Great Debate. *Education, 3–13*, vol. 7, no. 1, pp. 32–63.
Willis, P. (1977) *Learning to Labour*. Farnborough: Saxon House.
Willmott, A.S. (1977) *CSE and GCE Grading Standards*. London: Schools Council/ Macmillan.
Wilson, J. (1975) *Educational Theory and the Preparation of Teachers*. Windsor: National Foundation for Educational Research.
Wilson, R.A. (1983) *The Declining Returns to Becoming a Teacher*. Institute of Employment Research Paper 73. University of Warwick.
Wisconsin School of Education (1961) Wisconsin studies of the measurement and prediction of teacher effectiveness. *Journal of Experimental Education*, September, pp. 5–156.
Wiseman, S. and Start, K. (1965) A follow-up of teachers five years after completing their training. *British Journal of Educational Psychology*, vol. 35, pp. 342–361.
Woods, P. (ed.) (1980) *Pupil Strategies*. London: Croom Helm.
Wootton, G. (1978) *Pressure Politics in Contemporary Britain*. Lexington, Massachusetts: Lexington Books.
Workers' Action Teachers (1977) *A Manifesto for Socialist Teachers*. London: Workers' Action Teachers.
Young, M. (1961) *The Rise of the Meritocracy*. Harmondsworth: Penguin.

INDEX